SPEECH PHYSIOLOGY AND ACOUSTIC PHONETICS

Speech Physiology and Acoustic Phonetics: An Introduction

PHILIP LIEBERMAN

Department of Linguistics, Brown University

MACMILLAN PUBLISHING CO., INC.
New York

Collier Macmillan Publishers
London

MACMILLAN PUBLISHING CO., INC.
866 Third Avenue, New York, New York 10022
COLLIER MACMILLAN CANADA, LTD.

Library of Congress Cataloging in Publication Data

Lieberman, Philip.
  Speech physiology and acoustic phonetics.

  Bibliography: p.
  Includes index.
  1. Speech—Physiological aspects.   2. Auditory
perception.   3. Phonetics.   I. Title.
QP306.L52   612'.78   76–19003
ISBN 0–02–370620–1

Printing: 1 2 3 4 5 6 7 8   Year: 7 8 9 0 1 2 3

Preface

THE study of speech is relevant to a variety of different fields such as psychology, linguistics, anthropology, primatology, electrical engineering, and computer science, as well as the primary fields of speech science and speech therapy. In teaching introductory courses on the production and perception of speech, and on the procedures of acoustic phonetics and speech physiology, I have therefore encountered students with very different academic backgrounds. Some of these students have had a working knowledge of the acoustics of speech, electrical circuit theory, experimental psychology, or the anatomy of the vocal tract. Many of my students, however, have had very little quantitative knowledge of physics, anatomy, or psychology. Others may be familiar with one area but are deficient in all other aspects of the study of speech. I have felt for some time that there is a need for a text that guides students from different backgrounds to a quantitative understanding of speech without their having to take a two or three year sequence of specialized courses. This book thus provides a step-by-step introduction that starts with simple examples that put the subject into perspective. It ends with a detailed exposition of recent quantitative theories and data. The book assumes that the reader lacks any knowledge of physics or mathematics beyond the high school level. The background that is necessary for understanding the physics of sound, the source-filter theory of speech production, and the principles that underlie electrical and computer models of speech production is presented in stages and and is illustrated by means of simple examples.

The reader should be able to follow the primary research papers that are presented and understand the implications of their results on his or her own area of special interest, whether that is speech therapy, phonologic theory, psycholinguistics, anthropology, etc. The implications of quantitative studies involving techniques like cineradiography, sound spectroscopy, dichotic perception, electromyography, computer modeling, etc., are often unintelligible to the nonspecialist; this book should make these results accessible by providing a knowledge of relevant theories and techniques and also of the deficiencies of these theories and techniques. I have tried to convey some of the problems and some of the exhilaration that one encounters in doing research. Science is not the cut and dried gathering of "facts" that it sometimes seems to be in textbooks where theories are supported by armies of "facts" and "proofs" organised in divisions and battalions. Every theory has its deficiencies, and the "art" of science is in deciding which theories are most promising and how they may be tested. The chapter on the analysis of speech which notes the basic techniques of tape recording and the use of the sound spectrograph can serve as the basis of a course in experimental phonetics if it is integrated with laboratory exercises. The chapters on speech production, speech perception, and phonetic theory present various experimental techniques and unresolved questions. The text thus highlights problems that students can investigate. A number of original studies have been completed and published by undergraduate and graduate students using this text. Most of these students had no technical background before they started. The book is self-contained insofar as it has the range of information that is necessary for a student to move from unfamiliarity with the area to publishing a research paper. The reader obviously can and should supplement this material with primary research papers as he or she becomes more familiar with the field. Detailed charts and illustrations that can serve as reference material, as well as pedagogic aids, are therefore provided throughout the book, as well as references to primary research papers. The book may thus be useful as a convenient reference source. My basic aim, however, in writing this book has been to make more people aware of a very new and exciting field, and to start them working in it.

Although it is impossible to provide an inclusive list of all the people whose work I am indebted to, I would especially like to thank Arthur Abramson, Franklin Cooper, Morris Halle, Alvin Liberman, and Kenneth Stevens, who have over the years shared their insights and critical comments with me. I would also like to thank my colleagues at Brown University, especially Sheila Blumstein and Peter Eimas, for similar aid. I wish to thank Barbara Moslin, John Knapp, and Karen Landahl for their help in reading preliminary versions. Hope Fisher provided indispensable assistance in preparing the typescript. I also wish to acknowledge Kenneth J. Scott and J. Edward Neve of the Macmillan Publishing Company, Inc. However, I owe the most important acknowledgment to my students, from whose questions this book developed and to whom it is most appropriately dedicated.

P. L.

Contents

Illustrations

Tables

SPEECH PHYSIOLOGY AND ACOUSTIC PHONETICS

1
Introduction

THE study of language and the sounds of speech can be traced back at least to the Greek and Sanskrit grammarians of the third and fourth centuries B. C. The explicit study of speech science; began in the eighteenth century when Ferrein (1741) attempted to explain how the vocal cords produced phonation. Ferrein's studies were not an isolated event. Kratzenstein (1780) and von Kempelen (1791) attempted to explain how the vowels and consonants of human speech were produced by synthesizing sounds using artificial "talking machines." There indeed may have been earlier attempts at constructing talking machines; La Mettrie (1747) discusses some of these early attempts, but we lack detailed records. By the midnineteenth century Müller (1848) had formulated the source-filter theory of speech production, which is consistent with the most recent data and still guides research on human speech as well as the vocal communications of other animals. Although Müller's theory was further developed later in the nineteenth century, particularly by Hermann (1894), the modern period of speech science is really quite recent, dating back to the late 1930s, where devices like the sound spectrograph, and techniques like high speed photography, cineradiography, and electromyography made new data available. Quantitative studies like those of Chiba and Kajiyama (1941), Joos (1948), Peterson and Barney (1952), Stevens and House (1955), and Fant (1960) refined and tested the traditional phonetic theories of the nineteenth century and provided the framework for comprehensive, biologically oriented studies of speech production, speech perception, and phonetics. The advent and general availability of digital computers made quantitative modeling studies possible. New techniques for speech synthesis and psychoacoustic experiments made the encoded properties of human speech apparent. We are beginning to understand how human speech is produced and the properties of neural mechanisms of the brain that appear to be involved in the process of human speech perception. We also are beginning to understand how human language and human speech evolved and how other animals communicate. The development of speech and language in infants and children is being explored and new possibilities are opening for the diagnosis and amelioration of various speech pathologies.

The focus of this introduction to speech physiology and acoustic phonetics is thus to provide a background to the "new" speech science. An understanding of the acoustics of speech, the physiology of speech production, and the special factors that are involved in the perception of speech is a prerequisite for further study of the pathologies of speech production or the neurological impairment of either speech production or speech perception. It is also necessary for quantitative, predictive phonetic and phonologic studies. Linguists have been content to *describe* the process of sound change and other phonologic phenomena—for example, the ways in which sounds change as they go together in different combinations. Phonologic studies have also compared different languages and noted what sounds seem to occur more often than others. The aim of speech science must be to *explain* why certain sounds tend to occur and why some sounds seem to occur more often than others. This introduction is no substitute for a traditional phonetics text, focused on teaching people how to make auditory transcriptions of various languages and dialects. The training techniques that phoneticians use are not included in this book because our objective is to understand the biological mechanisms that are the basis not only of human speech but of vocal communication in many other animals.

Readers who have a good background in high school mathematics should have little difficulty in following the discussions of the acoustics of speech production or the source-filter theory of speech production. Readers who have a more advanced background may be able to skim appropriate chapters.

Although readers may find this book a useful reference source, its primary function is pedagogic. It should be viewed as an introduction to the physiology of speech and acoustic phonetics. Many current problems are not discussed in detail, and the advanced reader may be familiar with topics that have been omitted. Everyone, however, should encounter new material and indeed note that there are many gaps in our knowledge. These gaps follow, in part, from the comparatively recent nature of the field, but they primarily reflect the difficulties inherent in understanding the nature of language and intelligence of which speech forms a crucial part.

2
A Qualitative Introduction to the Physiology of Speech

P HYSIOLOGY is the science that deals with the function of biological systems. An anatomist, for example, could describe the bones and muscles of the human foot without considering how these elements work together in activities like bipedal locomotion. A physiologist would have to consider these same bones and muscles in terms of their functional value in locomotion and other activities. In fact, anatomists usually take account of the function of the bones, muscle, and soft tissue that they describe since the physiological or functional approach is inherently more integrated than a strictly anatomical one. The physiological method of describing the anatomy of human speech production indicates what elements have a functional value with regard to speech production and what anatomical elements are irrelevant. We thus do not have to catalogue every bone and variation in the soft tissue of the mouth, pharynx, and nose. We can focus on the elements that have a functional role in the production of speech. So instead of listing every bone, cartilage, and muscle, we will start with a broad outline of the physiology of speech and relevant anatomical structures. We will add more detail in later chapters when we consider specific aspects of the physiology of speech production.

The Three Physiologic Components of Speech Production

It is convenient and correct to consider speech production in terms of the three main physiologic components—1) the subglottal component, which consists of the lungs and associated respiratory musculature, 2) the larynx, and 3) the supralaryngeal vocal tract. The three components are sketched in the diagram in Figure 2-1. The diagram obviously does not attempt to present a realistic picture of the anatomy of speech production. The supralaryngeal vocal tract, which consists of the airways of the nose, mouth, and pharynx, is shown as a lateral (side) view of the air passages.

3

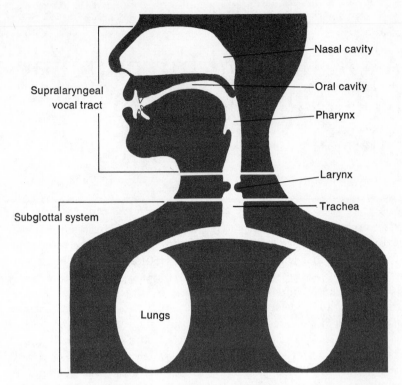

FIGURE 2-1. *The three physiologic components of human speech production.*

The supralaryngeal vocal tract acts as a variable acoustic filter that lets proportionately more acoustic energy through at different frequencies as the speaker changes the shape of the tract.

The larynx is sketched in Figure 2-1 in a sort of X-ray frontal view. We will use more realistic sketches and photographs when we discuss the anatomy, control, and activity of the larynx in more detail. The primary role of the larynx in the production of speech is to convert a relatively steady current of air out from the lungs into a series of almost periodic "puffs" of air. The puffs of air contain acoustic energy at audible frequencies. The larynx thus can act as a "source" of acoustic energy that the supralaryngeal vocal tract then "filters."

The subglottal system is sketched in Figure 2-1 as though it were a frontal X-ray view. The trachea or windpipe leads down from the larynx where it bifurcates into two airways that each lead into a lung. The subglottal component generates the air flow that powers speech production. It is important to note at this point that these three components all perform functions necessary to maintain life, quite apart from their activity relative to speech production. These primary vegetative, or life-supporting, functions have crucially affected the anatomical "design" of the tongue, larynx, nose, lungs, etc., and the physiology of respiration, chewing, swallowing, lung protection, etc. Over hundreds of millions of years there has been natural selection for mutations that facilitate these functions (Negus, 1949). Many of the characteristics of the anatomical mechanisms that we use to produce human speech reflect these adaptions. Human speech is thus, in part, structured by the constraints of physiologic mechanisms whose primary purpose is nonlinguistic.

Some of the characteristics of the larynx do appear to reflect adaptions that enhance communication in humans and other animals (Negus, 1949). There are also certain characteristics of the human supralaryngeal vocal tract that presently appear only in *Homo sapiens* (Lieberman, 1975). Together, these various physiologic constraints exert a strong force on the particular form that human speech has taken. In this chapter we will discuss these three components in a simplified manner in order to keep the total process of speech production in mind as we go into more detail in later chapters.

The Subglottal Respiratory System

The lungs and associated musculature often are not discussed with regard to their activity during the production of speech. Their activity during the production of speech is, however, very interesting because it derives from the general vegetative functions of the respiratory system without being completely similar. In other words, speech production for the most part is inherently structured in terms of the "normal," nonspeech characteristics of the lungs and respiratory muscles, but there are, in addition, some additional factors that appear to enter into the production of speech and activities like singing. The best way to approach the discussion of the subglottal respiratory system is to describe in simple terms how the lungs work. The respiratory system is put together in a manner that is not immediately obvious. Stetson (1951), for example, proposed a theory that attempted to explain the linguistic and physiologic bases of the syllable as a unit of speech. Stetson's theory is unfortunately flawed because he misinterpreted the function of the lungs during quiet respiration and speech.

In Figure 2-2 we have sketched a simple model of the subglottal respiratory system. The model consists of two bicycle pumps that have their push rods rigidly linked together. A crossbar and handle have been welded to the two push rods. Each pump contains a large rubber balloon attached to the inlet tube. The two inlet tubes are linked together and merge into a single tube. This single tube is analogous to the trachea of the human respiratory system. The air entering the two bicycle pumps

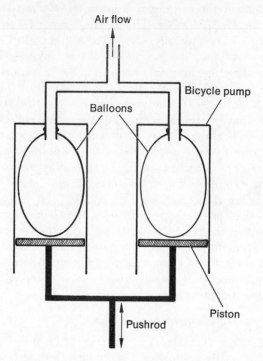

FIGURE 2-2. *A mechanical model of the subglottal respiratory system.*

flows through this inlet tube into the inlet tubes of the two bicycle pumps, where it goes into the balloons. The linked bicycle pump push rods are "volume change" rods. This mechanical model isolates some of the physiologic aspects of the subglottal respiratory system that are of interest for speech production.

The dynamics of changing the internal volume of the two balloons, which are the mechanical analogs of the lungs, are straightforward. If the push rod is pulled out, the internal volume of the two pumps will increase. Because the air pressure multiplied by the volume of the en-closed space within the pump body must equal a constant value,

$$P_{pl}(V) = C$$

where

$P_{pl} = $ the air pressure within the pump body
$V = $ the internal volume of the pump
$C = $ a constant value

the air pressure in the pump body will fall as the push rod is pulled out.

The air pressure within the pump body, outside of the balloon, labeled P_{pl} on Figure 2-2, will thus be less than it was before the push rod was pulled out. The outside air pressure is manifested on the inside of each balloon because the balloon is connected through the inlet tubes to the outside. The balloons therefore will expand as outside air enters. In other words, the two balloons will stretch and expand, storing more air as the push rod is pulled out. Note that it takes more energy to suck a given volume of air into this system than into a simple bicycle pump that did not have a balloon placed over its inlet tube. When you blow up a rubber balloon you have to stretch the rubber walls of the balloon. The rubber walls of the balloon are elastic and they store up energy as they expand. You therefore have to provide the energy that is stored in the stretched, elastic balloon walls. This stored elastic energy is, of course, released if you release a rubber balloon after you have blown it up. The *elastic recoil* force of the balloon walls will force the air out of the balloon under pressure. Everyone has probably played with a flying balloon. You blow it up and then release it; the power for flight comes from the energy that was stored in the balloon.

What will happen in our model of the subglottal respiratory system if we release the push rod with the balloons in their expanded state, i.e., after the push rod has been pulled down as far as it will go? The balloons obviously will collapse and air will flow out of the "tracheal" tube. The elastic recoil force of the balloons will force air out and the push rods will move inwards, following the collapsing balloons. It takes muscular force to get air into this model when you pull the rod out during inspiration. In contrast, during expiration air will go out of the system without your applying any force. You could force the air out faster during expiration if you also pushed the rod inwards, but you don't have to. The energy stored in the elastic balloons can provide the force that pushes the air out during expiration.

This model holds for the subglottal respiratory systems of virtually all air-breathing higher animals. The internal volume of the bicycle pump that is not taken up by the balloon is called the *pleural cavity*. Most of the energy that we expend to transfer air into and out of our lungs comes from the inspiratory muscles that expand the pleural space. As the pleural space increases its volume, the volume of the elastic lung-balloon increases. Energy is stored in the elastic expansion of each lung. During expiration the elastic recoil of the lungs furnishes much of the energy that is necessary to push air out of the lungs through the larynx and supralaryngeal air passages. The balance of force provided by the elastic recoil and various inspiratory and expiratory muscles is variable during the production of human speech and is an example of how the physiologic constraints that underlie the production of human speech ultimately structure the form of human speech. Other variable forces also act during the respiratory cycle. The force of gravity, for example, acts differently when a person stands up or lies down. The control problem is actually quite complex. We will return to the topic of the control of the sub-glottal respiratory system after we discuss the necessary background material in the chapters that follow; for the moment we will continue our preliminary discussion of the respiratory system.

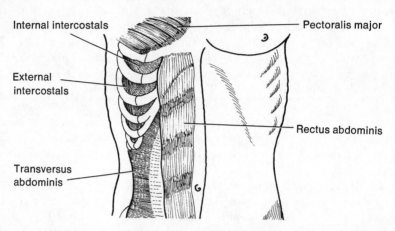

Internal intercostals

Pectoralis major

External intercostals

Rectus abdominis

Transversus abdominis

FIGURE 2-3. *Some of the muscles that control respiration.*

In Figure 2-3 some of the muscles that are active in the regulation of respiration are sketched. This view is more realistic than our first two diagrams. We have several different inspiratory muscles. The *intercostal* muscles, for example, which are interwoven with the ribs, can act to increase the pleural space by expanding the rib cage. The *external intercostals*, which are closer to the outside surface of the body, and most of the *internal intercostal* muscles are inspiratory muscles (Bouhuys, 1974). The *diaphragm* can move downwards to expand the pleural space. Part of the internal intercostals and the *abdominal* muscles can act to force air out of the lungs. They thus can act as expiratory muscles. These muscles are all used to maintain a steady pulmonary air pressure while we speak or sing. The term *pulmonary* here refers to the lungs. The pulmonary air pressure hence is the air pressure inside the lungs. The control pattern of the respiratory muscles that maintains a steady pulmonary air pressure while the lungs collapse during expiration is fairly complex. If we return to our simple balloon model the problem becomes fairly evident. Consider the results of the following simple exeriment that you easily can perform yourself. Blow up a balloon. When the balloon is full, release it. What happens? The balloon flies around. At the start it goes fairly fast but it rapidly slows down and finally falls to the floor.

The balloon is flying fast at first because the pressure of the air inside it is highest when the balloon is distended. As the balloon collapses, the air pressure falls and the balloon flies slower and slower. If you now perform some simple exercises you can sense the pulmonary control problems.

Start by taking a deep breath, i.e., a large inspiration. Put your hand a few inches in front of your open mouth and let your breath out while you relax. You will note that the air streaming out of your mouth has less force towards the end of the breath. This reflects the gradual release of the elastic recoil force of your lungs. Repeat the procedure a second time, wait until your breath ceases, and then push some more air out. You should be able to sense your rib cage and abdomen pulling inward. as you force some more air out of your lungs by means of your expiratory muscles.

Suppose that you now want to maintain a steady, moderate pulmonary air pressure throughout an expiration. How can you do this? The elastic recoil force of your lungs is high at the start of the expiration because that is when your lungs are most distended. The pulmonary air pressure generated by your lungs' elastic recoil therefore starts at a high value and then gradually falls as you let your breath out. You could augment the pulmonary air pressure at the end of the relaxed expiration by using your expiratory muscles at the end of the expiration, but what can you do to lower the pressure at the *start* of the expiration? What you do, in fact, every time you utter a fairly long sentence are the following muscular feats. You start by opposing the collapse of your lung "ballons" by using the inspiratory muscles to hold back the elastic lungs. As the lungs deflate, reducing the elastic recoil force, you gradually ease up on your inspiratory muscles. You then gradually switch to your expiratory muscles, maintaining an even pulmonary air pressure throughout the operation. Recent studies on the "programming" of the respiratory muscles during speech, which we will discuss in Chapter 6, indicate that speakers are unconsciously aware of these problems and that they unconsciously organize the control of their respiratory muscles in terms of the length of a sentence before they utter a sound.

The Larynx

The larynx is a device that transforms what would, in its absence, be a steady flow of air from the lungs into a series of puffs of air. The larynx is present in all terrestrial animals and derives from the valve that protected the lungs of primitive lungfish. Although it evolved from a device whose primary function was the protection of the lungs, the larynx is also adapted for phonation (Negus, 1949). The periodic series of puffs of air constitute the source of acoustic energy that characterizes phonation. The vocal calls of many air-breathing animals, even simple ones like frogs (Stuart, 1958), involve phonation. Sounds like the English vowels /a/ and

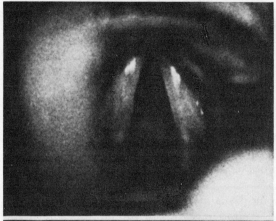

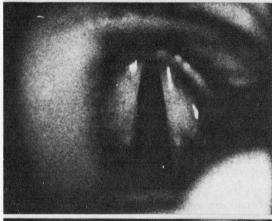

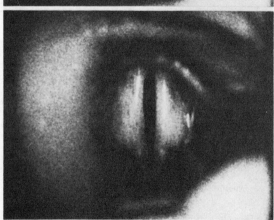

FIGURE 2-4. *Three frames from a high-speed movie showing the vocal cords gradually moving together before the start of phonation. A Fastax high-speed camera exposed these frames at a rate of 10,000 pictures per second (Lieberman, 1963). The posterior part of the vocal cords is oriented towards the bottom of each frame. The uppermost picture shows the vocal cords open wide for inspiration. The middle frame was exposed about 50 msec later. It shows the vocal cords partially closed. The bottom frame was exposed 50 msec later. It shows the vocal cords closed just before phonation started.*

/i/ usually are phonated, as are sounds like the English consonants /m/ and /v/. These sounds occur in the words *mama*, *meat*, and *vie*. The croak of a bullfrog is phonated, as is a sheep's bleat.

In Figure 2-4 a set of frames from a high-speed movie of the human larynx is presented. The photographs show the vocal cords gradually adducting, or moving together. The vocal cords consist of muscles, ligament on a cartilaginous support. Cartilage is a material that generally is rigid or semirigid. The vocal cords are complex structures that do not really resemble cords. The term *cords* was first used by the eighteenth century French scientist Ferrein (1741), who published one of the first theories that attempted to account for how phonation occurred. Ferrein thought that the vocal cords acted like the strings of a violin or a harp. His theory was not correct but his terminology, insofar as it has a functional derivation, is perhaps somewhat better than the term "vocal folds," which is often used to describe these complex structures. The opening between the vocal cords is called the *glottis*. Terms like "subglottal air pressure" therefore refer to the air pressure immediately below the glottal opening.

The first frame in Figure 2-4 shows the vocal cords at the moment when they began to adduct. The second photographic frame shows the same speaker's larynx about 50 msec later. (A millisecond or msec is 1/1000 of a second; it is a convenient unit of time for describing the events that occur during the production and perception of speech.) The third frame shows his vocal cords fully adducted at the start of phonation. Note that it took about 100 msec for this speaker's vocal cords to close before he could start phonation. The muscles of the larynx actively close the larynx, and tense the vocal cords before and during the act of phonation. They do not, however, furnish the power for phonation. That power comes from the airstream passing out from the lungs. The process of phonation involves an alternation of forces. The air flow out of the lungs first pushes the vocal cords apart, letting lots of air through. The vocal cords are then pulled together by the elastic properties of the stretched tissue of the vocal cords and the suction generated by the flow of air through the glottal constriction. The force generated by the airflow through the glottal constriction, the Bernoulli force, is similar to the suction that occurs when a bus passes close to a car at a high speed.

The pictures in Figure 2-5 show three frames for the same speaker from the same high-speed movie, but they show the vocal cords during phonation. Note that the change in opening is not as great and that it occurs very fast, within 7 msec. Phonation consists of the vocal cords rapidly opening and closing under the *control* of the laryngeal muscles, *powered* by the air flow from the lungs. The respiratory muscles can also exert control on phonation; we will go into the details later. If you purse your lips and blow through them you can simulate the process. The

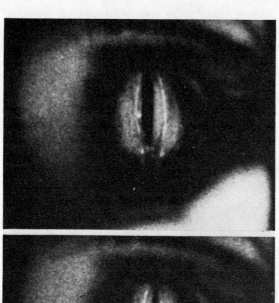

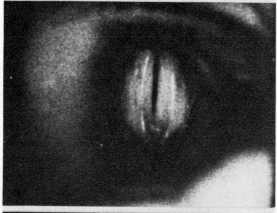

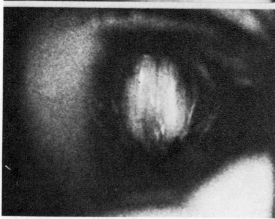

FIGURE 2-5. *Three frames from the same high-speed movie as Figure 2-4, exposed during phonation. The top frame shows the maximum opening during one cycle of phonation. The bottom frame, exposed 7 msec later, shows the vocal cords closed completely.*

force of air going out of your mouth furnishes the power that produces the sound. The sound comes from the acoustic energy generated by your lips interrupting the flow of air out of your mouth.

The Supralaryngeal Vocal Tract

Like the role of the larynx, the role of the supralaryngeal vocal tract in speech production was known in the eighteenth century. In 1779 Kratzenstein constructed a set of tubes that he supposed were similar to the shape of the human vocal tract during the production of the vowels of Russian. The Academy of Sciences of St. Petersburg, Russia, had offered its annual prize for explaining the physiological differences between the five vowels that occur in Russian. Kratzenstein (1780) used these tubes to filter the output of vibrating reeds and thereby "explained" the physiological differences that differentiated these vowels. In 1791 von Kempelen demonstrated his speech-synthesizing machine. The relationship between the sounds of speech and the supralaryngeal vocal tract is, in part, analogous to that between the pipes of an organ and musical notes. In a pipe organ the length and shape of each pipe (whether the pipe is open at both ends or closed at one end) determines the musical quality of the note produced by that pipe. The organ pipes act as acoustic filters that are interposed between the common source of sound, which can excite any particular pipe and the listener's ear. When we play a pipe organ we connect different pipes to the source. The production of human speech involves changing the shape and length of a "plastic" pipe, the airways of the human supralaryngeal vocal tract, as we talk. It would in principle be possible to make a pipe organ that had a single plastic pipe whose shape would change through the action of electrically controlled motors that distended or contracted the pipe. If we constructed such a pipe organ we would have a closer mechanical analog to the human supralaryngeal vocal tract.

We also can construct electrical analogs to the human supralaryngeal vocal tract. These analogs, which are the descendants of Kratzenstein's and von Kempelen's eighteenth century models, have yielded important insights on the nature of human speech and the vocal communications of many other animals. We will return to this topic.

The Neural Processing of Speech

Before we go on to introduce some of the physical and mathematical concepts that are necessary to explore the production and perception of speech in more detail, we should point out the match that exists between the production and the perception of sound. As we have already noted, frogs are among the simplest animals that produce calls by means of a laryngeal source. We never hear the laryngeal source directly because the frogs' supralaryngeal airways, like those of a human being, act as a filter. Electrophysiologic and behavioral experiments (Frishkopf and Goldstein, 1963; Capranica, 1965), which we will discuss in greater detail in Chapter 7, demonstrate that bullfrogs have "devices" in their auditory systems that are tuned to respond selectively to their mating calls. The acoustic characteristics of the mating calls are fully specified by the physiology of the frogs' larynges and supralaryngeal vocal tracts. Frogs thus have auditory systems that have, in part, been designed to respond to the vocal calls that frogs make. Similar though more complex systems may exist in human being. Since the late nineteenth century it has been evident that certain parts of the human brain appear to be especially involved with the production of speech (Broca, 1861) and the processing of language (Wernicke, 1874). Human beings also have a supralaryngeal vocal tract that differs from those of other living nonhuman primates as well as hominids like Neanderthal man who lived until comparatively recent times (Lieberman, 1975). These brief initial comments will be developed as we discuss the production and the perception of speech in relation to phonetic theory.

3
Basic Acoustics

THE principles that underlie the processes of speech production and speech perception are difficult to discuss without making use of the physical concepts of wave motion, periodicity, frequency, and amplitude. These concepts are, fortunately, fairly simple and straightforward. We will also discuss the use and the physical meaning of graphs as they relate to the description of physical measurements and we will conclude with an elementary description of the frequency analysis of acoustic signals and the properties of filters. Readers who have appropriate backgrounds in the physical sciences, mathematics, or engineering will undoubtedly find this chapter superfluous because we will introduce and explain these concepts by means of simple everyday examples, using a minimum of mathematical formalism. The examples that we will start with—the measurement of temperature, ocean waves, and so on—have nothing to do with the acoustics of speech but they illustrate in a direct manner the physical concepts that we want to develop.

Graphs and Physical Measurements

Let us start by considering the topic of graphs and their interpretation. Suppose that you were asked to read the temperature at 4-hour (hr) intervals from a thermometer mounted in the shade on the back of your house. You could record the temperature that you read at each 4-hr interval in the form of a list. The list, for example, might look like that in Table 3-1 for the 3-day period August 7 to August 9. An equivalent way of recording this temperature information would be to make a graph. The graph of Figure 3-1 is equivalent to Table 3-1.

The graph is organized as follows. The vertical scale records the temperature registered on the thermometer. The horizontal scale records the time at which the reading was made. The first observation of temperature of the graph of Figure 3-1 therefore must be interpreted as indicating a temperature of 80 degrees Fahrenheit at 9 A.M. The observation is marked by means of the black dot that lines up with 80 degrees on the vertical scales of the graph and with 9 A.M., August 7, on the horizontal scale. This fact is, of course, recorded in Table 3-1, which also indicates that the temperature at 9 A.M. on August 7 was 80 degrees. The next black dot on the graph indicates that the temperature was 90 degrees at 1 P.M. This fact is again indicated by the information in Table 3-1. The graph thus loses none of the information recorded in Table 3-1. If the graph did no more than display the information recorded in Table 3-1 in a different manner, there would be little point in bothering to make the graph. The graph, however, does much more. It allows us to derive

TABLE 3-1
LIST OF TEMPERATURES
RECORDED AT 4-HOUR
INTERVALS FOR 3 DAYS

Temperature (°F)	Time
80	9 A.M. August 7
90	1 P.M.
95	5 P.M.
80	9 P.M.
70	1 A.M. August 8
60	5 A.M.
82	9 A.M.
88	1 P.M.
94	5 P.M.
75	9 P.M.
60	1 A.M. August 9
55	5 A.M.
80	9 A.M.

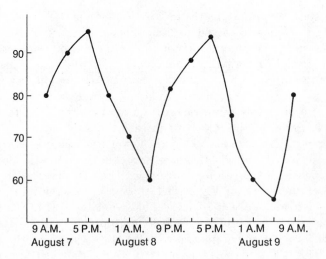

FIGURE 3-1. *Graph of temperatures plotted from data in Table* 3-1.

from the temperature readings interpretations that are not as apparent when we view the data in Table 3-1.

The first interpretation of the data on Table 3-1, implicit in the graph, is that the temperature changed gradually and in the same direction between temperature observations. The black dots that mark the actual temperature readings recorded are connected by a line and we, for example, would estimate that the temperature at 10 A.M. on August 7 was probably 82 degrees. Note that we did not really read the temperature at 10 A.M. We have derived this estimate of the temperature from the graph. We could have made the same estimate from the data of Table 3-1, but it is more apparent in the graph. The graph directly presents this "interpolation" between the actual temperature readings taken at 9 A.M., and at 1 P.M.

Waveforms and Periodicity

The visual pattern of this graph where we have plotted temperature as a *function of time* also throws into relief other interpretations of the temperature observations. The term function of time implies that there is a time dependency between the temperature readings and time. This is obviously true since the temperature readings were taken at 4-hr intervals. It is also true in a deeper sense since there is an over-all relationship or pattern between the temperature readings and the time of day. This is quite apparent from the shape, that is, the "form" of the graph of Figure 3-1. Note that the temperature goes up to a peak value at 5 P.M. each day and then descends to a minimum value at about 5 A.M. the next day. The temperature readings are not identical for the same hour of each day, but the pattern is quite similar. We can see from the graph that the temperature pattern over this interval of three days is *quasiperiodic*, or almost periodic. A periodic event is one that repeats itself. The periodicity or period of temperature cycle is 24 hours. In other words, the temperature variations tend to repeat themselves every 24 hours. It is obvious to everyone that the temperature variations are periodic, with a period of 24 hours, because the sun rises and sets each day. We do not need a graph to tell us this. However, the graph shows the periodicity in an obvious manner. The periodicity of the temperature variations tends to be buried in the data of Table 3-1.

Frequency

We can make graphs that present virtually any measurement. Graphs allow us to readily "see" periodic relationships. We could, for example, record the height of the water as it was measured against a ruler nailed to the side of one of the posts supporting the end of a pier at the Atlantic City beach. We could, in principle, record the height of the water every second and plot it, that is, record it on a graph. Figure 3-2 is a graph of

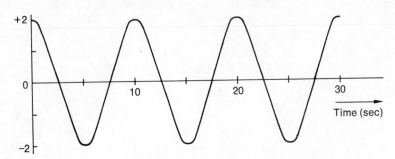

FIGURE 3-2. *Graph of water height showing 10-sec period of the waveform.*

these hypothetical measurements. Note that the height of the water *at this fixed point in space—the end of the pier*, is plotted as a function of time. The period of the *waveform* refers to the shape of the plotted data on the graph. The period is 10 seconds (sec), because the waveform repeats itself every 10 sec. A complete cycle from maximum to minimum, and back to maximum height occurs every 10 sec. In 1 minute (min) the waveform would repeat itself six times. If we wanted to note how often this waveform repeated itself, we could say that it had a period of 10 sec or we could alternately say that it repeated itself with a frequency of 6 cycles per minute. The term frequency thus refers to the number of times that a periodic event repeats itself for some standard interval of time. An ocean wave that had a period of 30 sec, that is, 1/2 min, would have a frequency of 2 cycles per minute. An ocean wave that had a period of 1/4 min would have a frequency of 4 cycles per minute.

Algebraically, periodicity and frequency have the relationship

$$f = \frac{1}{T}$$

where f = frequency and T = the duration of the period. An event that had a period of 1/50 sec would have a frequency of 50 cycles per second, an event that had a period of 0.01 sec (1/100 sec in decimal notation) would have a frequency of 100 cycles per sec. We will encounter the term *Hertz* (abbreviated Hz) as a measure of frequency when we discuss sound waves. A frequency of 1 Hz is, by definition, equal to 1 cycle per second, 50 Hz to 50 cycles per second, etc.

Amplitude-Sinusoidal Waves

Note that the vertical scale on the waveform plotted in Figure 3-2 has both positive and negative values. The value 0 in this particular graph corresponds to the height of the water in the absence of any waves.

The positive values thus represent water heights above this zero line, and negative values represent water height below this zero line. Note that the high and low points for each cycle of the waveform in Figure 3-2 have the same numerical value, 2 ft. The waveform plotted in Figure 3-2 is a sinusoidal waveform. Its *amplitude*, that is, the deviation of its peak and its minimum from the zero line, is 2 ft. The amplitude of a wave essentially is a measure of its size. The amplitude is independent of the frequency of the wave. The greater the amplitude, the "bigger" the wave. One can have either a big or a small ocean wave coming towards the beach at the same frequency.

The waveform plotted in Figure 3-2 is, as we have noted, *sinusoidal*. Sinusoidal waves, which always have this smooth shape, are extremely important mathematical constructs because it is possible to analyze any complex periodic waveform in terms of a set of sinusoidal waveforms. This is extremely useful since the behavior of devices like organ pipes or the human vocal tract can be calculated for sinusoidal sound sources. Since we may analyze any complex periodic wave in terms of sinusoids, we can thereby predict the response of a device like the human vocal tract to any periodic waveform. We will discuss these procedures later in this chapter. For the moment we will simply note that a sinusoidal waveform can be completely specified by noting its frequency, amplitude, and phase.

Phase-Sinusoidal Waves

The waveform plotted in Figure 3-2 had an amplitude of $+2$ ft when we started to measure it at $t = 0$ sec. It had an amplitude of -2 ft after 5 sec. Suppose that we had measured a wave that started off at $t = 0$ sec with an amplitude of -2 ft, and this second wave had exactly the same amplitude and period as the wave we actually measured. How could we convey this information? We could, of course, make a graph of the second wave. In Figure 3-3 the graph of this second wave is plotted. Note that this second wave could be obtained by shifting the wave plotted

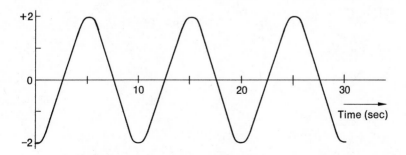

FIGURE 3-3. *Wave of Figure 3-2 shifted in phase.*

in Figure 3-2 1/2 period forward. In other words, the wave in Figure 3-3 is equivalent to that of Figure 3-2 shifted by half of its period. The two waves are by definition 1/2 period *out of phase*.

It is usual to quantify phase differences in terms of degrees. If we divide the total period into 360 degrees, then 1/2 period equals 180 degrees and the two waves plotted in Figure 3-2 and 3-3 are 180 degrees out of phase. The human auditory system is not very sensitive to phase. Slight shifts in the phase of a waveform are not usually perceptible, although large shifts can be heard. Telephone systems traditionally have been designed with this tolerance in mind because it simplifies some of the electronics and saves money. (In recent years the introduction of electronic data transmission devices that, unlike the human auditory system, are sensitive to phase differences has made changes in telephone system's design necessary.)

Wave Motion—Propagation Velocity

Wave motions are characterized by the transfer of energy. It is obvious that energy is transmitted by an ocean wave when it hits you. The motion of an ocean wave can easily be observed as it sweeps in toward the beach. The crest of the wave moves in with a certain speed. This speed is called the propagation velocity of the wave. The propagation velocity of an ocean wave could be determined by observing its crest. In Figure 3-4 we have sketched the crest of an ocean wave at two instants of time separated by 10 sec. We could have obtained these data by taking two flash pictures of the wave at night. The horizontal scale in these pictures, which are really graphs of the height of the water as a function of

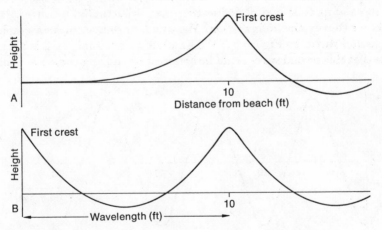

FIGURE 3-4. *Propagation of an ocean wave.* (*A*) *At first measurement.* (*B*) *10 sec later.*

distance, is the distance measured in feet from the edge of the beach. The vertical scale is the height of the wave. Note that the crest that is at 10 ft in Figure 3-4A is at 0 ft in Figure 3-4B. The velocity of propagation is therefore 1 ft/sec.

The fact that the crest has moved 10 ft in the 10 sec that separate the graphs of Figures 3-4A and 3-4B does not mean that any molecule of water actually moved 10 ft towards the beach. The energy in the wave has moved forward through the medium of the water. The wave that hits you at the beach at Atlantic City, New Jersey, may, for example, have started from the coast of Portugal, but no molecule of "Portuguese water" will touch you.

It is fairly simple to see the distinction between the transfer of energy in a wave and the motion of the particles of the medium. One traditional demonstration makes use of three coins placed on a table. If the coins are placed in a row and the coin on one end of the row is flipped against the center coin, the energy of the collision will be transmitted to the coin on the other end of the line. The center coin won't move very far. The first coin obviously won't move around the center coin. The energy derived from the motion of the first coin will, however, be transmitted through the middle coin to the last coin.

The transmission of energy in a sound wave is rather like the transmission of energy through the row of coins. The molecules of gas that form the atmosphere transmit forces as they collide with each other. The sound that you hear has been transmitted by a wave that has exerted a pressure on your eardrums. In a near vacuum, as in outer space or the moon, where there aren't any gas molecules, sound cannot be transmitted. The pressure that a sound wave exerts is no different from the pressure that is exerted on your finger when you press it down against the open end of an open water faucet. The water actually pushes against your finger. It exerts a certain force per unit area. A sound wave exerts a force against your eardrums.

In Figure 3-4B the crest of a second cycle of the wave has been drawn. Note that the distance between the two crests of the periodic wave motion is 10 ft. The wavelength of the periodic wave is thus 10 ft. The *wavelength* is, by definition, the distance between recurring events in a wave motion distributed over distance. The wavelength is *not* the same as the period. The wavelength can be seen when a waveform is plotted as a function of distance *at some particular instant of time*. Wavelength, frequency, and the propagation velocity are all related. Algebraically the following relationship holds:

$$\lambda f = c$$

where $\lambda =$ the wavelength, $f =$ the frequency of the wave, and $c =$ the propagation velocity.

The relationship between wavelength, frequency, and the propagation velocity is not difficult to visualize if we return to the simple case of ocean waves. If the wavelength in Figure 3-4B is 10 ft and the velocity of propagation is 1 ft/sec, then a person standing at a fixed point, e.g., the edge of the beach at the waterline, will be hit by the crest of a new wave at 10-sec intervals. The periodicity of the wave motion as noted by the observer standing at this fixed location, therefore, will be 10 sec. The frequency of the wave motion will be equal to 1/10 sec, or 0.1 Hz. We would arrive at the same frequency if we solved for frequency using the equation $f = c/\lambda$. This is, of course, to be expected since the algebraic equation is a formal statement that describes the physical world.

It is important to remember that the wavelength and period of a wave are quite different quantities. Much confusion can arise because the period of a wave is measured along the horizontal scale of a graph when a wave is plotted *as a function of time*. The wavelength also is measured along the horizontal scale of a graph when a wave is plotted *as a function of distance*. In one case the horizontal axis is measuring the course of time at a fixed location. In the other case the hozintal scale is measuring the amplitude of the wave along the dimension of distance for a particular instant of time.

Complex and Sinusoidal Waveforms—Fourier Analysis

At first glance there would appear to be very little in common between sinusoidal waveforms like that plotted in Figure 3-2 and the sawtooth crested waveform plotted in Figure 3-4. A fundamental principle of mathematics, however, shows that it is always possible to analyze a "complex" periodic waveform like that of Figure 3-4 into a set of sinusoidal waveforms. Any periodic waveform, no matter how complex it is, can be closely approximated by adding together a number of sinusoidal waveforms. The mathematical procedure of *Fourier analysis* tells us what particular set of sinusoids go together to make up a particular complex waveform. We won't go into the details of Fourier analysis except to note the important fact that the set of sinusoids that one adds together to approximate a particular complex waveform are harmonically related. What does this mean?

Fundamental Frequency

In Figure 3-5 we have plotted a complex waveform and its first two sinusoidal Fourier components. All three graphs have the same horizontal time scale and same vertical amplitude scale. The complex waveform could, for example, be the sound waveform recorded by a microphone monitoring a loudspeaker. Note that the complex waveform is *not*

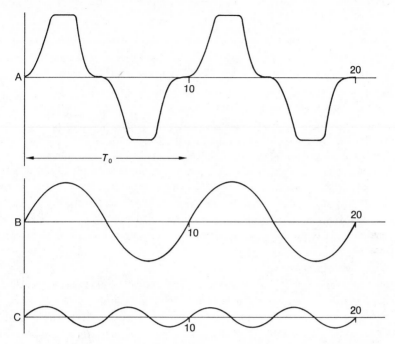

FIGURE 3-5. (*A*) *A complex waveform.* (*B*) *and* (*C*) *Its first two sinusoidal Fourier components.*

sinusoidal. Its leading edge, for example, rises sharply; it has a flat top, etc. It is, however, a periodic waveform and the duration of its period is, as Figure 3-5 shows, 10 msec. As noted in an earlier chapter, milliseconds are convenient units for the measurement of the periods of audible sound waves. The first two sinusoidal components are plotted beneath the complex waveform. The first component's period, T_0, is equal to the period T of the complex waveform. This is always the case. This period, which is the time that it takes for the complex waveform to repeat itself, is called the fundamental period. The frequency of the first component is called the fundamental frequency. The symbol f_0 is usually used to represent the fundamental frequency. Algebraically:

$$f_0 = \frac{1}{T_0} = \frac{1}{T}$$

Harmonics

The period of the next possible component is always equal to one half of the period of the fundamental. Period T_1 of wave B on Figure 3-5 thus is equal to 5 msec. The frequency of wave B is twice that of the fundamental frequency since f_1, the frequency of wave B, must equal

$$f_1 = \frac{1}{T_1} = \frac{\dfrac{1}{T_0}}{2} = \frac{2}{T_0} = 2f_0$$

These two sinusoidal components, if they are added together, approximate the complex waveform. To achieve a better approximation of the complex waveform it would be necessary to add other components that had still higher frequencies to the sum of the first two sinusoids. The frequencies of these higher sinusoidal components would all be harmonically related to the fundamental frequency. The frequency of the third sinusoidal component, for example, would be equal to $3f_0$; the frequency of the fourth component would be $4f_0$; etc. The frequency of the nth component would be equal to nf_0.

The fundamental frequency of the complex wave of Figure 3-5 thus is 100 Hz. The frequency of the second sinusoidal component is 200 Hz; the third component, which is not plotted would be 300 Hz; etc. The components are said to be *harmonically* related since they are integral multiples of the fundamental frequency. Sinusoids, when heard in isolation, are perceived as "pure tones." The sound produced by a tuning fork or certain bird calls (Greenewalt, 1968) are simple sinusoids. The higher the fundamental frequency, the higher the perceived tone is. Adult human beings generally can perceive sounds from 20 to about 15,000 Hz. That means that human listeners can hear the sinusoidal components of complex sounds for frequencies between 20 and 15,000 Hz. A sudden "sharp" sound, like a door slamming, may have higher sinusoidal components, but we can't hear them. Children and many adults can hear frequencies higher than 15,000 Hz. The upper limit is generally about 20,000 Hz, but it falls with age. The meaningful sinusoidal components that constitute human speech are, for the most part, below 7,000 Hz; hence, telephone systems that transmit frequencies no higher than 5,000 Hz are adequate for most purposes (Flanagan, 1972).

Spectrum

In the Fourier analysis of a complex waveform the amplitude of each sinusoidal component depends on the shape of the particular complex wave. It therefore is necessary to keep track of the amplitude of each component if one wants to specify a complex wave in terms of its sinusoidal components. We can conveniently keep track of the frequencies and amplitudes of the sinusoidal components that go together to make up a complex wave by means of graphs like that in Figure 3-6.

The horizontal axis is the frequency scale; the vertical axis is the amplitude scale. The amplitude of each component is represented by a

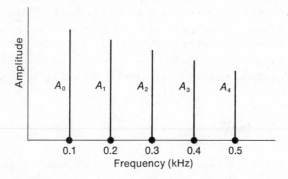

FIGURE 3-6. *Graph of a spectrum.*

line at the frequency of each sinusoidal component. The units plotted on the vertical axis would most likely be units of sound pressure when sound waves are analyzed. This type of graph is known as a graph of the spectrum. We have plotted the amplitudes of the first two sinusoidal components shown in Figure 3-5 as well as the next three higher components. Note that the graph consists of vertical lines at each sinusoidal frequency. This signifies that there is sound energy present only at these discrete frequencies. This type of spectrum is sometimes called a *line* spectrum. It differs from spectra that have energy distributed over a broad, continuous range of frequencies. We have not kept track of the parameter called *phase* that we would need if we were actually to add up a number or sinusoidal components to make up a particular complex waveform. Phase, as we noted, is not particularly important in the perception of the production of speech. The conceptual value of representing a complex waveform as a spectrum will be apparent in Chapter 4.

Amplitude and Frequency Scales for Speech

The perceptually relevant metric for the amplitude of a speech wave is, as we've noted, its pressure. Pressures are always measured in terms of a force per unit area. If you look at a gas station's tire pressure gauge it will be calibrated in pounds per square inch. The metric units of dynes per square centimeter are by convention the basic units for speech signals. However, it is rare to see the amplitude of a speech signal directly measured in these units. The signal's amplitude will instead be given in decibels, abbreviated db. The decibel is a logarithmic unit. Logarithmic units relate quantities in terms of the "power" ratios. The logarithmic ratio between a sound pressure of 1000 dynes and one of 10 dynes would be equal to 2 if we took the log to the base ten, i.e., $1000/10 = 100$ which equals 10^2. The logarithm is the power 2, the number of times that the base, 10, would have to be multiplied by itself. It is obvious that a logarithmic scale would be useful if we had to make a graph of a function that encompassed a great range. If a sound pressure varied over a range of 10 to 1,000 dynes it would be difficult to plot the range on any reasonable sized paper. If we convert the pressures to a logarithmic scale, the graph becomes feasible. The decibel is defined in terms of a fixed air pressure reference, it is equal to

$$20 \log_{10} \frac{P}{0.0002 \text{ dynes per square centimeter}},$$

where P = the pressure measured. It is not necessary to memorize this number because relative values are what is usually important. The decibel scale is a convenient scale for the measurement of sound. Some useful indices to what various decibel measurements "mean" perceptually can follow from the following examples of average sound pressures:

A "quiet" average room—30 db

A noisy average room—70 db

A few inches in front of someone shouting—80 db

"Inside" a rock band—100 db

Ten ft to the side of the rear of a jet engine at full power—115 db

A sound perceived as being roughly twice as loud as another is usually about 6 db greater. The decibel scale is a more suitable scale in terms of perceived loudness than a linear scale. The relative "loudness" of sounds is roughly in accord with a logarithmic or "power" scale to the human auditory system (Flanagan, 1972). There are differences between a logarithmic and power scale but these differences are not particularly germane to our understanding of the perception of speech.

Filters

In the next chapter we will discuss speech production in terms of the source-filter theory. Before we discuss this theory, which involves an understanding of some of the specific properties of acoustic filters, we'll briefly introduce some of the general properties of filters. Perhaps the simplest example of a filter is a sieve or strainer, so we'll return to our hypothetical demonstration site at the beach where we looked at ocean waves. This time we'll stay on the sand for our examples and examine some of the general properties of filters as they are exemplified in the properties of beach sieves.

In Figure 3-7 the uppermost sketch shows what we would see if we looked down at the top of a child's sieve. We would see a pattern of holes, each with approximately the same diameter. Let's call this diameter d_h, the average hole diameter. Obviously the holes will not all have

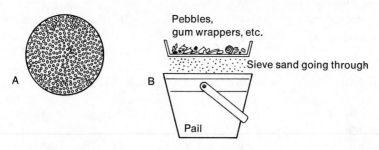

FIGURE 3-7. *Sieve as mechanical filter.* (*A*) *Top view of sieve of average hole diameter* d_h. (*B*) *Side view of sieve in action.*

exactly the same diameter. Children's beach sieves are not precision-machined to have holes of uniform diameter. The next lower sketch on Figure 3-7 shows the sieve in action.

Sand particles of diameter less than that of the holes in the sieve flow through the sieve into the child's pail below. Larger objects like pebbles, candy wrappers, and sand particles of large diameter are left in the sieve. The sieve is acting as a mechanical *filter* that affects the transfer of particles into the pail. If the sieve were not placed above the beach pail all of the large-diameter particles, pebbles, and candy wrappers would have entered the pail. We can quantitatively describe the filtering properties of the sieve placed above the pail by means of the graph in Figure 3-8.

The graph plots the *transfer function* of the sieve. The vertical scale denotes the per cent of material that will pass through, i.e., transfer through, the filter. The horizontal scale denotes the size of the particle. The

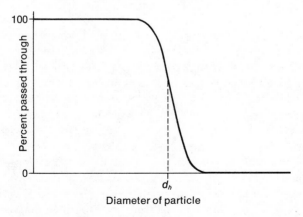

FIGURE 3-8. *Transfer function of sieve as "small-diameter pass through" filter.*

graph thus shows that 100 per cent, i.e., all, particles that are very much smaller than the average hole diameter d_h will pass through the sieve. Zero per cent of the very large objects will pass through. Particles that have diameters close to the average hole diameter d_h may or may not pass through. It will depend on whether a particular particle is above one of the smaller or one of the bigger holes. Some particles that are larger than the average hole diameter will get through if they happen to be positioned above a hole whose diameter is also larger than the average diameter d_h. Some particles that have smaller diameters likewise won't get through if they are positioned above smaller holes. The filter thus does not abruptly "cut off" the flow of sand at some exact particle diameter; its transfer function instead exhibits a gradual cut off.

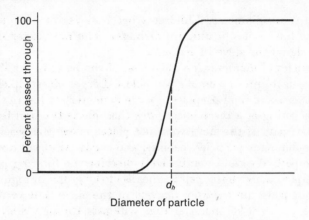

FIGURE 3-9. *Transfer function of sieve as "large-diameter pass through" filter.*

The mechanical filtering system exemplified by the sieve and pail constitute what we would term a "small-diameter pass through" filter. Small particles will go through; bigger particles will be trapped above. We could, using the same pail and filter, collect the material that was trapped in the filter. If we periodically collected the material trapped in the top of the sieve and put that material in the pail, discarding the small particles that flowed through the sieve, we would have a "large-diameter pass through" filter with the transfer function sketched in Figure 3-9. The same sieve and pail permit us to filter for either large- or small-diameter particles depending on how we arrange them.

We obviously could filter out a small range of particle sizes by sequentially using two sieves that had different average hole diameters. If we first placed the sieve with the larger average hole diameter above the pail, collected the material that accumulated in the pail, and then poured this material through the sieve with the smaller diameter we would be left with particles in the sieve that were restricted to a small range or "band" of diameters. The transfer function plotted in Figure 3-10 quantitatively represents the result of this sequential process for a case where the average hole diameters of the two sieves are close, although not identical, in size. Note that maximum transfer through the complete filter system occurs about particle diameter d_c and that there exists a range of particle sizes d_w, for which most, e.g., 70 per cent will get through the filter system to be collected.

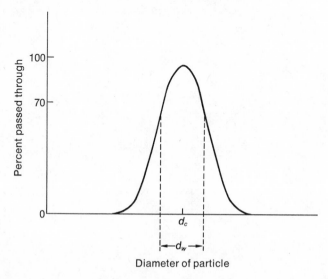

FIGURE 3-10. *Transfer function of sieve as "band pass" filter.*

We have presented this discussion of the filtering properties of beach sieves and pails because the supralaryngeal vocal tract—the air passages of the mouth, pharynx, and nose—acts as an adjustable acoustic filter that allows certain bands of wavelengths of sound to pass through. Wavelength sensitive filters are analogous to the particle diameter "band pass" filter whose transfer function is sketched in Figure 3-10.

We can describe the properties of the acoustic filters formed by the supralaryngeal vocal tract by noting the wavelengths at which maximum sound energy will pass through as well as the range of wavelengths that will mostly get through (the acoustic analogs of d_c and d_w.) The product of the wavelength and frequency of a wave is equal to the propagation velocity (the algebraic relationship $\lambda f = c$) and the velocity of sound is constant for normal atmospheric conditions. It therefore is appropriate to describe the transfer function of the supralaryngeal vocal tract filter in terms of frequency. The *center frequencies* at which maximum sound energy will pass through the filter systems are called *formant* frequencies. We will discuss the supralaryngeal vocal tract filter in the following chapters because the controlled variation of formant frequencies is perhaps the single most important factor in human speech.

4

Source-Filter Theory of Speech Production

I N this chapter we will discuss the basic aspects of the source-filter theory of speech production that we introduced in Chapter 2. In the chapters that follow we will consider the acoustic characteristics that differentiate many of the sounds of speech and the articulatory gestures that underlie speech. The source-filter theory makes it possible to relate the acoustic and articulatory levels in a quantitative and coherent manner.

The Laryngeal Source

Let us start by considering the production of a *voiced* sound, i.e., one in which the vocal cords interrupt the air flow from the lungs, producing *phonation*. The larynx can serve as a source of sound energy. It can produce a periodic wave through the process of phonation, as for example, in the words *mama* and *able*. It can also generate a "noise" source, e.g., the source during the [h] sound of *Hop!* The source of sound energy when we whisper is the noise generated through air turbulence at the glottal constriction. The vocal cords do not have to move during a whisper. Many of the sounds of speech involve sources of sound that are generated through turbulent air flow through constrictions at other parts of the airways of the vocal tract. However, it will be useful to begin our discussion of the source-filter theory of speech production by considering voiced sounds in which the larynx produces a periodic source.

In Figure 4-1 we have plotted three cycles of a possible pattern of periodic air flow from the larynx. Note that the period of the complex waveform is 10 msec. The fundamental frequency of this periodic glottal air flow is 100 Hz. (The term *glottal* refers to the air flow through the opening between the two vocal cords, which is called the glottis.) The spectrum of this glottal air flow is plotted in Figure 4-2. Note that the glottal spectrum shows that the waveform of Figure 4-1 has energy at the fundamental frequency (100 Hz = 0.1 kHz) and at higher harmonics. Note that the amplitude of the harmonics gradually falls. We have not drawn the complete spectrum, but there is perceptible acoustic energy to at least 3,000 Hz present in the typical glottal air flow of a male speaker

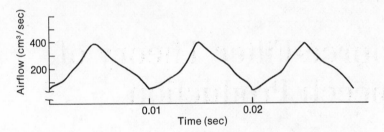

FIGURE 4-1. *Three cycles of a waveform typical of the air flow through the glottis during phonation.*

phonating at a fundamental frequency of 100 Hz. The vertical amplitude scale is a decibel (db) scale.

The rate at which the vocal cords open and close during phonation determines the period and, hence, the fundamental frequency of the glottal air flow. Within broad limits a speaker can vary this rate, which is determined by the shape and mass of the moving vocal cords, the tension of the laryngeal muscles, and the air pressure generated by the lungs. Adult male speakers can phonate at fundamental frequencies that range between 80 and 300 Hz. Adult females and children normally phonate

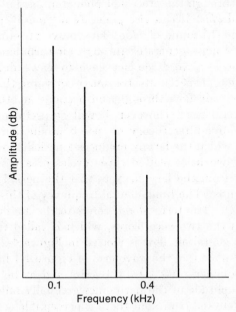

FIGURE 4-2. *Spectrum of typical glottal air flow.*

at fundamental frequencies that range up to about 500 Hz. The longer vocal cords of adult males, which are a consequence of secondary sexual dimorphism in *Homo sapiens*, yield a lower range of fundamental frequencies. (The thyroid cartilage grows differentially during puberty in males, cf. Kirchner, 1970, pp. 15–17.)

The perceptual interpretation of fundamental frequency is *pitch*. When a human speaker sings a sustained vowel sound and changes the fundamental frequency of phonation, we perceive the difference as a change in pitch. Musical performances consist, in part, of singing at controlled, specified fundamental frequencies. If the singer sings at the wrong fundamental frequency, the performance is marred since we will perceive it as being "offpitch." Controlled changes in fundamental frequency also can be used for linguistic purposes. In many languages, for example, in Chinese, the same vowels and consonants will signify different words when different fundamental frequency patterns are employed. In most human languages controlled changes in fundamental frequency at the end of a breath-group also can signify differences in the sentence's meaning, e.g., whether the sentence is a question or a statement (Lieberman, 1967; Atkinson, 1973; Collier, 1975). The vocalizations of many other animals also appear to involve modulations of fundamental frequency. The controlled variation of fundamental frequency is therefore one of the phonetic parameters that may be employed in speech communication.

The Supralaryngeal Filter

We all know that a trained singer can sing an entire sequence of vowel sounds at the same pitch. The differences in vowel quality are independent of the activity of the larynx. They are the consequences of changes in the shape of the supralaryngeal airway. During the production of human speech the shape of the supralaryngeal airway continually changes. The supralaryngeal airway always acts as an acoustic filter, suppressing the transfer of sound energy at certain frequencies, letting maximum energy through at other frequencies. The frequencies at which local energy maxima may pass through the supralaryngeal air passages are called *formant frequencies*. The formant frequencies are determined by the damped resonances of the supralaryngeal vocal tract, which acts as an acoustic filter. Vowels, like [a], [i], [æ], and [ʌ], owe their phonetic quality to their different formant frequencies.

In Figure 4-3 we have plotted the "transfer function" of the supralaryngeal airway for the vowel [ə] (the first vowel in the word *about*). This is the idealized supralaryngeal filter function for a speaker having a supralaryngeal vocal tract of approximately 17 cm. The length of the supralaryngeal vocal tract for this vowel would be measured along the centerline of the air passage from the lips to the glottal opening of the

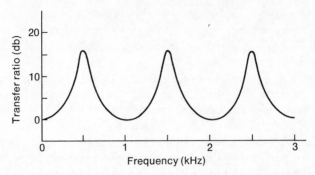

FIGURE 4-3. *Transfer function of the supralaryngeal vocal tract for the vowel* [ə]. *For our purposes, the term* transfer function *is equivalent to* filter *function. Note the locations of the formant frequencies at 0.5, 1.5, and 2.5 kHz.*

larynx, excluding the nasal cavity (Fant, 1960). The formant frequencies for this vowel are 500, 1,500, and 2,500 Hz. The symbols F_1, F_2, and F_3 are usually used to denote the formant frequencies of speech sounds. F_1 denotes the lowest formant frequency, which is 500 Hz in this example: F_2, the second formant, 1,500 Hz in this example. The formant frequencies are essentially the center frequencies of the supralaryngeal vocal tract acting as a complex filter that lets maximum sound energy through in several bands of frequency. The frequency bands of each formant have an appreciable bandwidth, from 60 to 100 Hz. Other vowels would have different formant frequencies. The formant frequencies of the vowel [i], for example, would be about 240 Hz for F_1, 2,200 Hz for F_2, and 3,200 Hz for F_3 for this particular speaker. The first three formants of vowels play the major role in specifying these sounds. Higher formants exist, but they are not necessary for the perception of vowel differences. The bandwidths of the formants of different vowels also do not markedly distinguish different vowels (Fant, 1960; Flanagan, 1972).

In Figure 4-4 we have plotted the spectrum that would result if the laryngeal source with the spectrum plotted in Figure 4-2 were filtered by the transfer function plotted in Figure 4-3. The resulting spectrum would describe the speech signal at the end of the air passages of the vocal tract. Note that sound energy would be present at each of the harmonics of the glottal source, but the amplitude of each harmonic would be a function of *both* the filter function and the amplitude of the particular harmonic of the glottal source. A human listener hearing a speech signal having the spectrum plotted in Figure 4-4 would recognize the signal as a token of the vowel [ə] that had a fundamental frequency of 100 Hz.

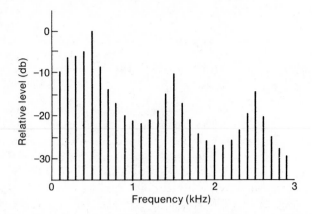

FIGURE 4-4. *The spectrum that would result if the transfer function plotted in Figure 4-3 were "excited" by the glottal source plotted in Figure 4-2. The sound is the vowel* [ə].

In Figure 4-5 we have plotted the speech waveform that corresponds to the spectrum of Figure 4-4. Figure 4-5 is a plot of the air pressure of the sound wave as a function of time. Note that this waveform resembles the glottal source waveform that was plotted in Figure 4-1 only insofar as it has the same period, 10 msec. The interposition of the supralaryngeal vocal tract has modified the glottal waveform and we can see that the laryngeal source is only one factor in the production of speech. The source-filter theory of speech, which formally takes account of these two factors, the source and the filter, was first proposed by Johannes Müller (1848). It has been developed on a quantitative basis in recent years. Studies like those of Chiba and Kajiyama (1941), Fant

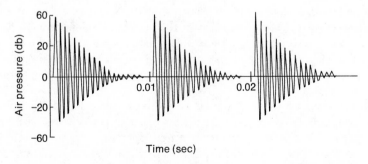

FIGURE 4-5. *Speech waveform as measured by a microphone sensitive to air pressure variations. The human ear is itself sensitive to air pressure variations.*

(1960), and Stevens and House (1955) make possible a quantitative prediction of the filtering effects of particular configurations of the supralaryngeal air passages.

The Perception of Fundamental and Formant Frequencies

The perception of speech in human beings appears to involve specialized neural mechanisms. The perception of fundamental frequency by the human brain appears to be made primarily through waveform measurements that derive the period (Flanagan, 1972). The neural procedures used in making these measurements appear to be fairly complex and they can be simulated only through the use of elaborate computer programs (Gold, 1962). The computer program has to "know" (i.e., the programmer must insert subroutines that take account of) the variation in the rate of change of fundamental frequency that normally occur from one period to the next (Lieberman, 1962). The computer program must also "know" how different supralaryngeal vocal tract transfer functions will affect the speech waveform; it must "know" the probable variations in the glottal spectrum that can occur at the onset and end of phonation as the larynx responds to transient conditions in air flow, air pressure, and laryngeal muscle tension. Despite the persistent application of the most advanced engineering techniques, a satisfactory "pitch extractor" is still not available although there have been important commercial applications since 1937 (Flanagan, 1972).

The procedures that the brains of human listeners use in deriving the formant frequencies of speech from the acoustic signal appear to be even more complex. These perceptual "recognition procedures" must involve the analysis of the speech signal in terms of its spectrum, but they go far beyond the simple examination of a spectrum for local energy maxima. The formant frequencies plotted in Figure 4-4, for example, are manifested as local energy maxima at 500, 1,500, and 2,500 Hz. This is, however, fortuitous, because the fundamental frequency of the glottal source was 100 Hz, which placed harmonics at each of the formant frequencies. A human listener who heard a speech signal having the spectrum plotted in Figure 4-6 would also say that it was a token of the schwa vowel [ə].

Note that the listener would have to deduce the location of the formant frequencies from a spectrum that actually lacked peaks at the formants. Formant frequencies are not always directly manifested in the acoustic signal that has been filtered by the supralaryngeal vocal tract. The formant frequencies are really the frequencies at which the supralaryngeal filter *would* let maximum energy through (Hermann, 1894). If the glottal source lacks acoustic energy at a particular formant frequency then

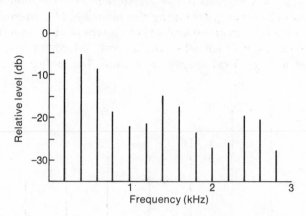

FIGURE 4-6. *Spectrum of the sound* [ə] *produced with a different fundamental frequency of phonation. The speech signal still has the phonetic quality of the vowel* [ə] *although it has a different fundamental frequency than the* [ə] *whose spectrum is plotted in Figure 4-4.*

there will be *no* acoustic energy in the output signal at that frequency. The graphs plotted in Figure 4-7 illustrate this point. The uppermost graph is the line spectrum of a glottal source with a fundamental of 500 Hz. This is a possible fundamental frequency for many children and some adult women. The second graph is a transfer function of the vowel [i]. The formant frequencies are appropriate for an adult female (Peterson and Barney, 1952). The lowest graph is a plot of the speech signal that results from the filtering of the 500 Hz fundamental frequency source by the [i] filter. Note that there is no energy at the formant frequencies marked by the circled X's in the bottom graph.

The electronic instrument that is most often used for the analysis of speech, the sound spectrograph, will not "show" formant frequencies for signals like the one represented in the bottom graph of Figure 4-7 (Koenig et al., 1946). In contrast, human listeners do not appear to have any difficulty in deriving formant frequencies from signals like this, despite the paucity of acoustic information. Human listeners, for example, do not make any more errors when they are asked to identify short syllables when these stimuli are produced by high-pitched female voices than when these stimuli are produced by low-pitched male voices (Moslin and Cowper, 1975). Human listeners appear to derive formant frequencies through a procedure that makes use of their unconscious, internalized knowledge of the mechanisms and physics of speech production. It is possible to program digital computers to "recognize" vowels using this sort of procedure (Bell et al., 1961). The computer program has access to a memory in which the acoustic consequences of various possible vocal tract shapes are stored. The computer systematically generates internal spectra using this memory. The internally generated spectra are then matched against the spectra of the incoming speech signal. The process does not select the individual formant frequencies on the basis of a single local energy maximum, but rather on the match

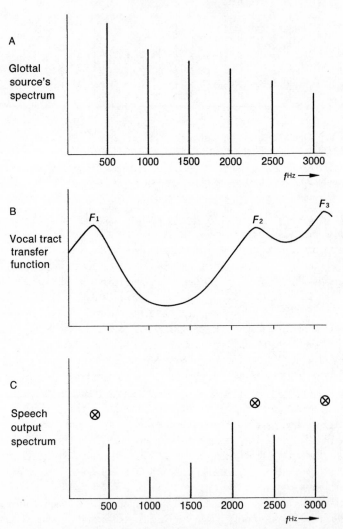

FIGURE 4-7. (A) Spectrum of glottal source. (B) Transfer function for vowel [i]. (C) Spectrum of the speech signal that would result if transfer function (B) were excited by glottal source (A). Note that the formant frequencies of the transfer function are not directly manifested in the speech signal by acoustic energy at the points labeled X.

between the total spectrum of the incoming speech signal and the internally generated signal specified by all three formant frequencies. The computer program is relatively complex because it must model the performance of human listeners who appear to have neural mechanisms that are especially adapted to the perception of speech. The computer program, for example, "knows" that the relative amplitude of formant peaks for vowels is determined by the frequency value of each formant frequency and that the over-all shape of the spectrum is thus largely specified by the positions of the formants (Fant, 1956).

Speech scientists are able to use instruments like the sound spectrograph to derive formant frequencies by making use of their knowledge of where the formant frequencies of various sounds *should* be. In other words, they make use of the knowledge that has been acquired by looking at a great many speech samples when they interpret a particular sound spectrogram. Despite this prior knowledge it is very difficult to determine the formant frequencies of a signal like that plotted in Figure 4-7 with a conventional sound spectrograph, although a human listener will have no difficulty in recognizing the vowel. We will return to this topic when we discuss the analysis of speech and the sound spectrograph in Chapter 5.

Formant Frequency Calculation

We have stated that the shape and length of the supralaryngeal air passages cause them to act as an acoustic filter. Although the calculations that are necessary to determine the transfer function that corresponds to a particular supralaryngeal vocal tract shape often are complex and difficult to follow, the relationship between the vocal tract shape and the formant frequencies is straightforward and simple in some cases. It is useful to get an appreciation or "feel" for the problem from these simple cases since the general principles that govern the relationship between vocal tract shape and formant frequencies apply for both simple and complex vocal tract shapes. The physical basis of the relationship between the formant frequencies and the shape and size of the supralaryngeal vocal tract is perhaps easiest to see for the unnasalized vowel [ə].

The vowel [ə] called schwa (the first vowel in the word *about*) is perhaps the "simplest" and most basic vowel sound. In Figure 4-8 a sketch of the supralaryngeal vocal tract is presented for this vowel. The sketch shows a stylized midsagittal view of the supralaryngeal vocal tract as derived from X-ray movies of speech for this vowel. The speaker's velum is raised, closing the nasal cavity off from the rest of the supralaryngeal airways. The speaker's lips are neither advanced nor retracted. The speaker's tongue is in a fairly unperturbed position with respect to the shape that it assumes during quiet respiration (Perkell, 1969).

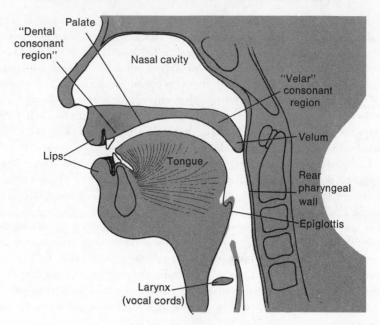

FIGURE 4-8. *The adult human vocal tract.*

We can calculate the formant frequencies of the supralaryngeal filter function of this vowel fairly simply. The area function is acoustically equivalent to a uniform tube open at one end. The area function is plotted in terms of the cross-sectional area as a function of distance from the glottis. The vocal tract is thus open at the speaker's lips. The glottis is represented as a complete closure because the average glottal opening is quite small during normal phonation. The speaker's nasal cavity would be sealed by the velum during the production of an unnasalized vowel so we have only one tube in the supralaryngeal airway for the vowel [ə]. The supralaryngeal vocal tract for this vowel behaves rather like an organ pipe and we can see how the formant frequencies are related to the shape and length, i.e., the area function of the pipe.

In Figure 4-9 we have sketched a uniform pipe open at one end. We have superimposed on the sketch of the pipe a dotted line that represents the pressure-waveform of the lowest frequency sinusoidal sound wave that could be sustained in this tube. Sound waves are air pressure waves. At a given instant of time a sinusoidal air pressure wave will be distributed in space. It will have a peak pressure at one point, zero pressure at a distance of 1/4 wavelength from the maximum, a peak pressure at one wavelength from the first peak, etc. We have sketched a pressure wave, marking these points in Figure 4-10. How does the pressure waveform sketched in Figure 4-9 relate to the waveform sketched in Figure 4-10?

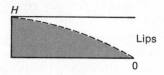

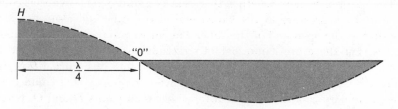

FIGURE 4-9. *A uniform tube open at one end, showing pressure waveform at the first formant frequency.*

FIGURE 4-10. *The relation of quarter-wavelength "inside" the tube to the air pressure wave waveform outside the tube.*

Let us imagine that we are trying to "match" the physical constraints of the pipe sketched in Figure 4-9 with the power required to sustain a sinusoidal air pressure wave. In other words, we are trying to take advantage of the physical dimensions of the pipe to minimize the amount of power (or energy) that we would need to generate an air pressure wave. The pressure in an air pressure wave comes from the constant collision of the air molecules. It is obvious that maximum air pressure could most easily be sustained at the closed end of the tube where air molecules would bounce off the rigid wall of the tube to hit other molecules. The letter H therefore represents the position of the highest air pressure in Figure 4-9. The closed end of the tube is the place where we could most easily generate a high air pressure. The walls and closed end of the tube, the "boundaries," aid in maintaining a high air presssure because they constrain the air molecules and build up the number of collisions between the air molecules as they bounce off the closed end. When you put your finger over the end of a water faucet when the water is on, you can feel the pressure against your finger. The molecules of water are hitting against your finger.

The open end of the tube presents the reverse situation. Zero air pressure is, by definition, the atmospheric air pressure. It is obvious that, in the absence of any sound, the air pressure outside of the tube would be at atmospheric pressure. It logically would be easiest to sustain an air pressure wave that had "zero pressure," i.e., just atmospheric pressure, at the open end of the tube. The letter O therefore appears in Figure 4-9 at the open end of the tube. Note that the examples that we have used to explain the basis for the H and O pressure points are quite simple. We could use any of a number of other simple examples; 20 people bouncing balls off a wall would be hit more often by the balls than 20 people throwing balls off the end of a ship. The examples can be simple because the physical principle that we are attempting to illustrate is also simple. It is that the boundaries of the tube provide "constraints" that best match certain air pressures. Open ends best match the atmospheric pressure while a closed end will match a pressure maximum.

The question is now whether there exists a sinusoidal wave that could have its high pressure at the closed end of the tube and also have zero pressure at the open end of the tube. The answer to this rhetorical question is that there are a number of sinusoidal waves that would satisfy these "boundary" conditions. The interrupted line in Figure 4-9 represents the sinusoidal wave that has the lowest frequency that could meet these boundary conditions. The distance between points H and O, which is one quarter of the total wavelength, separates the high point of the wave from the "zero" value.

The tube open at one end thus will lend itself to sustaining a sound wave at a frequency whose wavelength is four times the length of the tube. The physical attributes of the tube—the fact that it has a closed end that is 17 cm away from its open end—make it possible to generate, with minimum energy input, an air pressure wave whose wavelength is equal to four times 17 cm. If the glottal source were exciting the tube at the closed end, then it would generate a wave pressure wave at the frequency corresponding to this wavelength with minimum input energy. For a given input energy an air pressure wave would be generated at this frequency with maximum amplitude.

The frequency of the pressure wave at which maximum amplitude will be generated is equal to 500 Hz for a 17-cm tube at sea level in a normal atmosphere. This follows from the relationship that we discussed in Chapter 3, $\lambda f = c$. The velocity of sound in air at sea level is approximately 33,500 cm/sec. Since the length of the tube is 17 cm, the wavelength is four times 17 cm, i.e., 68 cm. The frequency of the wave at which a maximum amplitude will be generated is therefore equal to 33,500/68 or about 500 Hz. This frequency is the first formant frequency, F_1. It is the lowest frequency at which maximum sound energy would be generated by a source at the closed, glottal end of the tube.

Air pressure waves at higher frequencies also would satisfy the boundary conditions of the tube, maximum pressure at the glottis, zero pressure at the open lip end. In Figure 4-11 we have sketched a sinusoidal wave that has three times the frequency of the first formant frequency and also meets these conditions. Its wavelength would be one third that of the first formant. The second formant frequency for this tube, which is an idealized model of the vowel [ə], would be 1,500 Hz for supralaryngeal

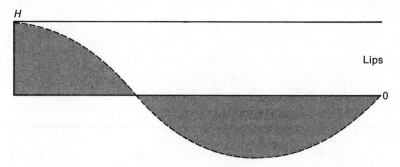

FIGURE 4-11. *The uniform tube of Figure 4-9 showing the second formant frequency, which is three times higher than the first formant frequency.*

vocal tract that was 17 cm long. The third formant for this tube would be 2,500 Hz, five times the first formant frequency. The physical dimensions of the 17-cm tube open at one end thus yields the formant frequencies $F_1 = 500$ Hz, $F_2 = 1,500$ Hz, $F_3 = 2,500$ Hz. The transfer function of this vowel was plotted in Figure 4-3.

The formant frequencies of a uniform tube open at one end will occur at intervals of

$$\frac{(2k+1)C}{4L} \tag{1}$$

where C is the velocity of sound, L is the length of the tube, and k is an integer $= 0$ (i.e., $k = 0, 1, 2, 3, \ldots$). It is, moreover, not important that the tube be exactly uniform. A tube shaped like a slightly flared trumpet would have similar slightly higher formant frequencies (Fant, 1960). The walls of the tube could also have slight irregularities and it is not too important what they're made of. Some corrections are necessary in the calculations to take account of the absorption of sound energy by the walls, but the effects are predictable (Fant, 1960). Formant frequencies are always determined by the size, length, and shape and ends of the supralaryngeal vocal tract, i.e., the cross-sectional area function. It is harder to calculate and visualize the physical situation in speech sounds that involve more complex shapes than the vowel [ə]. The formant frequencies are also usually not integral multiples of each other and there are some additional factors that influence the total spectrum that we have not considered, e.g., the "radiation impedance" of the lips (Flanagan, 1972). However, the formant frequencies always are determined by the shape and dimensions of the supralaryngeal vocal tract.

Formant Lowering and Vocal Tract Length

Suppose that instead of having a fixed-length tube in Figure 4-9 we had a tube whose length was adjustable. If we increased its length while phonation was sustained the formant frequencies would all fall because the denominator of Equation (1) would increase. The velocity of sound would be constant so the formant frequencies would fall as the length of the tube increased. There are two ways in which the human supralaryngeal vocal tract can rapidly increase its length. One of these articulatory gestures is quite obvious. You can protrude your lips. This can add a centimeter or so to the length of the vocal tract (Fant, 1960; Perkell, 1969). The shift in the frequency of F_1 would be about 27 Hz, which would be perceptible to a human listener (Flanagan, 1955). Most traditional phonetic theories are thus correct in claiming that two sounds can be differentiated if the minimal articulatory distinction rests in whether the speakers protrude their lips or not.

Normal human speakers can also lengthen their supralaryngeal vocal tracts by lowering their larynges. In Chapter 6 we will discuss in greater detail the musculature and anatomy of the larynx and the muscles and ligaments that connect it to the rest of the body. The muscles that support and position the larynx can pull it up or down about 2 cm during the production of fluent speech (Perkell, 1969; Ladefoged et al., 1972). If a speaker lowers his larynx 1 cm, the formant frequency shift will be identical to that which would have resulted from a 1-cm protrusion of his lips. The change in length of the supralaryngeal vocal tract is the physiologically relevant phenomenon. If you were listening to this speaker over the telephone or if you were not intently looking at his lips you would not be able tell how he effected the formant frequency shift. Roman Jakobson stressed the linguistic equivalence of articulatory gestures that have similar acoustic consequences (Jakobson et al., 1963). Traditional phonetic theories often fail to take into account the possible equivalence of different articulatory gestures or indeed the irrelevance of certain articulatory gestures.

The source-filter theory of speech production enables us to evaluate the possible communicative significance of other articulatory gestures. We can, for example, see that the offset of constricting the lips is acoustically equivalent to lengthening the vocal tract. The sketch of Figure 4-12 shows a uniform tube similar to the previous tubes except for a constriction at its "open" end. The partial block of the open end results in a slight increase in the air pressure behind the constriction. The physical basis for this pressure increase is equivalent to the basis for the increase in pressure that you would feel on your finger as you partially blocked off a water faucet from which water was flowing. The "boundary constraint" for air pressure at the open end thus would best match a

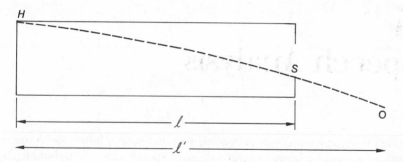

FIGURE 4-12. *Formant frequency lowering that results from a constriction at the end of a uniform tube.*

pressure S which would be higher than the zero 0 atmospheric pressure. The interrupted line on the sketch is the fraction of a sinusoidal waveform that connects the maximum pressure H with pressure S. Note that this sinusoidal waveform will not reach its zero pressure 0 inside the tube. The wavelength of this sinusoid, which is the lowest frequency sinusoid that can connect the air pressure H and S, is equal to $4(\ell')$. Since ℓ' is greater than ℓ, the formant frequencies of the tube, which are still determined by Equation (1), all are lowered. The effect of constricting one's lips[1] is thus equivalent to protruding one's lips, which is again equivalent to lowering one's larynx. All of these articulatory gestures result in lower formant frequencies and we would need telescopes, X-ray machines, and videotelephones to tell how speakers were generating particular sounds that were differentiated by falling formant frequency patterns. The acoustic result of all of these articulatory gestures is *formant frequency lowering*.

The formant frequencies of a uniform tube can likewise be raised by shortening its length. The larynx can move upwards and the lips can be retracted. Both of these gestures can shorten the tube's length, although the lips cannot shorten the vocal tract's length as effectively as they can protrude and lengthen the tube. The lips can open and the jaw can also drop to effectively "flare" the vocal tract and raise the formant frequencies. The extent that the vocal tract can be flared, however, is not as great as the extent to which it can be constricted by closing one's lips. We will return in Chapter 6 to discussing the relationship that holds between the acoustics of speech and particular articulatory maneuvers.

[1] The shape of the lip constriction is also secondary (Beranek, 1949).

5
Speech Analysis

INSTRUMENTAL analysis is necessary to understand how vocal communication works. Auditory transcriptions of speech can never isolate the acoustic cues that specify the sounds of speech. We can, for example, listen to as many carefully transcribed tokens of the syllables [di] and [du] as we care to, without ever discovering that different acoustic cues specify the "identical" sound [d] in these two syllables. As listeners, we have no more direct knowledge of the process of speech perception than we, as eaters of ice cream, have of the enzyme systems that are involved in the digestion of sugar. If we want to study the digestion of sugar we have to make use of instrumental techniques. We likewise have to make use of instrumental techniques for the analysis of speech. In this chapter we will discuss some of these techniques and the acoustic correlates of various speech sounds. Our discussion will, hopefully, provide the background material that will enable you to apply these techniques yourselves.

The Sound Spectrograph

The sound spectrograph is probably the single most useful device for the quantitative analysis of speech. The sound spectrograph was developed at Bell Telephone Laboratories in connection with work on analysis-synthesis speech transmission systems like the Vocoder, which we will discuss in Chapter 7. The sound spectrograph can be used to make various types of analyses of acoustic signals; we will discuss the most useful applications for speech analysis. Detailed discussions of the circuitry of the machine and other applications can be found in Koenig et al., (1946), Potter et al., (1947), and Flanagan (1972).

The output that the machine yields is a piece of paper called a spectrogram. The relation between the name of the machine and its output is like that which holds between the telegraph system and a telegram. (The rareness of telegrams in recent years makes the analogy somewhat archaic.) There have been recent attempts to use spectrograms to identify people's voices. The promoters of these endeavors have applied the term "voiceprint" to the spectrogram (Kersta, 1962). The term voiceprint, of course, brings to mind the term, fingerprint. However, further research is necessary to demonstrate that people can be identified through the use of spectrograms with the certainty of fingerprints (Bolt et al., 1973; Tosi et al., 1972). There apparently have been several independent attempts to develop the use of sound spectrograms for voice identification. The central project of the scientists imprisoned in the Soviet slave labor camp in Alexander Solzhenitsyn's novel, *The First Circle*, is, for example, the development of a voice identification device.

The sound spectrograph essentially performs two sequential operations. The first step in an analysis is to record a speech signal on the machine. The usual "input" is from a magnetic tape recorder, because the first step of a real analysis is to record the speech signals of interest. We will discuss later in this chapter some of the precautions that one should take when making tape recordings. The *speech input* thus usually is from a tape recorder that is playing a signal that has previously been recorded. The sound spectrograph machines that are commercially available, for example, the model of the Kay Elemetrics Corporation, have a number of input channels, which are controlled by a switch. You thus can connect both a tape recorder and a microphone to the machine and select the input that you want. The sound spectrograph records the input signal on a magnetic medium that goes around the outside edge of a thin drum or "disk." The recording head, which is similar to the recording head on a conventional tape recorder, records on this magnetic recording medium. When you switch the sound spectrograph into its "Record" mode, you convert the input signal from the tape recorder or microphone into a magnetic "image" on the edge of the magnetic recording disk.

The recording head converts the electrical signal that corresponds to the speech signal into a magnetic field that is impressed on the magnetic recording medium. This is, of course, similar to the process that is the basis of practically all magnetic tape recorders. As is the case in a conventional tape recorder, the "level" of the input signal mut be kept within a range appropriate for the machine and recording medium. If the electrical signal that is being recorded is too large, the magnetic image is likely to be distorted. If the electrical signal is too small the magnetic image will not be discernible when it is reproduced. The *record level* thus has to be kept within certain limits. This is not very difficult because there is a meter on the machine and a "Record Level Adjustment" knob. You simply set the record level to the value specified in the machine's instructions. The problem is similar to setting the brightness control on a television set. If the control is set at too high a value, the image on the television set will be "washed out"; if it is too low you won't be able to see the image. The sound spectrograph level setting problem is in some ways simpler than setting the brightness level of a television set because you have a calibrated meter on the sound spectrograph. Most tape recorders have level meters or level-indicating devices. These meters or devices take into account the acoustic properties of human speech and the recording electrical and magnetic properties of the recorder, and good recordings of speech signals can be made by keeping the level at or slightly under the value specified in the instructions. As in interstate driving, you have to keep under a maximum and over a minimum "limit."

There are, however, some important differences between recording an input signal on a sound spectrograph and on a conventional tape recorder. The most obvious difference is that the drum magnetic disk on the spectrograph will only record a 2.2-second sample of speech. If the spectrograph is left in its "Record" function, it will record a new message signal, erasing the material that was previously recorded on it, as the magnetic disk rotates past the recording head. The proper technique in using the spectrograph is thus to set the machine into its "Record" function, record a 2-sec sample of speech, and then immediately switch the machine from its "Record" to its "Reproduce" function. If you have set the correct record level on the meter you will then have a 2-sec sample recorded on the magnetic disk. The spectrograph has a monitor loudspeaker so it is possible to listen and to verify that you have recorded the appropriate material. It is easy to set the appropriate record level when a tape recording is the speech input source. If the level is not correct you can adjust the record level control, stop the tape recorder, rewind, and play it back again.

The meter that is used to adjust the record level is adjusted to yield a good recording when the *peak* signal does not exceed 0 VU. The VU scale is an old method of measuring sound levels that originated in the days of radio network AM broadcasts. The dimensional term VU signifies "volume units" and the meter is designed to respond to speech signals in a manner that will produce deflections of the meter's needle that are easy to follow when the input to the meter is a speech signal. It is easy to make tape recordings or sound spectrograms that are distorted when the VU meter readings of "odd" signals like bird calls are interpreted as though they were human speech signals.

There is one additional control on the spectrograph which is specially adapted for the analysis of speech signals. The spectrograph has an *input shaping* control which can be set to either a "Flat" or "HS" position. The HS position is usually used when speech signals are being analyzed. It switches in an electrical network that emphasizes the high frequencies of the speech signal. As we noted in Chapter 4, the amplitude of the glottal source falls off at the rate of 6 db per octave. This means that there is less energy in the acoustic speech signal at higher frequencies. The HS circuits compensate for this decrease in energy and compensate in part for the limited dynamic range of the paper that the spectrograph uses to make spectrograms. These circuits are used whenever the machine is being used to make normal spectrograms of adult humans. The Flat setting is sometimes useful for the analysis of the speech of infants, who have proportionately more energy at high frequencies, or for the analysis of nonspeech signals. It is also useful for making spectrograph "sections," which we will discuss later.

The way in which the spectrograph performs an analysis may be clearer if we first consider a simpler form of frequency analysis. Suppose that someone asked you to provide a graph that showed the frequencies at which FM radio stations were broadcasting in Providence, Rhode Island, at or about 12 noon on December 10, 1975, and the relative amplitude of each station's broadcast as received in your home. The request would be very easy to satisfy if you had a radio receiver that had a "tuning meter" that measured signal strength. The "dial" on a radio is a control that adjusts the frequency of a variable electronic filter. As you turn the dial the filter lets electromagnetic energy within a certain range of frequencies through into a series of amplifiers and other devices that ultimately produce an audible signal. The variable electronic filter that you "set" to "select" the appropriate radio station has a fixed bandwidth and an adjustable center frequency. When the dial is set to 88.5 the electronic filter's center frequency is 88.5×10^6 Hz. When the dial is moved to 100, its center frequency is 100×10^6 Hz, etc. If you systematically tuned to each station in Providence and wrote down the "signal strength" that the radio's meter noted you would be able to make the graph that appears in Figure 5-1. The signal strength meter of the radio (probably only a relatively expensive "high fidelity" tuner would have this type of meter) measures the amplitude of the received signal and is plotted on the vertical scale. The horizontal scale

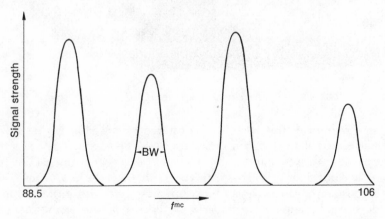

FIGURE 5-1. *A plot of signal strength of FM radio stations. BW refers to bandwidth.*

represents the settings of the tuner's dial. Note that there is a range of frequencies for each radio station that corresponds, in part, to the bandwidth of the tuner's filter. The bandwidth of the tuner's filter also roughly matches the band of frequencies that each station broadcasts.

The graph of Figure 5-1 is a sort of spectrum of the FM broadcast frequencies in a particular location at a particular time. It was made by taking a single variable filter and moving it through the frequency range of interest and keeping track of the amplitude of the signal at each setting of the variable filter. The sound spectrograph operates in essentially the same manner. Displays that are similar, in principle, to that of Figure 5-1 can be made for a speech signal for a particular interval of time. These displays are called "sections." The usual spectrograph display provides information on the intensity of energy in the speech signal as a function of both frequency and time over the full 2.2-sec interval recorded on the spectrograph's magnetic disk.

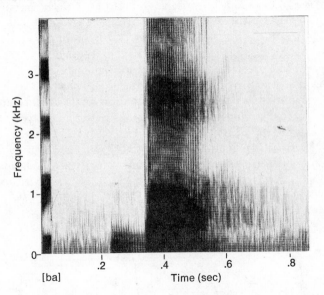

FIGURE 5-2. *Wide-band spectrogram of the sound* [ba]

A spectrogram of the syllable [ba] uttered by an adult male speaker of American English is shown in Figure 5-2. The vertical scale is a frequency scale. Note that it is a linear scale, i.e., a given interval of frequency is equivalent to a fixed interval throughout the frequency scale. The spectrograph can be set to make spectrograms with either a linear or a logarithmic scale. The linear scale is best if one wants to make quantitative measurements from the spectrogram. Note that the frequency scale runs from 0 to 4,000 Hz. The spectrograph was equipped with a "Scale Expander" unit that allows one to match the vertical scale of the spectrogram to the frequency range of interest. The formant frequencies of the sounds on the spectrogram all fall below 4,000 Hz so the frequency scale was "expanded" to cover the range 0–4,000 Hz. If the "Scale Expander" had not been used, the vertical scale would have encompassed the range 0–8,000 Hz, but the upper half of the spectrogram would not have contained any useful information and we would have half the detail in the 0–4,000 Hz range where the useful acoustic material is displayed. Note also the short, straight "bars" that occur at 1, 2, 3, and 4 kHz near the vertical scale. These bars are frequency-calibrating signals that can be placed on the spectrogram. Their use is strongly recommended since they reduce the likelihood of measurement errors.

The dark "bands" of the sound [ba] indicate the presence of local energy peaks in the spectrum of these sounds as functions of time. In other words, there are local peaks at about 700 Hz, 1,100 Hz, and 2,800 Hz at 0.4 sec. There is also a very low frequency peak at about 140 Hz. The dark bands at 700 Hz, 1,100 Hz, and 2,800 Hz are the spectrogram's response to the formant frequencies of the vowel [a]. The dark band at 140 Hz reflects the fundamental frequency of phonation. The fundamental frequency can be determined more accurately by counting the number of vertical striations that appear in the dark bands per unit of time. Note that all the dark bands actually consist of vertical striations. This spectrogram is a "wide band" analysis that was made using the 300-Hz bandwidth analyzing filter of the spectrograph apparatus. The 300-Hz bandwidth filter obviously does not have a good frequency resolution. You can see this in the width of the bands that correspond to the frequency calibrations of the spectrograph machine. The bands are about 300 Hz wide although the calibration signals actually consist of "pure" sinusoids, i.e., single frequencies. The wide-bandwidth analyzing filter, however, responds rapidly to changes in the energy of the acoustic signal. It therefore shows the fluctuations in the energy of the speech signal that occur as the vocal tract is excited by the glottal output.

In the spectrogram in Figure 5-2 you can see that the spacing between these striations varies in the course of time. In the interval between 0.35 and 0.45 sec, 14 striations occur. The average fundamental period in that interval therefore is 0.07 sec, i.e., 70 msec. The "average" fundamental frequency for this interval of speech is therefore equal to 140 Hz. The calculations that lead to this result are quite simple. Since 14 striations occur in 100 msec the average period must be approximately equal to:

$$T = \frac{100}{14} = 7 \text{ msec}$$

If we recall the definition of fundamental frequency from Chapter 3,

$$f_0 = \frac{1}{T} = \frac{1}{70/1,000} = 140 \text{ Hz}$$

The fundamental frequency rapidly falls in the interval between $t = 0.5$ sec and $t = 0.6$ sec. A "narrow-band" spectrogram of the same utterances is shown in Figure 5-3. Note the different appearance of this spectrogram. The only difference in the analysis is the substitution

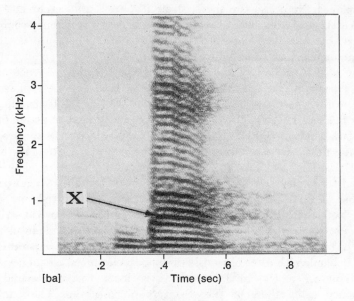

FIGURE 5-3. *Narrow-band spectrogram of the same sound* [ba] *analyzed in Figure 5-2. The symbol X denotes the fifth harmonic of the fundamental frequency.*

of a 50-Hz bandwidth analyzing filter. The dark "bands" of this spectrogram now reflect the energy that is present in the fundamental frequency and each harmonic of the glottal excitation. Note that the fundamental frequency is 140 Hz at $t = 0.4$ sec. It is easier to "read" the value of the fundamental frequency by looking at the fifth harmonic, which is marked by an X in this figure. The frequency of this harmonic is by definition equal to $5 f_0$. If you wanted to derive the fundamental frequency of phonation for this syllable as a function of time you could mark the fifth harmonic on the spectrogram and then trace it through the syllable. If you transferred the time scale and remembered to divide the vertical frequency scale by 5, you would have a plot of the fundamental frequency. You would gain two advantages by tracing the fifth harmonic:

(1) it is easier to see than the fundamental frequency and (2) variations in fundamental frequency are "magnified" five times. If the fundamental frequency, for example, fell 10 Hz, the fifth harmonic would fall 50 Hz. It would be almost impossible to see a 10-Hz variation on the spectrogram; the 50-Hz fall is easy to see. Still higher harmonics can be traced for more detail. The limit arises from the decreasing energy in the higher harmonics, which is a characteristic of the glottal source. The spectrogram may not always mark the higher harmonics. The narrow-band filter also does not respond to rapid changes in the fundamental frequency. At the end of phonation there typically are a few long glottal periods that have less energy in their higher harmonics. These transients occur because the speaker is opening his vocal cords at the end of phonation and also lowering his pulmonary air pressure (Lieberman, 1967). We'll discuss the mechanisms that regulate fundamental frequency in detail in Chapter 6, but you can see these transient conditions in the wide-band spectrogram. Note the longer spacing of the "voicing" striations, which reflects the long glottal periods, and the absence of darkening at higher frequencies in the wide-band spectrogram at the end of the syllable.

Interpreting Spectrograms—How the Spectrograph Works

The difference between the appearance of the spectrograms in Figures 5-2 and 5-3 is obvious, and it is essential to know why these two displays of the same signal look so different; this entails knowing how the spectrograph apparatus works. If you don't know how the spectrograph makes these displays, you can easily misinterpret sound spectrograms. Spectrograms are always difficult to interpret, but you can make absurd errors if you don't know what the machine is doing. This does not mean that you have to be a graduate electrical engineer and know the electronics of the sound spectrograph, but that you simply understand the general principles of the machine. If you know how the spectrograph works, you can avoid introducing artifacts into your data. You can also learn how to circumvent some of its limitations and analyze sounds that you otherwise couldn't.

In Figure 5-4 the functional elements of a "photo-output" narrow-band spectrograph machine have been sketched. The variable analyzing filter has a 50-Hz bandwidth, and its center frequency can be shifted to cover the frequency range between 0 and 8 kHZ. The filter feeds into an amplifier and then into an averaging device, which removes small fluctuations in the filter's output. The averaged output, in turn, goes into a small light bulb. The brightness of the light bulb thus is a function of the electrical current from the filter. If the filter responds to a peak in the acoustic spectrum, the light bulb will burn brighter. A low level

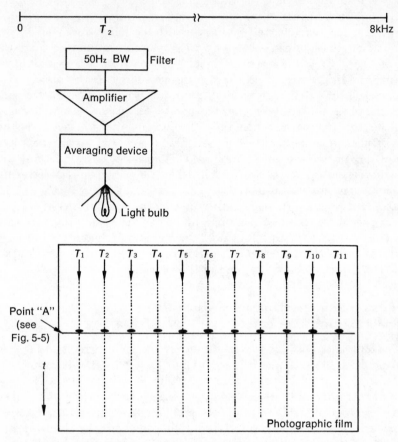

FIGURE 5-4. *Sketch of a hypothetical "photo-output" narrow-band sound spectrograph machine.*

acoustic signal will result in a slight glow, an intermediate acoustic level in an intermediate brightness, etc. If the light bulb's output were focused on a photographic film, the film after development would be darker for a high acoustic level and lighter when the acoustic level was lower. The darkness of the film would reflect the level of the acoustic signal within the range of frequencies that the variable input filter was "set" to cover. If we provided a suitable mechanical system we could pull a piece of film past on a "track" T_1 while the filter that was set to a particular frequency range "scanned" a speech signal. The density of the film along that track would correspond to the presence of acoustic energy within that range of frequencies as a function of time. If we then adjusted the frequency range of the variable filter to a higher range of frequencies, moved the light bulb to track T_2, and repeated the process with the same speech sample, we would record a second track of variable density on the film.

The sound spectrograph is functionally very similar to this photo-output spectrograph. The acoustic signal is recorded on the magnetic disk, which also holds a piece of special paper. The paper is darkened by the current that flows through the wire stylus of the spectrograph. The current that flows through the stylus is a function of the acoustic energy that the spectrograph's variable filter admits. As the spectrograph's disk turns round and round in its "Analysis" mode, a mechanical system adjusts the range of frequencies that the variable filter admits, while it simultaneously moves the stylus up the sensitized paper. The darkening of the spectrogram paper at a particular location thus shows when the filter has admitted acoustic energy at a particular frequency range at some particular point in time. The sound spectrograph does not have the dynamic range of a photographic film. This means that the range of dark-to-light gradations on the spectrogram can not encompass the range of that intensity that actually occurs in a real speech signal. The sound spectrograph therefore makes use of additional electronic processing to compensate for this deficiency.

In Figure 5-5 the spectrum of the sound [ə], which was shown in Figure 4-4, is shown at the top of the diagram. The plot beneath it is a hypothetical plot of the light output that might be measured for our photo-output spectrograph as a function of frequency at a particular point in time. This would be a "section" of the signal at point A in Figure 5-4. The "width" of each of the bars on the light output graph is, of course, 50 Hz wide because of the bandwidth of the spectrograph's analyzing filter. The vertical height of these bars would correspond to the density of the developed film on our hypothetical photo-output spectrograph. However, we have noted that we cannot handle this range of density with the paper that is used on the actual spectrograph machine. The spectrograph machine solves this problem by a two-stage process. The amplitude range of the output of the analyzing filter is first "compressed" by an "automatic gain control" system. This is equivalent to a little man sitting inside the machine who rapidly turns a volume control, "turning up" the lower level signals and "turning down" the high level signals. The spectrograph machine thus has a control labeled "AGC" which controls the degree to which this adjustment is carried out. In Figure 5-5 the third graph down shows this output with a moderate amount of AGC action. There still are differences between the amplitudes of different harmonics but they are reduced. The range of densities that the spectrograph paper can handle is about 12 db. The setting of the "Mark Level" control on the spectrograph machine, which is indicated by the dashed line that goes across the third graph in Figure 5-5 shows this control set to produce a spectrogram in which the relative amplitude of each har-

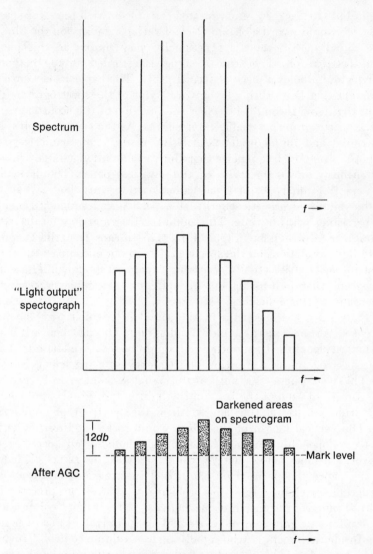

FIGURE 5-5. *Spectrum of a speech signal and two stages of processing in the spectrograph machine.*

monic of the spectrum is portrayed on the spectrogram *after* AGC action. Amplitudes less than the value of the dashed line will not be marked at all; levels above it will be proportionately darker.

It is obvious that the darkness of any "bar" on the spectrogram is affected by the setting of the AGC control and the Mark Level control. If the Mark Level were set to the level shown in Figure 5-6 the spectrogram would not "show" any energy present at harmonic Y although,

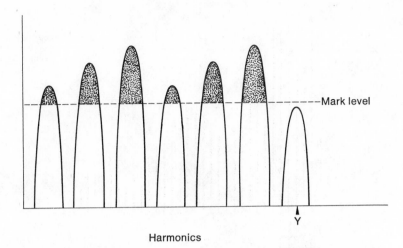

Mark level

Y

Harmonics

FIGURE 5-6. *The effect of Mark Level on a spectrogram. Note that the machine would not darken the spectrogram at harmonic Y although acoustic energy is actually present there.*

in fact, energy was present there. The interpretation of a spectrogram is, on this count alone, a difficult undertaking since what you see depends on the setting of the AGC and Mark Level controls. Some spectrograph machines do not offer a choice of AGC and Mark Level settings, but the problem still remains. The only difference is that the manufacturer has set the controls inside the machine. It sometimes is tempting to conclude that there is no energy at some harmonic of the fundamental because no line appears on a particular spectrogram at the expected frequency. This conclusion might not be warranted; it might be an artifact of the settings of the AGC and Mark Level values. Before one can conclude that a harmonic has "disappeared" at some instant of time, it is wise to make additional spectrograms with different AGC and Mark Level values.

Measuring Formant Frequencies

It is possible to determine formant frequencies in some narrow-band spectrograms if conditions are optimal. However, the wide-band spectrogram is generally more accurate and sometimes is the only way in which one can get even an approximate idea of the formant frequency. It is best to make use of both the wide- and narrow-bandwidth filters to locate a formant frequency, but the wide-band spectrogram is usually the starting point. In Figure 5-7 the spectrum of the [ə] sound (cf. Figure 4-4) is again displayed at the top of the sketch. The fundamental frequency

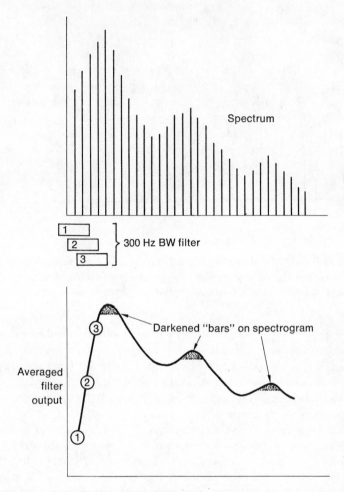

FIGURE 5-7. *Functional operation of wide-band filtering of spectrograph. The input spectrum is averaged by the wide-band filter and the formant frequencies appear as darkened bars on the spectrogram.*

of phonation is 100 Hz, and harmonics thus occur at 100-Hz intervals. The analyzing bandwidth of the 300-Hz bandwith filter is shown schematically as the filter just begins to admit the acoustic energy at the fundamental frequency in the uppermost (number 1) block. The averaged output of the filter is sketched below. Note that the output of the filter will continue to rise as it moves upwards in frequency from block 1 to block 2 to block 3, because the filter will admit additional harmonics of the speech signal. The filter's output will continue to increase as its center frequency (cf. Chapter 3) moves upwards in frequency until it is at 500 Hz. There is no point at which the filter's output is zero, because the filter's bandwidth is so wide that it is always admitting at least three harmonics once its center frequency is past 150 Hz. As the amplitude of the harmonics falls after 500 Hz, the filter's output also falls. The output of the filter approximates the "envelope" of the spectrum of the sound [ə]. (The "envelope" is the function that connects the peak of each harmonic with the peak of the adjacent harmonic.)

If appropriate AGC and Mark Level settings are used on the spectrograph apparatus, the final spectrogram will have darkened "bars" at the three peaks that are shaded in the graph of the filter output in Figure 5-7. The wide-band spectrogram thus provides information on the local peaks in the spectrum's "envelope," which reflects, in part, the formant frequencies of the sound.

The wide-band spectrogram will "show" the approximate location of a formant even when there is no energy present at the actual formant frequency *if* the fundamental frequency is at least half the bandwidth of the analyzing filter. In Figure 5-8 the low frequency end of the spectrum of an [i] sound (the vowel of *meet*) is sketched. The frequency of F_1, the first formant is 200 Hz, the fundamental frequency is 125 Hz, so no acoustic energy occurs at F_1. The graph of the wide-band filter output shows that a peak in the envelope will still occur near 200 Hz, because the analyzing filter will, if it is centered at that frequency, pass the two harmonics at 125 and 250 Hz. These two harmonics have the greatest amplitudes, so the peak in the filter output function will be centered at 200 Hz, the frequency of the first formant. The darkened area on the spectrogram will, of course, be about 300 Hz wide, but it will be centered on the formant frequency. Note that a narrow-band spectrogram would *not* show the formant frequency. It would introduce an additional source of error into the measurement of the formant frequency because it would produce dark bars at the harmonics. We might be able to see that the harmonic at 250 Hz was darker than those at 125 and 375 Hz. This would indicate that the formant frequency was near 250 Hz, but we would not be able to tell that it was at 200 Hz. The frequency resolution of the narrow-band spectrogram is greater than that of the wide-band spectrogram, but it does not necessarily yield greater precision in the measurement of formant frequencies. This follows from the point that we stressed in Chapter 4, that the formant frequencies are properties of the filter function of the supralaryngeal vocal tract. *The formant frequencies are the frequencies at which the supralaryngeal filter would let maximum acoustic energy through.* The electronic processing of the sound spectrograph is a means whereby we can often derive useful information that can help us locate formant frequencies. It does not directly "show" formant frequencies.

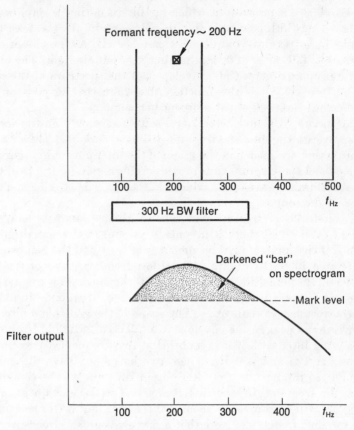

FIGURE 5-8. *Operation of wide-band filter when a formant frequency does not coincide with that of a harmonic of the fundamental frequency.*

Variations in the settings of the AGC and Mark Level controls of the spectrograph apparatus can also produce wide-band spectrograms of the same acoustic signal that look very different and we cannot assume that a formant frequency has "disappeared" because it is not marked. We likewise have to be very careful to avoid interpreting every dark bar as though it reflects the presence of a formant frequency. The fundamental frequency of phonation of normal adult male human beings often exeeds 200 Hz during connected discourse. Normal adult females usually have average fundamental frequencies in excess of 200 Hz. In Figure 5-9 the uppermost spectrogram is a wide-band spectrogram made by using the usual 300-Hz bandwidth setting. The sound that is being analyzed is the word *bad* transcribed [bæd]. Note the wide bars on the spectrogram that are spaced apart at intervals of 300–250 Hz. Do these bars show the

formant frequency variations of this sound? Should we rush to our typewriter and send off a communication to a scholarly journal announcing
the "discovery" of a sound that has at least ten formant frequencies
between 250 Hz and 3,000 Hz?

The answer to this question is, of course, No! The narrow-band, 50-Hz
bandwidth spectrogram of this same utterance, which appears beside the
spectrogram made with the 300-Hz bandwidth analyzing filter in Figure
5-9, shows the same set of darkened bars. The width of the bars made
with the 50-Hz bandwidth analyzing filter is less, and the bars do not
show some of the variations that are evident in spectrograms, but it is

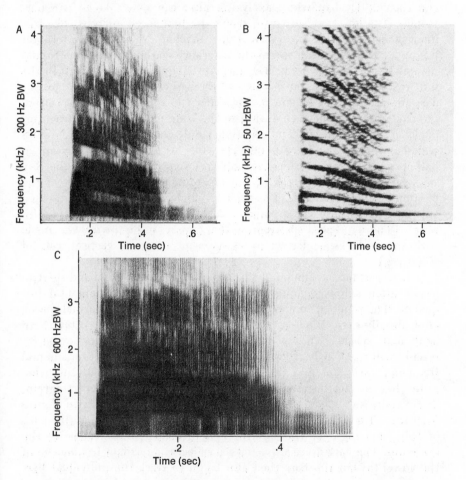

FIGURE 5-9. *The spectographic analysis of a speaker whose fundamental frequency exceeds 200 Hz. (A) 300-Hz bandwidth spectrogram. (B) 50-Hz bandwidth spectrogram. (C) 600-Hz bandwidth
spectrogram.*

evident that the dark bands of both spectrograms primarily reflect the *harmonic* structure of the glottal source. The fundamental frequency of the utterance exceeds 250 Hz and is so high that the 300-Hz bandwidth filter can not "take in" at least two harmonics. The output of the analyzing filter thus is *not* a measure of the envelope of the spectrum and the dark bands on the spectrogram do not manifest the formant frequencies.

We can increase the bandwidth of the spectrograph's analyzing filter by a simple artifice. If we present the speech signal to the analyzing filter at half speed, we will divide all the frequencies on the recording by one half. The fundamental frequency of phonation now becomes 125 Hz, and the 300-Hz bandwidth analyzing filter can now take in two harmonics. The lowest spectrogram shows the half speed analysis. The formant structure of the utterance is now evident. Note that the formant frequency pattern at the end of the utterance does not match the fundamental frequency variation. The formant frequencies do not fall in the interval between 0.2 and 0.4 sec, whereas the fundamental frequency does in spectrograms *A* and *B*. Note that the time scale of the bottom spectrogram is expanded compared to the scale for the two spectrograms made at normal speed. The effective bandwidth of the spectrograph's wide-band analyzing filter is 600 Hz when we make a spectrogram at half speed. It is simple to make half speed spectrograms with the Kay spectrograph by recording with the recording speed selector set at the position labeled 16,000 Hz. The Scale Expander unit is very useful when you do this because the frequency scale can be adjusted to a useful range. (The half speed spectrogram that appears in Figure 5-9 was made with the Scale Expander set to 25 per cent to get a vertical scale of 4,000 Hz.)

It is important to remember that the dark bars on wide-band spectrograms often simply manifest the harmonics of the fundamental frequency. The range of fundamental frequency variation in normal speech often usually exceeds one octave and sometimes reaches two octaves. An adult male speaker whose "average" fundamental frequency is 100 Hz usually will reach at least 200 Hz in connected speech. The fundamental frequency variations may not be perceived as being especially high because they are not sustained, but they will show up in the spectrogram. The "staircase" effect that you can see in the spectrogram in Figure 5-10 at $t = 1.0$ sec occurs when the fundamental frequency is at the point of being too high for the spectrograph to derive the envelope of the spectrum. The dark areas at $t = 0.2$ sec reflect the formant frequencies of the vowel [a] but the bars then also begin to track the individual harmonics.

The formant frequencies of the utterances of speakers who have extremely high fundamental frequencies can often be more readily determined by selecting for analysis an utterance that is "breathy," i.e., whispered, or produced with mixed noise and phonation. The spectrum of a noise source has energy throughout a range of frequencies rather than at discrete, harmonically related, frequencies as is the case for the glottal

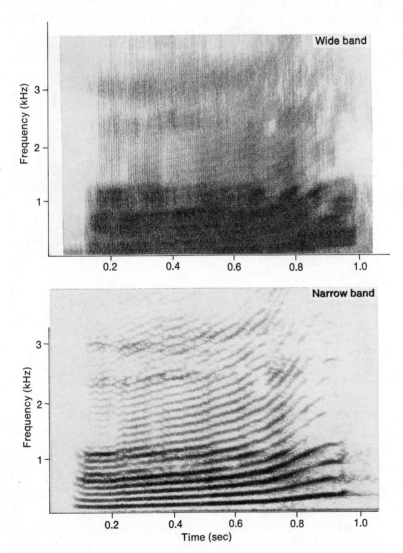

FIGURE 5-10. *Note the "staircase" effect on wide-band spectrogram. The fundamental frequency is at the point of being too high for the spectrograph to resolve the formant frequencies.*

source during phonation. Energy is present at all frequencies within the range that characterizes the noise source, so the analyzing filter of the spectrograph can derive the spectrum envelope during the breathy part of an utterance. In Figure 5-11 a breathy utterance of a newborn infant is shown. The formant frequencies are evident at 1.1, 3.3, and 5.8 Hz. The fundamental frequency of phonation is about 400 Hz. If the cry did not have a breathy, noisy quality (i.e., noise mixed with phonation), it would not have been possible to derive the formant frequencies in this way.

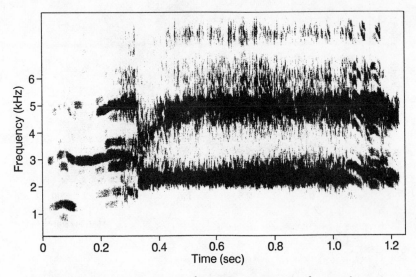

FIGURE 5-11. *Spectrogram of breathy utterance of a newborn infant. The "noise" excitation makes it possible to resolve the formant frequencies although the fundamental frequency is very high.*

If the AGC and Mark Level controls of the spectrograph are carefully adjusted, it is possible to determine the approximate locations of formants for voices that have high fundamental frequencies. This is done by looking at the relative darkness of the harmonics. In Figure 5-12 the formant frequencies of the sound are near 500, 1,200, and 2,500 Hz. There is obviously a great deal of inherent uncertainty here because we don't have acoustic information at intervals closer than 300 Hz, which is the fundamental frequency of phonation for this utterance. The spectrographic "section" which would show the relative amplitude of each harmonic for a 100-msec-long sample of time would not really provide much more information. Energy still would be present at intervals of 300 Hz. As we noted in Chapter 4, human beings have no difficulty in deriving the formant frequencies of sounds like this.

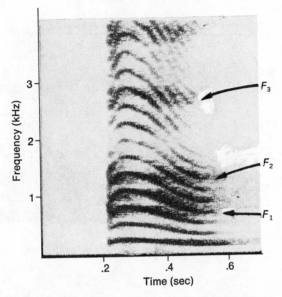

FIGURE 5-12. *Using a narrow-band, 50-Hz bandwidth spectrogram to estimate formant frequencies.*

The different analyzing filter bandwidths and sectioning device of the spectrograph can all be used together to determine the formant frequencies of sounds like the vowel [a], where two formants are close in frequency. It is easier to determine these formant frequencies if you have all three displays, but the combination of the wide-band and the narrow-band spectrogram is sufficient to determine the formant frequencies with reasonable accuracy. As we have noted there are definite limits on the precision that is necessary to specify the formant frequencies. Psychoacoustic experiments, which we will discuss in Chapter 7, show that it is not necessary to specify the position of F_1 and F_2 with better than 3 to 5 per cent accuracy (Flanagan, 1955).

Some Precautions and Techniques for Measuring Formant Frequencies

In Figure 5-13 a line is traced through the center of the dark bands that reflect F_1, F_2, and F_3 in the spectrogram. It is useful to trace the presumed position of each formant directly on the spectrogram with a pencil line before you attempt to measure the frequency value. If you make a mistake or arrive at an odd result later you then can trace back through the

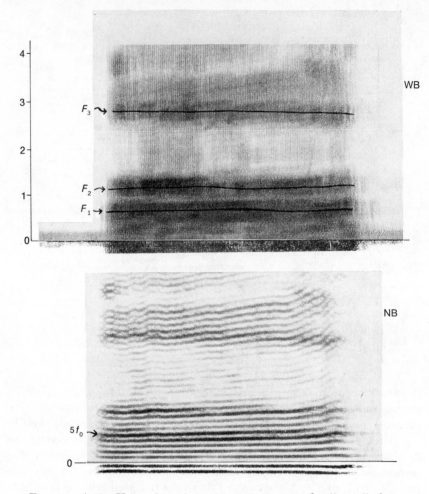

FIGURE 5-13. *Using the mirror-image technique for "zero" frequency calibration. The formant frequencies are noted on the upper wide-band spectrogram. The fifth harmonic of the fundamental frequency is marked on the lower narrow-band spectrogram.*

measurement process step by step. If you were to measure the formant frequency from the spectrogram by means of a calibrated scale without marking the spectrogram, you might not be able to trace the point at which you were in error. Note that the "zero" frequency line in the spectrogram has some dark traces beneath it. These traces are a mirror image of the display above the zero line. The spectrograph can be adjusted to eliminate this "mirror image" effect, but it is safer to set the zero frequency line for each spectrogram by means of the mirror image. The spectrograph's electronic circuits, like all other electronic circuits, tend to change their properties with time as they "warm up." If you do not use the mirror image technique, it is possible to introduce systematic errors as the zero line drifts to some new unknown nonzero value.

The Acoustic Classification of Speech Sounds

The sound spectrograph was the instrument that lent impetus to the modern era of speech research. Studies like those of Potter and Steinberg (1950) and Peterson and Barney (1952) demonstrated that speech sounds could be classified through formant frequency measurements derived from spectrograms. Peterson and Barney (1952) demonstrated that the vowels of American English could be classified on the basis of F_1 and F_2 measurements. They recorded the utterances of 76 different speakers (33 men, 28 women, and 15 children) who spoke 1,520 words. In Figure 5-14 we have reproduced the plot of the frequencies of the first and second formant frequencies, F_1 and F_2, of the vowels of these utterances. The speakers represented a sampling of American English dialects although most were from the Middle Atlantic speech area. A few of the speakers were not native speakers of English. They each recorded two lists of ten words twice. The words all had the form [h] V [d], where V stands for "vowel." The words were *heed* [i], *hid* [I], [ɛ], *had* [æ], *hod* [ɑ], *hawed* [ɔ], *hood* [U], *who'd* [u], *hud* [ʌ], and *heard* [ɝ]. The formant frequencies for the vowels of these words were measured and plotted. The phonetic context of the word-initial [h] resulted in a reasonably steady formant frequency pattern for these vowels, which simplified the measurements.

The individual symbols of Figure 5-14 represent the first and second formant frequencies of one of the ten word lists for all the speakers. The graph, for example, includes an [i] that had a first formant frequency of 210 Hz and a second formant frequency of 2,100 Hz. The data points all are labeled with the phonetic symbols of the vowels that the speakers intended to convey. The labeled "loops" in Figure 5-14 encompass about 90 per cent of the data points for each phonetic category. Some of the data points for each vowel spill out into other vowel loops. Note that some of the vowel loops overlap. This means that the vowel loops alone work almost, but not quite as well, as the judgments of human listeners to classify the vowels of American English. Many attempts were made after the publication of this study to devise mechanical procedures that would work as well as human listeners. The problem, however, has eluded a solution until recently (Nearey, 1976), because it involves an appreciation of some of the basic properties of human speech production and perception. We will return to this question in the chapters that follow.

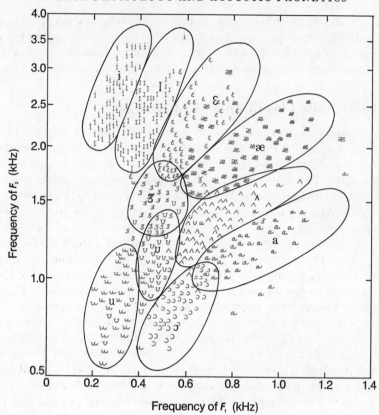

FIGURE 5-14. *Classifying vowel sounds in terms of their first and second formant frequencies. Each letter represents a vowel that has an F_1 plotted on the abscissa (horizontal scale) and F_2 on the ordinate (vertical scale). (After Peterson and Barney, 1952.)*

Tape-Recording Techniques

Some of the precautions that apply to tape recording in general apply with special force to recording speech samples for or on the spectrograph. In making a tape recording that you expect to analyze, it is essential to avoid overmodulating the tape. If you overmodulate the tape, you will introduce electrical energy that will look like acoustic energy on the spectrograms. It may be impossible to sort out the recording artifacts from the recorded acoustic signal. The recording level thus should be lower than the red area that marks the overload region on many tape recorders. The meters on conventional tape recorders are as we noted earlier, designed with human speech in mind. Signals like bird calls call for special recording techniques (Greenewalt, 1968).

The use of a low recording level helps to avoid the problem of tape "print through" in which the magnetic field recorded on one layer of tape produces an image on the adjacent layers of tape. The tape then has an echolike sound quality. It is advisable to use magnetic tape that is at least 1.0 mil (.001 inch) thick to avoid print through. Extra thick, 1.5-mil tape is still better. The guiding rule in recording speech for analysis on the spectrograph is to keep the level low if in doubt. The low level will increase the signal-to-noise ratio, and the tape might not be up to the standards necessary for high fidelity music recording. However, a signal-to-noise ratio of 25 to 30 db is more than adequate for good quality spectrograms. The choice of microphone for recording will depend on the goals of the particular research project. If you simply want to determine the formant frequencies or fundamental frequency pattern of an utterance, then almost any microphone that will cover the frequency range between 100 and 8,000 Hz with reasonable fidelity is adequate. It will be more important to make the recordings in a quiet environment, and, directional microphones may be helpful. If the details of the spectrum and relative amplitudes of noise bursts, etc., are the focus of the research, quality condensor microphones and an echo-free acoustic environment may be necessary. Tape recorders likewise don't have to be laboratory-standard instruments for most studies. Perhaps the most important consideration in a tape recorder is the stability and accuracy of the tape speed. In well-controlled studies it is essential to record test signals on the tape recordings that you will be analyzing. If you record a series of sinusoidal signals from a calibrated signal generator on the tape, you can compensate for any variations that may exist in the tape recorder and spectrograph by making narrow-band spectrograms of these calibrating signals.

Waveform and Computer-Implemented Analyses

The spectrograph is not the only tool available to analyze speech. The speech waveform can be recorded by photographing an oscilloscope tube or by using devices known as oscillographs. Oscillographs, which record the speech waveform, are useful if one wants to determine the fundamental frequency of phonation. In Figure 5-15 a speech waveform is shown. The period of the waveform is about 10 msec, although it is evident that it varies slightly from one period to the next. Measurements of the fundamental frequency on a period to period basis can be affected either visually (Lieberman, 1961) or by means of computer programs (Gold, 1962). The fundamental frequency of phonation typically varies from one cycle to the next and measurements of "pitch perturbations," i.e. pitch variations, can be used to differentiate normal larynges from certain pathologies (Lieberman, 1963) and the emotional quality of speech. Pitch

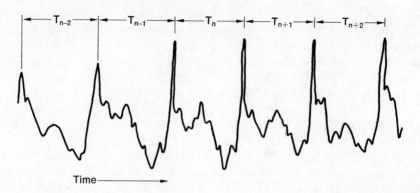

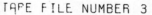

FIGURE 5-15. *Oscillographic record of speech waveform, showing its periodicity. Visual measurements can be used to derive the duration of each period of the fundamental.*

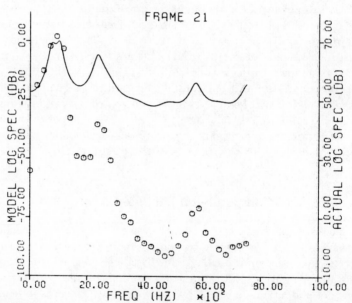

FIGURE 5-16. *Computer analysis of a speech signal. The data and scales were plotted automatically. Two computer programs were used to derive a spectrum (plotted with the open circles) and an estimate of the vocal tract transfer function (the solid line) that was used to produce this speech signal. The computer analyzed a 700-msec speech sample, which it segmented into contiguous 25-msec "frames." The vertical scale at the right is a decibel scale for the spectrum. The vertical scale to the left, which is also in decibels, is the scale for the*

perturbation measurements also have been used as a measure of psychological stress.

There have been many research projects that have developed methods for the analysis of speech by computer-aided techniques. In Figure 5-16 the plot of a computer-implemented formant analysis is shown. The technique is fairly complex. Many of these techniques are discussed by Flanagan (1972). A background in engineering or physics and computer programming is necessary to follow the details of these procedures. However, the basic elements that are "extracted" by these techniques are the fundamental and formant frequencies and the spectrum. We will discuss specific procedures in the chapters that follow, as they are germane to particular topics.

estimated (model) supralaryngeal vocal tract transfer function. Note that the peaks in the spectrum (the open-circle plot) and the peaks in the estimated supralaryngeal vocal tract transfer function (the formant frequencies) almost, but don't exactly, coincide in frequency. The speech signal analyzed was produced by a 4-month-old infant. Such young infants have very short supralaryngeal vocal tracts. Note that F_1 is about 1 kHz, F_2 about 2.5 kHz, and F_3 about 6 kHz. The computer program estimated the supralaryngeal vocal tract transfer function by means of a technique of "linear prediction" (Atal and Hanauer, 1971).

6
Anatomy and Physiology of Speech Production

In Chapter 5 we discussed the sound spectrograph in detail because the data derived from this instrument have been so important. Our "knowledge" ultimately depends on the nature and quality of the data available, as well as the theories that attempt to interpret these data. Techniques like high speed cinematography, radiographs (X rays), cineradiographs, and electromyography have made new forms of data available which speech scientists and phoneticians have used to synthesize and test new theories. We will focus on these new techniques and data in this chapter as they bear on the anatomy and physiology of speech production. However, we also have to keep in touch with classical data and theories. The anatomical basis of speech production, for example, has been studied in much detail (Zemlin, 1968) and much of our understanding still rests on the classical techniques of anatomical observation and inference.

We will develop the systems approach that we introduced in Chapter 2. The subglottal, laryngeal, and supralaryngeal components of the vocal tract obviously must be treated as a complete system, but different experimental techniques are appropriate for the measurement of relevant physiologic data on these components, and different physiologic principles are necessary to understand how these systems function. The anatomical charts that we will present will bear a number of terms that identify various morphological features. Although these features must be labeled, our discussion will not necessarily involve all of these structures. It is necessary to know your way around the anatomy of the vocal tract because you cannot always predict what structures may become relevant as new studies investigate various aspects of speech production. However, it is not necessary to memorize all the names that appear on each chart. Hopefully you will begin to remember the important features as you follow the discussion.

The Lungs

The discussion in Chapter 2 stressed the role of the elastic recoil force of the lungs. In normal inspiration the inspiratory muscles expand the lungs. Some of the force that is necessary for inspiration is stored in the elastic lungs. During expiration the elastic recoil of the lungs can provide the force necessary to push air out of the lungs. The bicycle pump and balloon model of Chapter 2 illustrated the dynamic behavior of the subglottal respiratory system, and we noted that maintaining a steady pulmonary air pressure during speech requires a complex pattern of muscular activity.

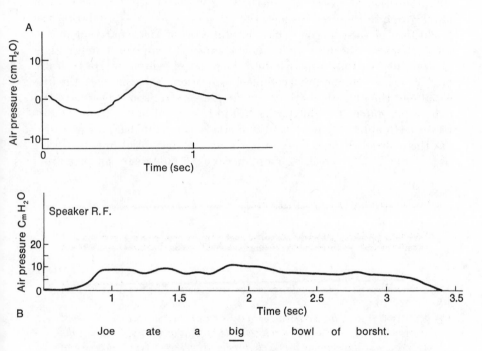

FIGURE 6-1. (*A*) *Pulmonary air pressure during quiet respiration.* (*B*) *Pulmonary air pressure during speech. The speaker was instructed to emphasize the underlined word in the sentence. Note the air pressure peak.*

The two graphs in Figure 6-1 illustrate the air pressure contours that result. The upper graph shows pulmonary air pressure during "quiet" respiration, i.e., the subject is not talking. The vertical scale is the air pressure in the lungs measured in centimetres of H_2O. Air pressure is often measured in terms of the force that a column of water will exert if it is 2, 3, 5, 6.4 cm, etc., high. The higher the column, the higher will be the force that it exerts.[1] The horizontal scale is one of time. The

---

[1] Air pressures are traditionally measured in terms of the height a column of liquid, for example water or mercury, will exert.

graph thus shows how the pulmonary air pressure varies as a function of time over the course of the respiratory cycle. Note that the air pressure is negative (lower than atmospheric air pressure) during inspiration and positive during expiration. It is possible to generate pressures of 70–100 cm H_2O during expiration; musical instruments like the trumpet require these high air pressures for the production of loud tones (Bouhuys, 1974). However, the pulmonary air pressures that usually are encountered during the production of speech are in the neighborhood of 10 cm H_2O. The lower graph in Figure 6-1 shows the pulmonary air pressure during the production of speech. Note that the duration of the expiration in the lower graph has been extended to encompass a complete sentence. The speaker in this study was reading a long list of sentences. He typically produced each sentence on a complete expiration. Note that both the fine detail and the over-all shape of the air pressure functions plotted in the two graphs differ. The differences in the fine detail follow from the different techniques that were used to measure the pulmonary air pressure, but the over-all shape is a result of the special pattern of muscle control that occurs during speech to maintain an even pulmonary air pressure.

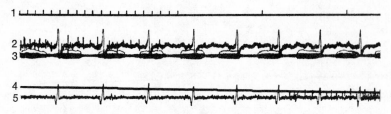

FIGURE 6-2. *The electrical activity of several muscles of the chest during speech. The traces were recorded on an oscilloscope during the repetition of the syllable* [ma]; (1) *time marker, seconds;* (2) *decreasing electrical activity of the external intercostals;* (3) *acoustic signal recorded by microphone;* (4) *volume of air in the lungs gradually decreasing;* (5) *increasing activity of the internal intercostals.* (*After Draper et al., 1960.*)

In Figure 6-2 a recording of the electrical activity of several of the muscles of the chest is reproduced (Draper et al., 1960). As we noted in Chapter 2, the regulation of air pressure during the production of speech involves a fairly complex sequence of muscular maneuvers. At the start of the expiration the force of the elastic recoil of the lungs is very high. If the elastic recoil force were not opposed, the pulmonary air pressure would be much higher than 10 cm H_2O. The speaker whose muscle activity is monitored in Figure 6-2, therefore, initially opposed the elastic recoil force by tensing his external intercostal muscles. This shows up in

Figure 6-2 in terms of the height and number of electrical "spikes" recorded by the electrode that was inserted into this muscle. The electrode was thinner than a standard hypodermic needle and is not itself dangerous or painful if inserted carefully. Medical supervision is, however, obviously mandatory for this procedure.

The external intercostal muscle is an inspiratory muscle in the sense that it functions during quiet respiration to expand the lungs during inspiration. The speaker, however, is using this muscle during the expiratory phase of speech to "hold back" the elastic recoil force and maintain a steady low pulmonary air pressure. Note that the activity of this muscle, as indicated by the frequency and amplitude of the electrical spikes, diminishes, and that the speaker gradually brings into play an internal intercostal muscle. The internal intercostal muscle monitored is an expiratory muscle, i.e., it contracts to deflate the lungs and force air out of the respiratory system. The speaker brings this muscle into play to keep the pulmonary air pressure steady as the elastic recoil force falls below the level necessary to maintain the initial level. In other words, there is a complex patterning of muscles that is necessary to maintain a steady air pressure during speech. The "scheduling" of these different muscles will depend on the length of the sentence that the speaker intends to produce, and the speaker's posture. If you are standing erect, the contents of your stomach will pull downwards and tend to expand the lung volume. If you are flat on your back or in an intermediate position, things will be different and a different pattern of muscular activity will be necessary to maintain the same pulmonary air pressure (Mead et al., 1968). The demands imposed by the need for different oxygen transfer rates in walking or running also interact with the constraints of speech (Bouhuys, 1974), but speakers are able to make all the necessary adjustments "automatically."

Linguistic Implications of Respiratory Control: Syllable and Sentence

Studies of the variation of pulmonary air pressure during speech (Draper et al., 1960; Lieberman, 1967, 1968; Atkinson, 1973) show that it is relatively steady over the course of a sentence-length expiration. There are no systematic variations that correspond to "syllable pulses" as Stetson (1951) claimed. Local "prominences" in air pressure sometimes occur when a speaker stresses or emphasizes a syllable or word, but this is not always the case (Lieberman, 1967, 1968; Atkinson, 1973). Different speakers, moreover, regulate their pulmonary air pressure in different manners. The single factor that is uniform is that the pulmonary air pressure must fall at the end of an expiration. This is obviously a necessary consequence of the speaker's initiating inspiration, which must involve a negative pulmonary air pressure. The terminal falling air pressure transitions in Figure 6-1 illustrate this phenomenon, which has linguistic significance.

The control of the muscles of respiration is interesting because it demonstrates that the muscular gestures that underlie speech are "programmed," i.e., organized in a global manner in terms of linguistically determined segments. A speaker seems to have some knowledge of the duration of the sentence that he is going to utter before he takes air into his lungs. The amount of air that a speaker takes into his lungs is usually proportional to the length of the sentence that *will be* uttered. The duration of an expiration is thus linguistically conditioned during speech production and it can vary between 300 msec and 40 sec. It usually marks the length of a sentence. In the recitation of certain types of poetry it is a function of the poetic structure (Lieberman and Lieberman, 1973). This contrasts with the usual 2-sec length of the expiratory phase during quiet respiration. The inspiratory phase of respiration is roughly equal to the expiratory phase in duration during quiet breathing. During speech production or during the excitation of woodwind or brass instruments the inspiratory phase stays short while the expiratory phase varies in duration. The physiology of the respiratory system that allows the inspiratory muscles to hold back the elastic recoil force of the lungs probably is the reason that speech takes place on the expiratory phase and the duration of the expiratory phase is the linguistically conditioned variable.

The physiology of the human subglottal respiratory system is not a uniquely human attribute. Its anatomy is essentially similar to that of other terrestrial mammals. The seemingly odd system in which the lungs essentially float in the pleural space (which gives rise to the elastic recoil force) follows from the fact that the lungs evolved from the swim bladders of fish (Darwin, 1859). Other animals, for example, wolves, whose vocal communications involve long passages of vocalization also produce their calls on the expiratory phase of respiration.

Humans appear to use feedback control mechanisms to regulate their respiratory muscles during speech and singing. Feedback control systems are essentially ones in which the output of the system is monitored in order to make necessary corrections. In a feedback-regulated cookie factory the final products would be constantly sampled and eaten. If their taste, texture, and so on, deviated from the desired standards of quality, necessary corrections would be taken at appropriate stages in the production process. In a feedback-regulated high fidelity amplifier for the reproduction of music, the electrical output of the amplifier is constantly monitored by means of electronic circuits that also apply signals that correct distortions. Feedback-regulated systems obviously differ with respect to how they are implemented, how they work, how fast they work, etc., but all feedback systems must have sensors that derive information on the output of the "device" that is to be regulated. The feedback system also must transmit, or *feed*, this information *back* to some point where corrections can be made (hence, the term feedback). In Figure 6-3 a schematic diagram of the intercostal muscles and a segment of the spinal cord illustrates some of the components of the feedback system that is involved in the regulation of respiration.

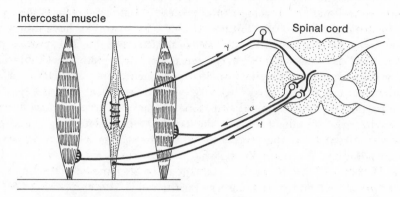

FIGURE 6-3. *"Feedback" system for regulation of a respiratory muscle. (After Bouhuys, 1974.)*

The middle muscle "fiber" in the diagram illustrates a *muscle spindle.* Muscle spindles are devices that signal the relative state of muscle contraction. A muscle applies a force as it contracts; its "output," therefore, is a function of the extent to which it has contracted. In the diagram of Figure 6-3 the pathway with the arrow labeled $\rightarrow\gamma$ transmits the electrical signal from the signal to the spinal cord. At the level of the spinal cord special regulatory mechanisms generate electrical signals that are transmitted back to the intercostal muscles by the pathways labeled $\leftarrow\alpha$ and $\leftarrow\gamma$. The symbols α and γ identify particular pathways. The physiologic function of these feedback systems in respiration is as yet still not understood but it is clear that they play an essential role (Bouhuys, 1974). They operate extremely rapidly; the regulation of respiration as a function of exercise, for example, takes place within the phase of the breath in which work begins (Dejours, 1963).

Muscle spindles are numerous in the intercostal muscles, which, together with the abdominal muscles, are active during speech and singing. The diaphragm, which traditionally is supposed to be an important muscle for the regulation of pulmonary air pressure during singing, has very few muscle spindles. Despite the claims made by many teachers of voice and singing, the diaphragm performs no active role in either speech or singing (Bouhuys, 1974). The absence of muscle spindles and the role of feedback control perhaps explain the inactivity of the diaphragm during speech production or singing. The diaphragm is used during quiet respiration but it does not appear to be used when we have to carefully regulate pulmonary air pressure.

"Learning" to Breath

Studies of the respiratory activity of human infants demonstrate that there is a well-defined developmental process. What is not clear is the role of learning in this process. Trained athletes, for example, have different respiratory patterns than do untrained healthy people. The process of "learning" is "unconscious" in the sense that the athlete is not told that he or she should use a specific muscle in a particular manner. However, a distinct pattern of "learned" activity emerges as the athlete is exposed to a particular environmental situation. The process by which we learn to produce the sounds of a particular language or dialect is not conceptually different from the process by which an athlete learns to breathe while running. We don't know what we are doing when we learn to talk. We simply learn to speak a language if we are exposed to the linguistic environment and start before we are too old. There appears to be a "critical" period or critical periods involved in language learning. If we start before a certain age (which may vary for different individuals), it is easy to learn to speak a second language fluently. For most people it becomes impossible or extremely difficult to learn to speak another language without a "foreign accent" after a certain age. Similar effects occur with respect to the "simple" act of breathing. Human beings appear to "learn" how to breathe effectively at high altitudes. If you're a native "lowlander" who ascends to 12,500 feet, exercise is at first very difficult. If you wait and acclimatize, after approximately 11 days, your respiratory pattern changes and it becomes easier to exercise. However, the native "highlanders," who have grown up living at that altitude will continue to breathe more effectively (Lefrancois et al., 1969). They will need to take in about 50 per cent less air than you do when you both perform the same task. The ability to learn the respiratory patterns that lead to more effective breathing at high altitudes appears to involve a critical period. Many of the coordinated patterns of muscular activity that structure various aspects of the behavior of humans and other animals appear to involve learning an automatic response pattern (Bouhuys, 1974; Lieberman, 1975).

The Measurement of Lung Volume and Volume Change

We have already discussed some of the techniques that are necessary to derive data on pulmonary air pressure during speech or singing. Measurements of lung volume and the rate of change of lung volume which is equivalent to air flow are easy to get without much discomfort to the subject. As the volume of air in your lungs increases or decreases, the volume of your body also increases or decreases. There is no "excess space" within your body. You, therefore, can measure changes in lung volume by measuring changes in the volume of your body that occur as you breathe. The device that is used to make this measurement is called the body plethysmograph. It consists of a sealed box in which a subject can sit with his head out and a seal around his neck. The air inside the box will be disturbed as the volume of the subject's body changes as he breathes in and out. It is not difficult to measure these changes in the air trapped inside the plethysmograph and compute the changes in lung volume (Bouhuys et al., 1966). It is not necessary to put a face mask on the subject or otherwise to interfere with his breathing.

The body box or plethysmograph, however, will not respond to rapid changes in air flow. The rapid changes in air flow that are associated with sounds like the consonants [p], [t], or [h] can be measured with face masks that incorporate wire mesh flowmeter screens (Klatt et al., 1968).

The Larynx

The larynx is an air valve that has two basic modes of operation. It can be set to a particular sized opening, which can vary from a complete closure of the airway from the lungs to minimum obstruction. The larynx is generally open widest during inspiration, when it is advantageous to have minimum interference with the air flow. The pictures of the larynx in Chapter 2 showed the larynx in an open position. The larynx can completely seal the airways. This frequently occurs when you are standing erect and lifting a weight. The larynx closes and seals air in the lungs, which stabilizes the rib cage. The larynx can also close to protect the lungs from the intrusion of harmful material. The larynx maintains particular openings during the production of certain speech sounds. We will discuss data that show that the larnyx opens wider during the production of a sound like [h] than it does during a sound like [f] (the first sound of the word *fat*). However, the speech function that the larynx is most directly associated with is the generation of quasiperiodic series of puffs of air. These periodic, or nearly periodic, air puffs constitute the source of acoustic energy that characterizes phonation. As we noted in Chapter 2, the vowels of English are usually phonated or, in the terminology that is usually used in linguistically oriented discussions, *voiced*.

The Myoelastic-Aerodynamic Theory of Phonation

In Figure 6-4 several views are sketched of the cartilages and intrinsic muscles of the human larynx. It is very difficult to visualize the larynx's separate parts. Our knowledge of how the larynx works derives from Joahnnes Müller's nineteenth-century studies. Müller excised larynges

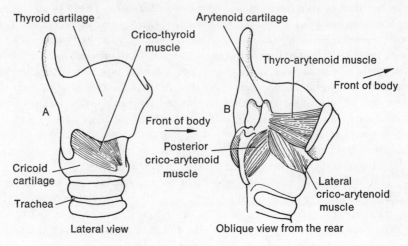

FIGURE 6-4. *Cartilages and intrinsic muscles of the larynx.*

from human cadavers, simulated the forces of various muscles by applying forces through strings fixed to various cartilages, and provided power to the system by blowing through the excised larynges (Müller, 1837). Van den Berg (1958, 1960, 1962) has quantitatively replicated Müller's original experiments.

The major structures of the larynx consist of a number of cartilages. Let us start from the bottom part of the larynx and work upwards. The first major cartilage is the cricoid, which is ring-shaped and sits on top of the trachea (Figure 6-4A). The trachea looks like a vacuum cleaner hose in most illustrations. Two small cartilages, the arytenoids each sit on one side of the cricoid towards its posterior (rear) (Figure 6-4B). The relationship between the arytenoid cartilages and the muscles that operate on them may be somewhat clearer in the schematic views that appear in Figure 6-5. The thyroid cartilage also sits on top of the cricoid. It is open at the rear and its closed solid front surface is positioned on the anterior (front) surface of the cricoid. When you feel your Adam's apple you are feeling your thyroid cartilage. The Adam's apple is usually more prominent in adult human males since their thyroid cartilages grow disproportionately large during puberty. The vocal cords consist of the conglomerate of ligaments, muscles, and tissue that run between the two arytenoid cartilages and the thyroid cartilage and the cricoid cartilage.

The thyroarytenoid muscle, which is sketched in Figure 6-4B, runs from the arytenoid cartilage to the thyroid. It is the muscle that constitutes the principal mass of each vocal cord. When it contracts, it applies force that tends to pull the arytenoids closer to the thyroid, as the arrows on Figure 6-5D show. The vocal ligaments also run above the thyroarytenoid muscles between the arytenoid and thyroid cartilages. The lateral cricoarytenoid muscles go between the arytenoid cartilages and the cricoid. When the lateral cricoarytenoid muscles tense, they swing the arytenoid cartilages inwards and adduct, i.e., close, the glottis. This is schematized in Figure 6-5. The interarytenoid muscles, which connect the two arytenoid cartilages, also adduct the glottis when they are tensioned. The combination of lateral cricoarytenoids and interarytenoids function to pull the arytenoid cartilages together and close the glottis. These two muscles also apply what Van den Berg (1958, 1960, 1962) has termed medial compression.

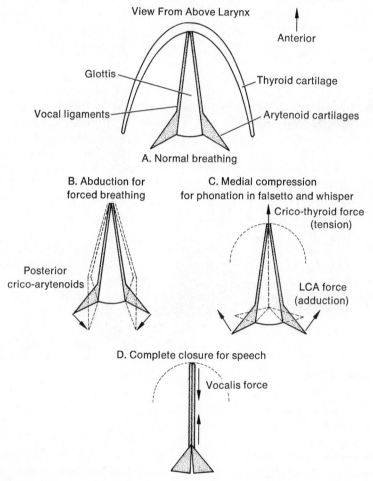

FIGURE 6-5. *Action of the intrinsic laryngeal muscles (the term Vocalis is often applied to the thyro-arytenoid muscle). (After Atkinson, 1973.)*

The posterior cricoarytenoid muscle (Figure 6-4B), in contrast, swings the arytenoid cartilages outwards and opens i.e., abducts, the glottis. The posterior cricoarytenoid muscle functions whenever you open your larynx. The cricothyroid muscle applies longitudinal tension. It lengthens and tenses the vocal cords (which consist of the vocal ligaments and thyroarytenoid muscles) by rocking the thyroid cartilage downwards and the cricoid cartilage upwards. Johannes Müller in his pioneering experiments was able to simulate the action of this muscle with the primitive technology that was available in the 1820s. This muscle is active in controlling the fundamental frequency of phonation, but is not its sole muscular determinant. The thyroarytenoids (vocalis muscle) upon contraction can either decrease or increase the tension in the vocal ligaments themselves, depending on the state of other muscles.

The Forces of Phonation

During phonation, the vocal cords move in response to a rapid alternation of aerodynamic and aerostatic forces generated by the flow of air. These forces are inherently nonlinear; they rapidly build up and then abruptly stop. The elastic forces of the larynx also interact with these forces during phonation. The basis of phonation is, however, the passive movement of the vocal cords under the influence of forces generated by the movement of air outwards from the lungs. The larynx itself adds no energy to the process. The laryngeal muscles serve to initiate and modulate phonation. The dynamic interaction of the aerodynamic, aerostatic, and muscle forces during phonation is very complex and is the focus of research projects that make use of computer-modeling techniques (Flanagan et al., 1970, 1975). It is however, useful to discuss qualitatively the process of phonation in order to get a sense of the process. Phonation is initiated by the laryngeal muscles swinging the arytenoid cartilages together and setting an initial phonation neutral position, medial compression, and longitudinal tension for the vocal cords. The interarytenoid and lateral cricoarytenoid muscles adduct, i.e., bring the vocal cords together and keep them medially compressed. Medial compression is necessary in some degree for phonation to take place. Imagine bringing your lips together and squeezing them together slightly. You have adducted your lips and applied some medial compression. If you now blow air out from your lungs, you can start your lips moving rapidly outwards and then inwards, producing a raspy noise, *if* you have applied the right amount of medial compression. If you squeeze your lips together too hard, they will stay closed. This is analogous to the production of a *glottal stop*, in which a great deal of medial compression is applied, stopping phonation. If, in contrast, you do not apply enough medial compression then you will simply blow your lips apart as you build up pulmonary air pressure. This is analogous to the production of turbulent or *strident* phonation. Newborn infants frequently do this, producing a characteristic quality to their cries. *Strident phonation* does not appear to be a phonetic feature of English, but it could be used. One point to remember here is that cutting back on medial compression is only one possible way of generating strident phonation. We will point out some other articulatory possibilities.

Now suppose that your vocal cords have swung together, partially or completely obstructing the air flow through the vocal tract. What happens? In Figure 6-6 a schematic view of a section made on a frontal plane is presented. A larynx in this plane is one sectioned from ear hole to ear hole with the saw blade running between the ear holes and then cutting down through the neck.

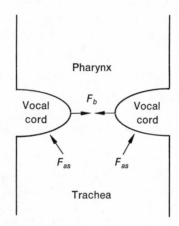

FIGURE 6-6. *Schematic view of vocal cords and some of the forces of phonation.*

The arrows labeled F_{as} represent the force generated by the air pressure impinging on the lower surface of the vocal cords. It is greatest when the cords are most nearly closed since $F_{as} = P_{pulmonary}$ (surface area of vocal cords). The arrow labeled F_b is the Bernoulli force that is generated by the air flow through the glottis. The Bernoulli force that operates on the vocal cords is a consequence of the increase in the speed of the air molecules as they move through the glottal constriction. As the glottal opening becomes smaller, the speed of the air molecules increases relative to their speed in the trachea and pharynx. The effect is similar to the motion of people when a crowd goes through a revolving door. When you are in the revolving door you are moving faster than you were in the crowd next to the door. The Bernoulli force is also the factor that piles up old newspapers in narrow alleys between buildings when the wind blows through the passageway. The Bernoulli force is greatest when the glottal opening is smallest, except that it disappears, i.e., equals zero, when the glottis closes completely because there then is no air flow whatsoever (Lieberman, 1967). Phonation is the result of the process wherein vocal cords are moved in and out by these alternating forces that ultimately depend on the air pressure generated in the lungs, the pulmonary air pressure. F_{as} pushes the vocal cords apart. F_b sucks them together.

The laryngeal muscles position the vocal cords and provide the medial compression that keeps the vocal cords from being blown apart or simply staying sealed. The laryngeal muscles also set up a "tissue" force that enters into the balance of forces that produce phonation. The tissue force will always act to restore the vocal cord to its phonation neutral position. It is analogous to the force exerted by the spring on a screen door. The screen door's spring acts to pull the door back to its "neutral" position when it is opened. If a simplified equation of motion is derived for the vocal cord, the important relationship that governs the rate at which the vocal cords move in and out becomes apparent.

$$F_{as} - F_b - F_t = ma$$

where m is the mass of the vocal cord, a is its acceleration, and F_t is the tissue force.

At the start of a glottal cycle the glottal opening is small because the phonation neutral position has closed or nearly closed the glottis. F_{as} is maximum. If F_{as} is greater than the sum of the tissue force and F_b, the vocal cords move outwards. The glottal opening becomes larger and F_b decreases, but F_{as} also decreases and F_t increases. When F_t is greater than F_{as}, the vocal cords begin to move inwards, and the process repeats itself.

What will increase the acceleration a of the vocal cord? Obviously the acceleration will vary as the various forces change their magnitude during the glottal cycle. However, if the individual forces are greater, the acceleration will be greater in some part of the cycle. Thus, increasing the tissue force, or increasing the pulmonary air pressure will increase the acceleration. (F_{as} is a function of the pulmonary air pressure.) The tissue force can be increased by tensing muscles like the lateral cricoarytenoid and interarytenoids, which generate medial compression, or by tensing the cricothyroid muscle, which stretches the vocal cords in their anterior-posterior plane (longitudinal tension). The thyroarytenoid muscles, which constitute the body of the vocal cords, also will increase the tissue force as they tense. So will the external thyroarytenoid muscles. Any one of a number of muscles can increase the tension on the vocal cords. So long as the vocal cords are phonating—this is important since the entire process can be stopped if some tension is set wrong, blowing the vocal cords apart or keeping them together—increases in tissue force will cause an increase in the acceleration of the vocal cord.

Since the velocity of the vocal cord is equal to the integral of acceleration with respect to time, the vocal cord will move faster if any of these forces increase. The fundamental frequency of phonation, which is the rate at which the vocal cords open and close, thus will increase if either the pulmonary air pressure or the tension set by the various laryngeal muscles increases. The laryngeal muscles as they tense also can change the vibrating mass that moves (Hollien and Curtis, 1960; Hollien, 1962; Hollien and Colton, 1969). If the forces that act on the vocal cords stay constant while the vibrating mass increases, the vocal cords will move slower. The fundamental frequency of phonation thus is a function of both the air pressure and the tension set by various laryngeal muscles.

Control of Fundamental Frequency: Electromyographic Data

Electromyographic data can be derived from the larynges of normal speakers by carefully inserting electrodes in appropriate muscles and amplifying and recording the signals (Sawashima, 1974). The techniques for inserting the electrodes are very complex and must be approached with the greatest caution by otolaryngologists trained in this technique. In Figure 6-7 electromyographic data for the cricothyroid muscle and the sternohyoid muscle (one of the laryngeal "hanger" muscles which we will discuss in the next section of this chapter) are presented together with a record of the subglottal air pressure obtained by means of a tracheal puncture and the audio signal. The speaker was an adult speaker of American English who was reading (with stress on the word *Bev*) the sentence *Bev loves Bob*. The fundamental frequency of phonation can be clearly seen both in the trace of subglottal air pressure and in the audio signal. Note that there is an increase in the subglottal air pressure on the initial stressed word *Bev*. If the speaker had not stressed this word, the subglottal air pressure would have about 8 to 10 cm H_2O. There was also increased electrical activity in the cricothyroid muscle, which correlated with the stressed word. The electrical activity of the cricothyroid muscle shows up in terms of the amplitude and frequency of the "spikes." Note that the subglottal air pressure falls at the end of this expiration while phonation still is taking place. The fundamental frequency of phonation also falls as the subglottal air pressure falls.

The "raw" electromyographic data of Figure 6-7 are difficult to interpret. It is hard to make quantitative statements concerning the relative activity of particular muscles or the total pattern of muscular activity. The electrical activity that the electromyographic electrodes record can also be misleading if only one token of an utterance is considered. Various artifacts can be recorded and the speaker may also produce a particular token in an anomalous manner. The most reliable technique for the evaluation of electromyographic data makes use of computer-implemen-

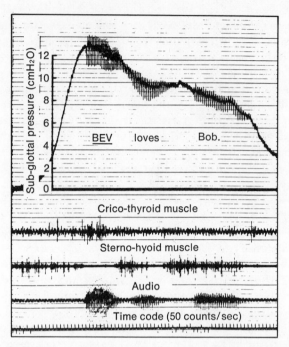

FIGURE 6-7. *Subglottal air pressure, acoustic signal, and electro-myographic activity of cricothyroid and sternohyoid muscles.* (*After Atkinson, 1973.*)

ted averaging of a large sample of tokens of a particular utterance from an individual speaker. The speaker reads a long list of utterances that includes many tokens of particular sentences. The particular sentences are read in a random order to avoid the "singsong" patterns that can occur when you repeat the identical sentence over and over again. The electromyographic signals and the acoustic signal are continuously monitored and recorded on magnetic tape using a multitrack instrumentation recorder. Special marker signals are also recorded that identify the individual tokens of each sentence in the computer program that is later used to integrate the electromyographic signals derived from the muscles under investigation and average the integrated data for the many tokens of each particular sentence. The integrating and averaging process reduces the possibility of electrical artifacts being interpreted as muscle activity (Harris, 1974).

In Figure 6-8 computer-averaged data for 38 tokens of the sentence *Bev loves Bob* are presented. The same speaker produced all of these utterances in two different recording sessions. The plot of fundamental frequency as a function of time that appears at the bottom of Figure 6-8

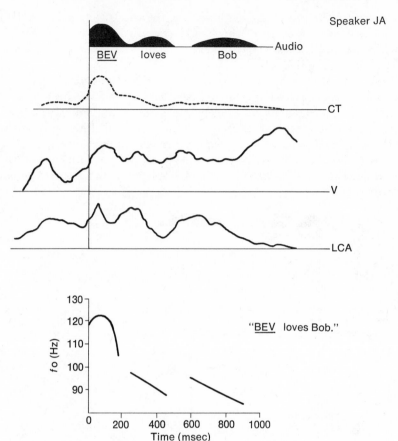

FIGURE 6-8. *Computer-averaged and computer-integrated electro-myographic signals and fundamental frequency of phonation as functions of time for 38 tokens of the sentence* Bev *loves Bob spoken by one speaker. The speaker stressed the word* Bev. *The activity of the cricothyroid muscles* (CT), *internal thyroarytenoid muscles* (V), *and lateral cricoarytenoid muscles* (LCA) *electrical activity are plotted.* (After Atkinson, 1973.)

was derived by a special computer program (Atkinson, 1973, p. 38) that uses an autocorrelation method and is accurate to within 2 Hz. The integrated and averaged plots for three muscles are shown in this figure, which is derived from Atkinson (1973). Atkinson also measured the electrical activity of the sternohyoid and sternothyroid as well as subglottal air pressure, lung volume, and air flow. Note that there is a peak in the cricothyroid muscle's activity, which is correlated with the peak in fundamental frequency for the stressed word *Bev*. The lower fundamental frequency of the rest of the sentence, i.e., the words *loves Bob*, is a consequence of lower activity of the lateral cricoarytenoid muscle acting in concert with the cricothyroid and the subglottal air pressure (which was plotted in Figure 6-7).

Figure 6-9 shows plots of these muscles and fundamental frequency for the same speaker reading the question *Bev loves Bob?* Note that the fundamental frequency rises sharply at the end of the sentence, when all three of the muscles show increased activity. A detailed statistical analysis of this data by Atkinson shows that the fundamental frequency of phonation is primarily controlled by the subglottal air pressure in utterances like that in Figure 6-8. Although laryngeal muscles can be used to enhance

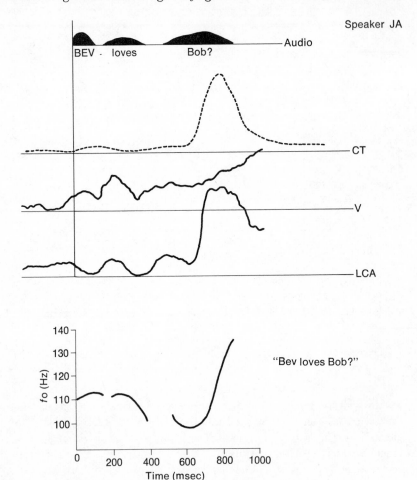

FIGURE 6-9. *Plots similar to those of Figure 6-8 for the same speaker's tokens of the question* Bev loves Bob?

the local prominences in the fundamental frequency function that are associated with the speaker's stressing a particular word (the word *Bev* in Figure 6-8), the primary determinant of f_0 variation is the subglottal air pressure. These utterances are produced with the larynx adjusted in a *register of phonation* that results in the fundamental frequency being fairly sensitive to air pressure variations. In contrast, the utterance plotted in Figure 6-9 was produced in a *register of phonation* in which the larynx was not very sensitive to variations in subglottal air pressure. The fundamental frequency contour throughout this sentence is primarily a function of the tension of the laryngeal muscles; the subglottal air pressure has very little effect on the fundamental frequency.

Registers of Phonation

Johannes Müller in the course of his pioneering studies with excised larynges found that the registers of phonation that singers had discerned were the result of the larynx phonating in different "modes." Singers had noted the presence of at least two basic modes of phonation, the "chest" and "falsetto" registers. A person singing in the falsetto register sounds quite different from the same person singing in the chest register. The fundamental frequency of phonation is higher in the falsetto register, but that is not the sole difference in voice quality. There is less energy present in the harmonics of the fundamental in the falsetto register than is the case of the chest register. A singer phonating at the same fundamental frequency in his falsetto register will have less energy present at higher harmonics of the fundamental than a singer phonating at the same fundamental in his or her chest register. A countertenor singing at the same fundamental as a contralto thus will have a different voice quality. Both singers will have the same fundamental frequency, but the glottal spectrum of the countertenor singing in his falsetto register will have less energy at the higher harmonics. The falsetto register sometimes is said to be "purer" in quality.

Müller believed that phonation would occur in falsetto register when high tensions were applied to the vocal cords by the laryngeal muscles. Van den Berg (1960) in his work with excised human larynges has been able to demonstrate quantitatively that this is the case. The vocal cords are stretched quite thin in the falsetto register. The role of the Bernoulli force in closing the glottis is negligible and the glottis typically does not close during phonation. The glottal waveform can become almost sinusoidal.

The "chest" register, which really doesn't involve using the chest in any unique way, may consist of several subregisters. The larynx does not behave in the same manner throughout the chest register. Van den Berg (1960) first noted that the sensitivity of the larynx to variations in subglottal air pressure varied for different adjustments of the laryngeal muscles. In other words, a change of, for example, 1 cm H_2O subglottal air pressure could result in as little as 2.5 Hz or as much as 18 Hz in the fundamental frequency, depending on how the vocal cords were positioned and tensioned. Van den Berg's data were derived from excised human larynges, so there was some question whether the muscular adjustments of this data actually occur in living human speakers. Measurements on the rate of change in fundamental frequency with respect to changes in sub-glottal (or transglottal) air pressure in living speakers are, however, con-sistent with Van den Berg's data (Lieberman et al., 1968; Ohala, 1970).

The muscular maneuvers that are involved in adjusting the larynx to achieve phonation in different registers are not completely understood. It looks as though the muscles that support the larynx are involved as well as the "intrinsic" muscles like the cricothyroid, interarytenoids, etc., that we have so far discussed. These muscles help to support the cartilages of the laynx. They also can move the larynx with respect to other parts of the body. The sternohyoid muscle (cf. Figure 6-14), for example, can pull the larynx downward if the muscles that connect the hyoid bone to the mandible and skull are not tensioned. A number of studies have measured the activity of the sternohyoid muscle and have attempted to correlate its activity with the fundamental frequency of phonation. Some have found that fundamental frequency tended to fall when it was active (Ohala, 1970; Ohala and Hirose, 1970), whereas others have not (Garding et al., 1970; Simada and Hirose, 1970). Atkinson's statistical analysis (1973) of the activity of the laryngeal muscles may explain these different results. The sternohyoid appears to function as a phonation register-shifting mechanism in the speakers whom he studied. The utterance plotted in Figure 6-8 was produced in what Atkinson terms the *low chest* register. The utterance plotted in Figure 6-9 was produced in the *high chest* register. The speaker appears to adjust his larynx to "set it up" in the appropriate register before he produces a sound. The sternohyoid muscle was active in Atkinson's data when the larynx was going through these register shifts.

FRY REGISTER. Much more research is necessary before we can state with reasonable certainty the muscular adjustments that are in-volved in effecting register shifts (Shipp and McGlone, 1971). Different individuals may use very different maneuvers and some register shifts may be more natural or prevalent than others. Trained singers, for example, are able to make smooth transitions from one register to another by means of adjustments that may involve bending their necks and upper torsos (Proctor, 1964). The old photos of Caruso, for example, often show him with his chin pulled sharply downwards. Some registers of phonation are not commonly used by speakers of English. The "fry" register appears to involve very slack tension and a large vibrating mass. Ingenious radiographic techniques reveal the vibrating mass (Hollien and Colton, 1969). The fundamental frequency of phonation in this register is in the order of 60 Hz for a male speaker. There also is a great deal of irregularity from one pitch period to the next. In certain pathologic conditions associated with cancer of the larynx this is all that a speaker can do. Normal speakers also can produce this register if they so desire.

BREATHY PHONATION. During normal phonation the glottal waveform has energy only at the fundamental and its harmonics. Noiselike "breathy" excitation of the vocal tract can, however, be generated by increasing the air flow through the larynx to the point where turbulence is generated. This can be done by introducing an opening that stays open throughout the glottal cycle (Timcke et al., 1958). If you think best in hydraulic terms think of the larynx during phonation as a water valve that is being rapidly opened and closed producing "puffs" of water. Opening a second valve and letting it stay open will increase the total air flow. There are several ways to do this. During normal phonation the larynx's posterior portion is held together while phonation takes place

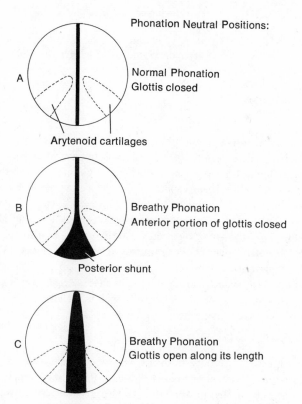

FIGURE 6-10. *Adjustments of the larynx that can produce normal (A) and breathy phonation (B) and (C).*

in the anterior portion. Looking down at the larynx, one sees the situation that is pictured in Figure 6-10A. If the posterior part is kept open during phonation as pictured in Figure 10B, a constant "shunt" will admit air through it. It is possible to open the posterior part by not tensioning the interarytenoid muscles. The glottal area waveform will be like that shown in Figure 6-11. Note that there is a constant steady opening through the larynx in addition to the periodic component.

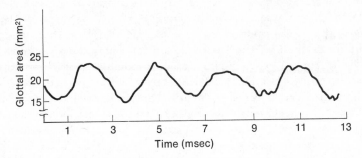

FIGURE 6-11. *Measurement of glottal area waveform derived from computer analysis of a high-speed movie (Lieberman, 1963). The waveform shows the glottal opening as a function of time. Note that the glottis is never completely closed in this particular example of breathy phonation.*

The effect of the different phonation neutral positions of Figures 6-10B and 6-10C will be equivalent insofar as both maneuvers will yield additional air flow. The high air flow will generate turbulent noise excitation if the air flow in any part of the supralaryngeal vocal tract or at the larynx exceeds that consistent with *laminar* flow.

In a sound like /h/ the air flow at the glottis is itself so great that noise-like excitation is generated. "Normal" English vowels also may be produced using breathy excitation generated at the larynx. Whispered vowels *without* phonation have this quality. It is also possible to produce sounds in which both breathy and periodic excitation co-occur. This is often the case for whispered speech in normal subjects. It also may be the case for breathy vowels that occur in other languages.

The Production of Voiceless Sounds

Studies of the total air-flow through the vocal tract show that voiced sounds are produced with significantly less air flow than voiceless sounds. Sounds like [h] and [s] are produced with the greatest air flow; voiceless stops like [p] with slightly less air flow. All of these voiceless sounds are, however, produced with significantly greater air flow than the voiced vowels (Klatt et al., 1968). The terms —*voiced* and *voiceless* can be used interchangeably to denote sounds that are produced with noise sources without any periodic phonation occurring. The distinction inherent in the contrast +*voicing* versus —*voicing* (or *voiced* versus *voiceless*) is binary. We are saying that sounds can be either voiced or unvoiced and that there is no intermediate in-between state. This binary distinction has a physiologic basis insofar as the larynx can either be adjusted to yield phonation when air begins to flow through it or alternately not yield phonation. The physiologic or functional contrast is thus inherently binary. However, the muscular maneuvers that are necessary to adjust the larynx so phonation will take place are not binary. The activity of a particular muscle depends on the activity of the total ensemble of muscles that adjust the larynx for phonation. It is not possible to derive a simple, binary muscle gesture that can be directly and uniquely related to phonation.

The situation is similar for the seemingly "simple" state of —*voicing*. The differences in air flow that are typical of the different sounds of speech are the result of subtle, graded adjustments of the glottal opening. Observations of the glottis derived from flexible fiber-optic bundles (which allow the larynx to be photographed during the production of normal speech)[2] show that the larynx opens more for the production of an [s] than for a [p] (Sawashima and Miyazaki, 1973). Electromyographic data furthermore show that the different-sized glottal opening is the result of a deliberate muscular maneuver (Hirose and Ushijama, 1974). It is not a secondary result of the greater air flow of the sound [s]. The speaker, in other words, deliberately opens his glottis a little wider to produce greater air flow for the sound [s]. The greater air flow of the sound [s] is necessary to generate noise at the constriction that is formed near the speaker's teeth in the production of the sound [s]. The size of the constriction near the teeth is greater for an [s] than it is for a [p] for the interval in which noise must be generated. It takes more air to generate noise at a constriction through air turbulence when the constriction is

---

[2] The fiber-optic bundle consists of a set of thin fiberglass filaments. Each filament conducts a beam of light along its length in the same manner as a plastic wand conducts light around corners. The fiber-optic bundle has thousands of filaments that each lie in a parallel, geometrically fixed relationship to the others. A lens projects an image on one end of the bundle and the image is conducted to the other end around bends, etc., to a camera (Sawashima and Hirose, 1968). The bundles are quite thin and flexible. If the bundles were inserted through the speaker's nose it would not interfere with articulatory maneuvers in the mouth. Other techniques for deriving information on the size of the glottis involve measuring the light that passes through. (A source of light is placed in contact with the speaker's throat against the front of the trachea and a photo cell that picks up light is lowered to a position above the larynx (Ohala, 1966; Lisker et al., 1969).) This method however, can introduce many artifacts. Ultrasonic scanning techniques (Minifie et al., 1968) and methods that measure the electrical resistance of the glottis have also been used with varying degrees of success (Sawashima, 1974).

wider (Flanagan, 1972). Noise will be generated at a constriction only if the air flow in the constriction is in excess of a critical value. If the constriction is small, the average air flow through the vocal tract does not have to be as high as when the constriction is relatively large. That is because the air flow is more concentrated in the constricted portion if the constriction is smaller.[3]

The "binary" quality of voicing as a phonetic contrast thus rests in the acoustic consequences of the total speech producing mechanism. In producing a "simple" — *voiced* sound the speaker takes into account the relative size of the constriction of the upper airway at which the noise excitation will be generated. At the articulatory and muscular levels (the levels that correspond to data derived by observing structures like the larynx or by monitoring the electrical activity of particular muscles) speech production is complex and no element of the vocal tract really operates in an independent manner.

Our discussion of the binary nature of the sound contrast *voicing* would not be complete if we did not note that some sounds, e.g., the sound [z] in the word *buzz* are produced by adjusting the larynx so that it is phonating and providing an air flow that will generate noise at the constriction that the speaker forms near his teeth. Sounds like [z] are often considered to be both voiced and "strident" by phonologists who want to maintain binary distinctions in their description of the sounds of speech (Jakobson et al., 1963).

Interactions of the Supralaryngeal Vocal Tract on Fundamental Frequency

The source-filter theory of speech production is generally interpreted to mean that the source and filter are completely independent factor. This is not really the case. The output of the larynx during phonation is affected by the transfer function of the supralaryngeal vocal tract. There is aerodynamic coupling between the first formant frequency and the glottal waveform. Low first formants result in a somewhat higher fundamental frequency of phonation, whereas a higher first formant frequency yields a lower f_0. Electrical analogs of the larynx (Flanagan et al., 1970, 1975; Atkinson, 1973), predict this response, which can be observed in the measurements of Peterson and Barney (1952) and other acoustic analyses that have since replicated the Peterson and Barney data. For an average f_0 of 120 Hz, the lower F_1's of /u/ and /i/ raise f_0 about 10 Hz. The higher f_0 of /a/ lowers f_0 about 8–10 Hz. These aerodynamic perturbations

---

[3] Think of a crowd of people moving through a narrow passage from a large room; they'll be moving faster in the narrow passageway. They would have to move still faster to maintain the same "rate of emptying" if they had to exit through a still narrower passageway. "Noise" would be generated as the people collided when they moved faster and faster.

probably most affect phonation in the low chest register. Careful measurements for different registers have not yet been made.

In addition to this aerodynamic coupling, aerostatic coupling between the larynx and the supralaryngeal vocal tract also takes place. Whenever the supralaryngeal vocal tract is obstructed, there must be a build-up in buccal (mouth) air pressure. Since the larynx is powered by the differential between the air pressure beneath and above it, the *transglottal air pressure*, f_0 will fall when, for example, a stop like /b/ is produced in intervocalic position. The fundamental frequency will fall until the transglottal air pressure falls to about 2 cm H_2O when phonation stops. The aerodynamic and aerostatic coupling between the larynx and the supralaryngeal vocal tract will induce fluctuations in f_0 that are a consequence of the inherent physiologic properties of the larynx. This has obvious implications for phonetic theories that attach linguistic significance to the small variations in fundamental frequency that continually occur during normal speech production.

The Supralaryngeal Vocal Tract

As we demonstrated in Chapter 4, formant frequencies are determined by the cross-sectional area function of the supralaryngeal vocal tract. In Figure 6-12, the adult human vocal tract is sketched in a stylized mid-

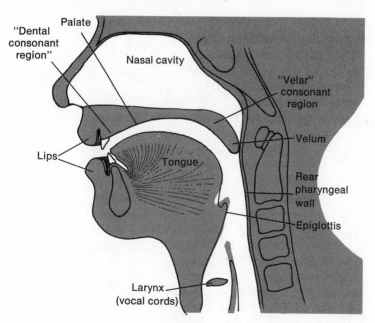

FIGURE 6-12. *Stylized midsagittal section of adult human vocal tract.*

sagittal section. Some of the principal landmarks are noted on the sketch. The lips are, of course, evident. The nasal cavity, which is quite large, is isolated from the oral cavity by the palate and velum. The palate, which forms the roof of the mouth, consists of two parts. The anterior (front) hard palate consists of bone. The posterior (rear) soft palate is made up of muscles and soft tissue. The "velum" or soft palate can move to help seal the nasal cavity from the oral cavity as these muscles tense, or to open the nasal cavity to the oral cavity and the pharnyx. The oral cavity is bounded by the palate and the upper surface of the tongue. The pharynx is bounded by the rear pharyngeal wall, which is positioned in front of the spinal column (the vertebrae are sketched in Figure 6-12) and by the posterior wall of the tongue, which forms the front of the pharynx. The larynx opens into the pharynx.

The open tube that is posterior to the pharynx is the entrance to the esophagus. It normally is closed during speech production and opens briefly while a person swallows. The larynx also moves upwards and forwards and the muscles of the pharynx propel the food into the esophagus, which briefly opens. Swallowing is a good example of a "programmed" act in which a complex series of motor acts proceed in a

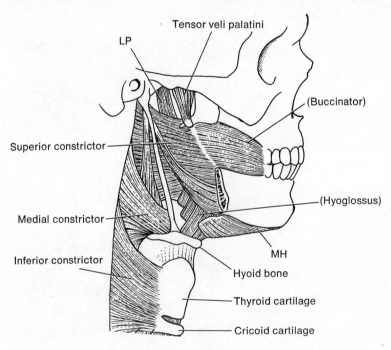

FIGURE 6-13. *The pharyngeal constrictor muscles.*

sequence of which the user is not consciously aware (Bosma, 1957). The muscles that are active during swallowing are also used for very different purposes in different patterns of activity in speech production. The process of "learning" to speak undoubtedly involves setting up new patterns of programmed activity.

In Figure 6-13 the sketches of the pharyngeal constrictor muscles, some of the muscles of the soft palate and the cheek muscles (the buccinators) are sketched. The superior constrictor (SC), medial constrictor (MC), and inferior constrictor of the pharynx propel food down the pharynx as they contract, one after the other. The stylopharyngeus muscle runs from the styloid process of the temporal bone of the skull; we will discuss the muscles that are inserted (i.e., attached) to the styloid process a little later. All of the muscles that we will sketch and discuss are noted in Table 6-1, which is keyed to these diagrams. The "strap" muscles that connect the larynx to the mandible (lower jaw), skull, and sternum (breastbone), some of which have already been discussed, are sketched in Figure 6-14, while the muscles of the tongue and suprahyoid muscles are sketched in Figure 6-15. Some of the muscles of the face and the muscles that close and move the jaw are sketched in Figure 6-16.

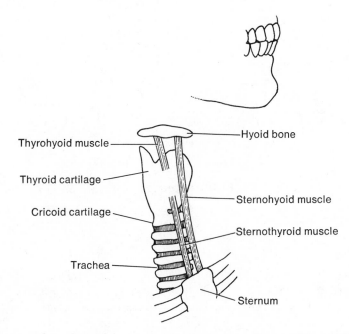

FIGURE 6-14. The "strap" muscles that connect the mandible, skull, larynx, and breastbone.

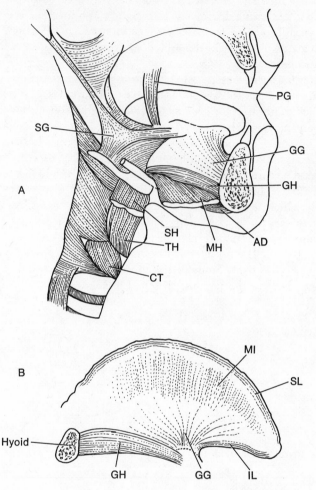

FIGURE 6-15. *Some of the muscles of the tongue. See Table 6-1.*

Electromyographic Studies of Supralaryngeal Muscles

These sketches do not show all of the muscles that can function during respiration, swallowing, chewing, or speaking. These muscles and the muscles that close and open the lips, however, constitute most of the muscles that appear to play a part in the production of speech. We have not included sketches of some of the smaller muscles like the paletoglossus, which runs between the soft palate and the tongue, but these diagrams should provide sufficient orientation for the reader to follow

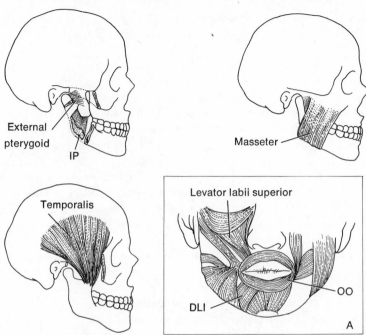

FIGURE 6-16. *Muscles of the face and jaw. See Table 6-1.*

discussions of muscle activity in papers reporting current research.[4] The patterns of muscular activity for different speakers are often quite different even when the speakers are producing the "same" sound in their native language. For example, the patterns of muscular activity for a "simple" act like sealing the nasal cavity from the oral cavity in the production of nasal-stop clusters like those of the nonsense words [fimpip], [fipmip], [futmup], etc., varies for different speakers. Bell-Berti (1973) in a detailed electromyographic study of velopharyngeal closure found that the muscle control patterns of the three speakers who she studied were very different. Two speakers consistently used their superior pharyngeal constrictors to help seal their nasal cavities during the production of the "oral," nonnasal stops [p], [t], [g]. The third speaker presented almost no activity in either the superior constrictor or middle constrictor muscles that could be identified with oral articulation. Electromyographic studies of the oral versus nasal distinction have shown that one particular muscle, the levator palatini, is consistently associated with the production of this distinction (Lubker et al., 1970). When the levator palatini tenses it tends to seal the nasal cavity. Other muscles of the supralaryngeal

[4] A survey of recent research on the electromyographic activity of the muscles of the supralaryngeal vocal tract is presented by Harris (1974).

vocal tract, however, act in concert with this muscle, but they don't behave as consistently. Different speakers exhibit different patterns of
activity.

These data are not consistent with traditional phonetic theories, which
are usually structured in terms of invariant articulatory gestures. If
different speakers use different patterns of muscular activity, it becomes
impossible to classify the sounds of speech this way. A determined phonetician might attempt to salvage the traditional theory (which only
dates back to the midnineteenth century) by defining the binary oral
versus nasal sound contrast in terms of the activity of the levator palatini
muscle. The electromyographic data show that this muscle always functions when a normal speaker produces an oral sound. The binary oral
versus nasal sound contrast cavity thus seemingly could be directly
related to the activity of this particular muscle. If the speaker tensions
his levator palatini muscle, the sound will be oral. If he doesn't tension
this muscle, the sound will be nasal. The distinction would be a binary
one *+levator palatini tensioning* versus *−levator palatini tensioning*.
However, this classificatory scheme won't work.

The aerodynamic phenomena that determine the degree of "coupling"
between the nasal cavity and the velopharyngeal port (the region of the
supralaryngeal vocal tract where the velum and pharynx meet, cf.
Figure 6-12) depend on the nature of the sound that is being formed in
the supralaryngeal vocal tract. The vowels [i] and [u] (in *meet* and *boot*)
require a better velopharyngeal port seal than the vowel [a] (the vowel
of *father*) when they are produced as *−nasal* vowels (House and Stevens,
1956). The three speakers of English who Bell-Berti (1973) monitored
consistently used more levator palatini activity for these vowels. The
speakers, in other words, used more muscle activity to effect a tighter
seal of the nasal cavity when it was necessary to do this to produce the
desired acoustic signal. The elevation of the velum (the soft palate) began
earlier and achieved a greater peak magnitude for the vowels [i] and [u]
than for [a]. The speakers in Bell-Berti's study, in fact, did not bother to
raise their velums for the vowel [a] after nasal consonants where the slight
nasal quality was not very evident at the acoustic level. These data are
consistent with a phonetic theory that assigns primary status to acoustic
contrasts (Lieberman, 1970; Ladefoged et al., 1972). The common phonetic distinction between the nasalized and oral vowel pairs [ã] versus
[a], [ĩ] versus (i), and (ũ) versus [u] (where the symbol ∼ indicates
nasality) is the presence of the formants and "zeros" that are the acoustic
correlates of nasality (Fant, 1960; Fujimura, 1962). The activity of the
muscles that generate these acoustic correlates vary for the different
vowels, even when we restrict our attention to a single speaker.

Electromyographic studies also demonstrate that it is impossible to
associate any particular muscle with a unique sound contrast. Although

the levator palatini muscle is closely associated with the nasal-versus-oral sound contrast, it also enters into the control of phonation in the production of stop consonants like [b] (Yanagihara and Hyde, 1966). The pharyngeal constrictors are also active in the production of the differences in anterioposterior width that enter into the production of sounds like vowels [i], [u], and [a].

Cineradiographic Studies

In Figure 6-17 a diagram is reproduced of a frame from an X-ray movie of the vocal tract of an adult speaker during the production of speech. The diagram is a reproduction of a tracing of a single frame of this movie. The subject was positioned in front of an image-intensifying apparatus that permits X-ray views to be made with reduced levels of exposure. The tracing was part of a quantitative study (Perkell, 1969) in which measurements of the displacements of various parts of the vocal tract were made for every frame of a slow motion, sound-synchronized

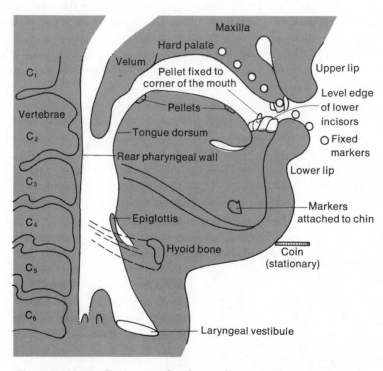

FIGURE 6-17. *Diagram of a frame from an X-ray motion picture of the vocal tract of an adult human male during the production of speech. Anatomical features are labeled. Reprinted from* Physiology of Speech Production, *by Joseph Perkell by permission of The M.I.T. Press, Cambridge, Mass. Copyright 1969.*

cineradiograph of a single adult speaker (Professor Kenneth N. Stevens of the Massachusetts Institute of Technology) carefully pronouncing a list of short syllables. The cineradiographic film was specially processed to enhance its quality. The subject's head was stabilized while he spoke and lead pellets were glued to his tongue to serve as reference points. The film's frames were numbered and measured and compared with sound spectrograms. In short, great effort was expended towards enhancing accuracy. In Figure 6-18 the midline contour of the tongue is sketched for the different vowels that occurred in this cineradiographic study. Note that the pharyngeal anterioposterior width of [a] is narrowest. The pharyngeal constrictor muscles tense, narrowing the pharynx in the production of an [a]. The pharynx is narrowed laterally as well as in its anterioposterior dimension. Changes in the lateral dimension of the pharynx do not show up in radiographs like that sketched in Figure 6-18 but they have been monitored by using pulsed ultrasound (a technique similar to the use of Sonar to locate the ocean floor). Movements of up to 5 millimeters (mm) of the lateral pharyngeal wall occur in the production of an [a]. There is little or no movement of the lateral pharyngeal wall in the production of an [i] or [u] (Minifie et al., 1970).

The sketches of tongue contour for each vowel that are presented in Figure 6-17 represent the most extreme movement of the tongue for

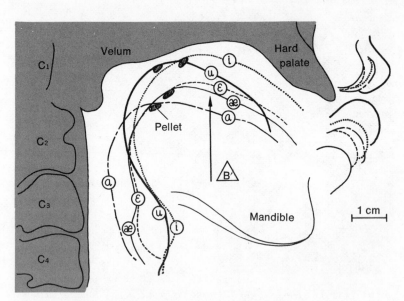

FIGURE 6-18. *Midline contours of the tongue for the same speaker as shown in Figure 6-17. Reprinted from* Physiology of Speech Production, *by Joseph Perkell by permission of the M.I.T. Press, Cambridge, Mass. Copyright 1969.*

each vowel at the approximate midpoint of each vowel. The tongue is constantly moving during the production of connected speech and the articulatory gestures that correspond to individual segments of speech are "melded" together (Daniloff and Moll, 1968; MacNeilage and De-Clerk, 1969; MacNeilage, 1970) as is the acoustic signal (Ohman, 1966; Liberman et al., 1967). It is possible to describe the process of speech production in terms of individual segments that are "coarticulated." The effect of a segment on the segments that occur before it can be viewed as "anticipatory coarticulation." Thus the position of the tongue in the production of the sound [t] in the word *tale* differs from the position for the [t] in the word *tile*. The position of the tongue in the production of the sound [l] likewise will differ in these two words because of "post coarticulation" effects. The effects of each "segment" on other "segments" of speech is, however, so pervasive that it is more realistic to view the movements of the articulatory apparatus as "encoded" sequences that encompass at least one syllable (Gay, 1974; Nearey, 1976; Lieberman, 1976). We will return to this topic in Chapter 7.

Cineradiographic data also demonstrate that the articulatory maneuvers that underlie speech are different between speakers of the same dialect when they produce the "same" sound, and that the particular articulatory maneuvers do not correspond with the hypothetical articulatory gestures that structure traditional phonetic theories (Houde, 1967; Perkell, 1969; Ladefoged et al., 1972; Nearey, 1976).

Supralaryngeal Vocal Tract Modeling

In Chapter 4 we calculated the formant frequencies for supralaryngeal vocal tract area functions that approximate uniform tubes. The formant frequencies of more complex supralaryngeal vocal tract area functions can be determined by various techniques. The simplest technique, in principle, is to construct a mechanical model of the supralaryngeal vocal tract and then excite it by means of appropriate acoustic sources. If we know the area function we can make a tube by hammering it out of brass, molding plastic, machining plastics, etc. If the area function that we're modeling is a vowel that is normally excited by a glottal source, we can place an artificial larynx at the glottal end and measure the formant frequencies of the sound that the tube produces. The transfer functions of consonants excited by noise generated at the constriction can be determined by passing air through the model. The material that is used to make the walls of the mechanical model does not have to match the sound absorbing and transmitting characteristics of the human supralaryngeal vocal tract since appropriate corrections can be made to compensate for differences (Fant, 1960). Mechanical models are particularly useful for simulating and analyzing the nonlinear vocal effects that are associated with the sound sources of —*voiced* sounds. A schematic of a

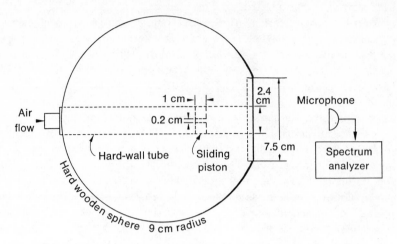

FIGURE 6-19. *A mechanical model for production of fricative consonants.*

model and the technique for making acoustic measurements is shown in Figure 6-19. The model makes it possible to assess the significance of the articulatory maneuvers that can be observed in cineradiographic data. It otherwise would be difficult to determine the acoustic consequences of different variations in the articulation of this sound.

The data that we can derive from a lateral X ray are not alone sufficient if we want to determine the acoustic consequences of articulatory maneuvers. The transfer function of the supralaryngeal vocal tract is a function of the cross-sectional area function. It, therefore, is necessary to derive an area function from the X-ray view. The procedures for deriving area functions from X-ray data are ad hoc and make use of whatever data are available. Dental casts of the oral cavity, photographs of the lips, X-ray views from the front, measurements from cadavers, and ultrasonic scans all are useful (Chiba and Kajiyama, 1941; Fant, 1960, Heinz, 1962).

Analog Models

Although it would be possible to use mechanical models of the vocal tract to determine the transfer function of any arbitrary area function, it is more convenient to use either analog or digital computer modeling techniques. The digital computer implemented modeling technique is most frequently used today but it is useful to understand the principles of analog modeling which underlie most of the computer techniques.

Suppose that you were in charge of an agricultural water distribution system and wanted to determine how to regulate the flow of water into different fields. You could construct a simple analog model of the system. The analog principle that you could make use of is the similar mathematical relationship that holds between the electrical parameters of *voltage, current,* and *resistance* and the hydraulic parameters of *pressure, flow,* and *resistance.* In Figure 6-20 the water supply system is sketched. It consists of a reservoir, which may be more or less full depending on weather conditions and use, a main supply channel, two branch channels, which go to the two fields in question, and two valves that can be set to introduce variable obstacles to the water flow into either field.

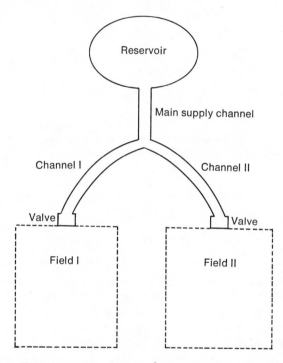

FIGURE 6-20. *Sketch of water supply system.*

The problem is how to regulate the water flow as the height of the water in the reservoir changes. The electrical analog of Figure 6-21 would solve this problem. The resistance of the main supply channel is represented by the fixed electrical resistor R_s, the two branch channels are represented by the fixed resistances R_1 and R_2, respectively, and the two valves by the variable resistors VR_1 and VR_2. The voltage V is set by adjusting the control of a variable voltage source. The analog works by measuring (by means of simple meters) the electrical currents i_1 and i_2 that flow through the two branch circuits for particular values of V, VR_1,

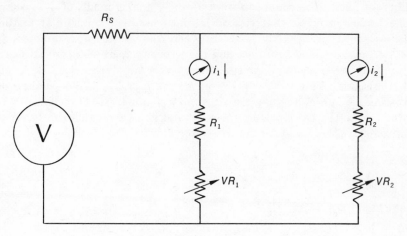

FIGURE 6-21. *Electrical analog of water supply system.*

and VR_2. Voltage is analogous to water pressure and current to water flow because Ohms law,

$$V = i(R)$$

which describes the relationship between electrical current, voltage, and resistance, also holds for the hydraulic variables,

$$\text{pressure} = \text{flow (resistance)}$$

The analog values appropriate for the resistors R_s, R_1, and R_2 can be determined by simple measurements once the system is set up. The usefulness of the analog system would become more apparent with more complex water distribution systems. It could be easily extended to very complex water distribution systems that had 50 or 100 channels.

The analog relationships that are appropriate for the construction of electrical analogs of the vocal tract involve relationships like that which hold between a force and the acceleration of matter, e.g., Newton's First Law of Motion, and the voltage change across an inductor. An inductor is an electrical device that can be constructed using a coil of wire. The analog between the Newton's First Law of Motion that applies to the acceleration of the air particles in the vocal tract and the voltage across the inductor is

$$F = m\frac{dv}{dt} \qquad \text{Newton's First Law of Motion}$$

$$V = L\frac{di}{dt} \qquad \text{Voltage across an inductor}$$

where dv/dt is the derivative with respect to time of velocity, F the force, m the mass in Newton's Law. The electrical analogs are V the voltage, L the inductance, and di/dt the derivative with respect to time of the current. Detailed discussions of electrical analogs like those contained in Flanagan (1972) are beyond the scope of this introduction. The essential point is that the principles of analog modeling are quite straightforward. The use of an analog model permits us to easily obtain quantitative measurements of variables that otherwise would be difficult or impossible to make.

" Terminal" Analog Studies of Speech

Several phases or trends are apparent when the results of analog studies of the supralaryngeal vocal tract are reviewed. The first phase used "terminal" analysis and demonstrated that the source-filter theory was an adequate description of speech production. Electrical analogs that specified formants and antiformants were excited by glottal or noise sources to synthesize speech signals (Stevens et al., 1953; Fant, 1960). Psychoacoustic tests which we will discuss in more detail in Chapter 7 demonstrated that human listeners perceived particular speech sounds if the appropriate formants and antiformants were specified. Since these synthesizers were designed by electrical engineers, the terminology of electrical circuit theory is often encountered when you read the research papers. The formant frequencies of the supralaryngeal vocal tract are essentially the frequencies at which a normal mode of vibration exists in the system. We illustrated this in Chapter 4 when we derived the formant frequencies of the uniform tube as the frequencies at which the physical system most readily supports a sinusoidal wave. This definition of the term formant is essentially that first proposed by Hermann (1894). It is equivalent to the way in which the term pole is used to characterize an electrical network (Stevens and House, 1961). The term resonance or damped resonance is often used to indicate the formants of a system.

The acoustic properties of the supralaryngeal vocal tract for unnasalized vowels, e.g., the vowels of English, involve only *formants* or *poles*, and they thus can be synthesized by "terminal analog" devices (Flanagan, 1957) that generate only formant frequencies. Sounds in which more than one airway is interposed between the source of acoustic energy and the outside environment, e.g., the nasalized vowels of Portugese, also have an antiformant at which energy is absorbed. The term zero is used to designate this characteristic of an electrical network and is used to denote the antiformants of speech sounds (Fant, 1960; Fujimura, 1962). Consonants that are excited by sources located at points above the larynx typically have both formants and antiformants. The experimenter using a "terminal analog" need only specify the frequencies of the formants and antiformants (and their relative amplitudes if a "parallel" analog synthesizer is being used (Lawrence, 1953; Stevens et al., 1953; Holmes et al., 1964)). In other words, the experimenters in theory don't have to know anything about the area function of the supralaryngeal vocal tract; they simply have to derive the formants and antiformants of the acoustic signal that they want to synthesize.

Area Function Analogs

Area function analogs of the supralaryngeal vocal tract model the vocal tract by using electrical networks that simulate the effects of changing vocal tract geometry. The first of these devices was constructed by Dunn (1950) and represented the vocal tract as a series of 1/2-cm-long sections. A sketch of a controllable vocal tract analog which includes a "nose" nasal section is shown in Figure 6-22. The effective cross-sectional area of each section can be electrically adjusted. Devices like this analog (Stevens et al., 1953; Rosen, 1958; Fant, 1960) and more recent

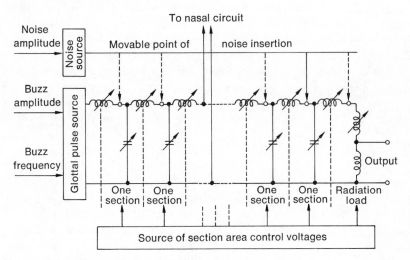

FIGURE 6-22. *Controllable electrical vocal tract model.* (*After Rosen, 1958.*)

computer-implemented models (Henke, 1966; Flanagan et al., 1970, 1975) permit experimenters to assess the acoustic significance of changes in the cross-sectional area of the supralaryngeal vocal tract.

Stevens and House (1955) controlled the cross-sectional area of an electrical analog of the vocal tract by systematically varying the effects of lip protrusion and lip opening, and the position and degree of tongue constriction. The diagram in Figure 6-23, which shows some of the area functions that they modeled, indicates the parameters that they used to specify the

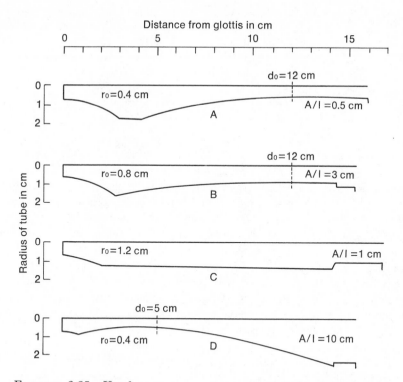

FIGURE 6-23. *Vocal tract parameters controlled by Stevens and House (1955).*

shape of the vocal tract. Note that there is no nasal section, so the results are relevant for — *nasal* vowels. The distance from the glottis appears as the scale at the top of the figure. The radius of the supralaryngeal vocal tract tube appears as the vertical scale for the four vocal tract configurations sketched. The notations at the right specifying the A/l values represent A, the cross-sectional area of the lips, divided by l, the length of the lip passage.

The effects of lip protrusion and lip opening are combined into this single parameter A/l for the reasons that we discussed in Chapter 4. A given value of A/l can be produced in different ways; for example, a mouth opening $A/l = 3$ could be 1 cm long with $A = 3$ cm², or could be 3 cm long with $A = 9$ cm². In either case the acoustic effect of the mouth opening would be approximately the same. The A/l values that Stevens and House used were derived from X-ray movies and high speed movies of lip opening and varied from about 20 cm for the vowel [æ] to about 0.1 cm for [u]. The point of constriction of the vocal tract by the tongue body was specified by the number d_0, the distance of the most constricted part of the vocal tract from the glottis, and r_0, the radius at the constriction. The values of d_0 and r_0 that they used were derived from X-ray data. The shape of the tongue was assumed to follow a parabolic function for all constrictions. There are some additional constraints on these control parameters that involve the effects of large constriction near the glottis and the effects of the mandible and lips.

Supralaryngeal Vocal Tract Modeling and Phonetic Theory

The results of the Stevens and House modeling study complement the acoustic analysis of vowel formants by Peterson and Barney (1952) which we discussed in Chapter 5. Traditional phonetic theories (e.g., Bell, 1867; Heffner, 1949; Chomsky and Halle, 1968) specify vowels in terms of hypothetical articulatory data. The system introduced by Bell (1867) specifies vowels in terms of the anterioposterior location of the constriction that is formed by the body of the tongue and the "height" of the constriction. The vowel [i], for example, is a high front vowel, [u] is a high back vowel, [I] is a slightly lower front vowel than [i], etc. The Stevens and House modeling study demonstrates that it is possible to generate most vowels by means of very different area functions which may, or may not, correspond with shapes consistent with traditional phonetic theory. Different combinations of tongue position, tongue height, and A/l can produce identical acoustic signals. The only vowels that "require" particular area functions are [i], [u], and to a lesser extent, [a]. The values of F_1 and F_2 that specify a vowel like [I] (the vowel in *bit*) in the Peterson and Barney formant frequency study (1952) can be produced by many different combinations of lip opening and rounding (as specified by the parameter A/l) and tongue position (the parameters d_0 and r_0). The Stevens and House modeling study thus suggests that acoustic factors may play a primary role in classifying vowel sounds. The auditory nature of traditional vowel diagrams has been discussed in many studies (Russell, 1928; Jones, 1932, Jakobson et al., 1963; Peterson, 1951; Ladefoged et al., 1972); we will take stock of the controversy in Chapter 8. The question of the auditory versus the articulatory classification of vowels is part of the more general question of the physiologic basis of phonetic theory.

Table 6-1 is not a comprehensive list of all of the muscles that can be involved in speech production. There is no general agreement on the function or functions of many of these muscles. It is apparent that different speakers use their muscles differently when they produce the "same" sounds. It is also apparent that these muscles are developed to a greater or lesser degree in different individuals. A more detailed listing of muscles and their possible activity may be found in Zemlin (1968).

TABLE 6-1

Muscle	Figure Reference	Function
LARYNX		
A. INTRINSIC		
1. Thyroarytenoid (TA)	6-4	Vocal cord tensor, forms body of vocal cord; is active during f_0 change. Acts to change thickness of vocal cord for register changes; also may act to change overall tension of vocal cord for phonation in different registers.
2. Posterior cricoarytenoid (PCA)	6-4	Opens the glottis for either breathing or the production of —voiced sounds.
3. Lateral cricoarytenoid (LCA)	6-4	Adducts the vocal cords; applies medial compression; is active during f_0 changes, always active in onset of phonation, when it adducts vocal cords, setting phonation neutral position.
4. Cricothyroid (CT)	6-4, 6-15	Applies longitudinal tension to vocal cords; is active during f_0 changes.
5. Interarytenoid	—	Adducts the vocal cords; applies medial compression. May be active in setting phonation neutral position.
B. EXTRINSIC		
1. Sternohyoid (SH)	6-14, 6-15	Lowers the hyoid *if* muscles that go from hyoid to skull and mandible are slack. Also stabilizes hyoid when muscles like digastric tense to open mandible. May be active in initiating phonation register shifts.

TABLE 6-1—*cont.*

Muscle	Figure Reference	Function
2. Thyrohyoid (TH)	6-14, 6-15	Decreases distance between thyroid cartilage and hyoid bone.
3. Sternothyroid (ST)	6-14	Lowers the thyroid cartilage.

PHARYNX

Muscle	Figure Reference	Function
1. Superior constrictor (SC)	6-13	Constrict the pharynx; active during swallowing and in the production of sounds like the vowel [a].
2. Medial constrictor (MC)		
3. Inferior constrictor (IC)		
4. Palatopharyngeus		Constricts the pharynx; also can lower the soft palate.

SOFT PALATE

Muscle	Figure Reference	Function
1. Levator palatini (LP)	6-13	Raises soft palate, sealing nasal cavity in the production of oral sounds. The SC also is active in some speakers when they seal their nasal cavity.
2. Palatoglossus (PG)	6-15	Raises tongue body or lowers soft palate.

TONGUE

INTRINSIC

Muscle	Figure Reference	Function
1. Superior longitudinal (SL)	6-15B	Turns up the tip of tongue.
2. Inferior longitudinal (IL)		Turns the tip of tongue down.
3. Transverse (MI)*	6-15B	Narrow the tip of tongue.
4. Vertical (MI)*	6-15B	Flattens the tip of tongue.

*MI includes both Transverse and Vertical.

TABLE 6-1—*cont.*

Muscle	Figure Reference	Function
EXTRINSIC		
1. Genioglossus (GG)	6-15	Pulls tongue body forward; depresses the tongue body; can elevate the hyoid. Is active in production of sounds like [i] or [u], where pharynx is widened by tongue body moving forward.
2. Styloglossus	6-15	Pulls tongue body towards styloid process. Is probably active in production of sounds like [u] and velar consonants.

SUPRAHYOID

1. Anterior belly of Digastric (AD)	6-14, 6-15	Opens the jaw *if* the hyoid is stabilized by tensioning muscles that connect hyoid to sternum; raises hyoid otherwise. Can be used in the production of sounds like [a].
2. Geniohyoid (GH)	6-15	Opens jaw if hyoid is stabilized; raises hyoid and pulls it forward.
3. Mylohyoid (MH)	6-13, 6-14, 6-15	Raises tongue body.

MANDIBLE (lower jaw)

1. Masseter (MAS)	6-16	Closes the jaw.
2. Temporalis (TEM)	6-16	Closes the jaw; pulls lower jaw backwards.
3. Internal pterygoid (IP)	6-16	Closes the jaw.

Table 6-1—*cont.*

Muscle	Figure Reference	Function
LIPS AND FACE		
1. Orbicularis oris (OO)	6-16A	Closes the mouth; puckers the lips; acts to close and round lips in sounds like [u]
2. Depressor labii inferior (DLI)		Opens and retracts lips. Active in the release of sounds like [p] and [b].
3. Levator labii superior		Opens lips; sometimes active in release of sounds like [p] and [b].

7
Speech Synthesis and Speech Perception

T Vocodor Synthesizers

HE pace of research on the perception of speech corresponds in a meaningful way with the development of speech synthesizers. The initial impetus for work on speech synthesis was commercial. In the 1930s Dudley and his colleagues at Bell Telephone Laboratories developed the Vocoder (Dudley, 1936, 1939). The Vocoder is a device that first analyzes a speech signal by means of a set of electronic filters and a fundamental frequency extracting device. The electronic filters derive an approximation of the spectrum of the speech signal as a function of time while the fundamental frequency extractor simultaneously derives the fundamental frequency, or in the case of — *voiced* sounds indicates a noiselike source excitation. The electrical signals derived by the spectrum channels and the fundamental frequency extractor are then transmitted to a synthesizer in which the acoustic signal is reconstructed.

The diagram in Figure 7-1 illustrates a Vocoder system. The signal from the fundamental frequency extractor is used to drive a pulse generator in the Vocoder synthesizer. The output of the Vocoder synthesizer thus has the same periodicity as the input signal. The Vocoder was developed to serve as a speech transmission system that would reduce the frequency bandwidth that is necessary to transmit a speech signal. Although the Vocoder equipment might be expensive it would more than pay for itself if it, for example, allowed the telephone company to "squeeze" twice as many messages into the frequency channel of a transoceanic telephone cable. The frequency channel of any electronic transmission system is always subject to some finite limit. In the case of a transatlantic cable the bandwidth of the channel is comparatively limited and the channel's cost is very great. Systems like the Vocoder thus were very attractive; if successful they would save millions of dollars. Vocoders, however, have never become widely accepted because the quality of the speech signal is degraded by the process of analysis and synthesis. The fundamental frequency extractors, in particular, do not work very well.

Dudley and his coworkers realized that the Vocoder's synthesizer could be used as a synthetic speaker (Dudley et al., 1939) by supplying

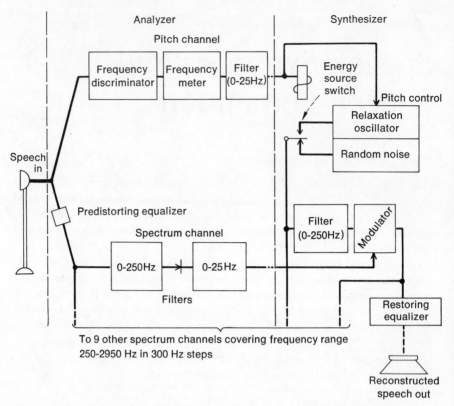

FIGURE 7-1. *Vocoder block diagram. (After Dudley, 1936.)*

artificially generated control signals in place of the signals that would have been derived by the analyzer. The synthesizer thus could be used to generate speechlike signals that, in fact, were never spoken. By precisely specifying the control signals, experimenters could systematically generate artificial speech signals and present these signals to human listeners, who could be asked to identify the signals and discriminate between slightly different versions of the signal, etc.

Various ingenious methods for controlling speech synthesizers derived from the Vocoder principle have been devised. Perhaps the most wideranging and seminal series of experiments came from the Haskins Laboratories group. A system was devised that would convert sound spectrograms or simplified sound spectrograms into acoustic signals (Cooper et al., 1952). In Figure 7-2 a sound spectrogram made with a narrow-bandwidth filter (*A*) and a simplified tracing of the formant frequency patterns of the same spectrogram (*B*) are presented. The formant frequencies which typically change as functions of time are

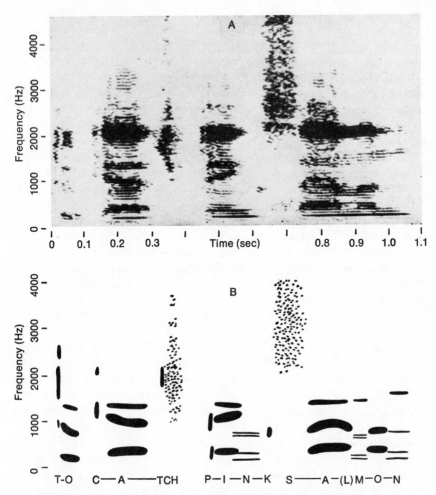

FIGURE 7-2. (*A*) *Sound spectrogram.* (*B*) *Simplified version of the same phrase that serves as input to pattern playback.* (*After Cooper et al., 1952.*)

represented as the dark areas on tracing (*B*). The stippled areas represent noise excitation. The simplified spectrogram when converted to an acoustic signal is intelligible, although it doesn't sound very natural.

Speech Synthesis and Segmentation

The practical goal of the Haskins Laboratories group was to devise a machine that would "read aloud" to blind people. The machine was to identify alphabetic characters in printed texts and convert these symbols into sounds that a blind person could listen to. It isn't too difficult to devise a print-reading device, although such would not be necessary if the machine's use were to be restricted to the "reading" of new books and publications. At some stage in the preparation of a manuscript a machine with a keyboard is used. The talking machine could be connected to the keyboard so that it produced a different sound, or combination of sounds, for each letter. The sounds would not have to be speech sounds, tones, buzzes, etc., could be used. The sequence of sounds could be tape recorded, and blind people could listen to the tapes or records made from the tapes. A number of different systems were developed. They all were useless although various schemes for slowing down the tapes, editing them, etc., were tried. Listeners had to slow down the tapes to rates that were about one tenth the rate of normal speech. The blind "readers" would forget what a sentence was about before they heard its end. It didn't matter what sort of sounds were connected to the typewriter keys; they all were equally bad. The basic rate of transmission and the inherent difficulty of these systems was about the same as the traditional "dots" and "dashes" of the telegrapher's Morse code, which is very difficult to follow and demands all of your attention.

The solution to this problem seemed to rest in producing speechlike signals. The obvious approach was to make machines that would "glue" the phonetic elements of speech together to make words and sentences. Linguists have traditionally thought of phonetic segments as "beads on a string." There seemed to be no inherent problem if the beads were isolated, collected, and then appropriately strung together. The medium of tape recording seemed to be the solution. Speakers could be recorded while they carefully pronounced words in which the full range of phonetic elements would occur. The phonetic elements could then be isolated by cutting up the magnetic tape (preferably with electronic segmenting devices that were functional equivalents of very precisely controlled scissors). A speaker, for example, would record a list of words that included *pet*, *bat*, *cat*, *hat*, and so on. The experimenters would than theoretically be able to "isolate" the sounds [p], [b], [h], [k], [e], [æ]. The isolated sounds would be stored in a machine that could put them together in different patterns to form new words, for example, *get* and *pat*. Systems of this sort were attempted (Peterson et al., 1958), but they did not work. It was, in fact, impossible to isolate individual sounds.

Studies with Vocoder speech synthesizers demonstrated why it was impossible to isolate sounds like the stop consonants [p], [b], [g], and [d]. Figure 7-3 shows a series of synthetic spectrograms that yield the voiced stops [b], [d], and [g] in initial position with various vowels in CV (consonant–vowel) syllables when they are converted to sound on a speech synthesizer (Delattre et al., 1955). The synthesizer was controlled with only two formant frequencies and a fundamental frequency control

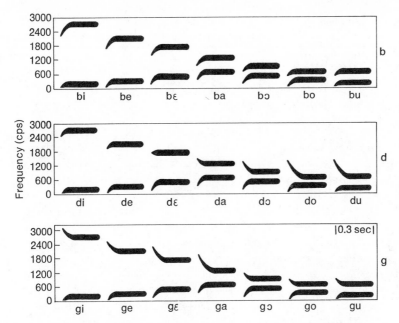

FIGURE 7-3. *Synthetic spectrograms using only F_1 and F_2 information that produce the voiced stops before various vowels. (After Delattre et al., 1955.)*

which was uniform for all the stimuli and is not shown in Figure 7-3. The acoustic cues that caused the listeners who identified these stimuli to "hear" the consonants [b], [d], and [g] were the formant transitions, i.e., the changing formant pattern that occurred at the start of each syllable. Note that the formant transitions of the "same" consonant are different for different vowels. It would be impossible to piece together the formant transitions of the [d] of [de] with the vowel [u] to get the syllable [du]. The data of Figure 7-3 show that there are no acoustic segments in these signals that correspond in any way to segmentable "beads." The acoustic realization of a [d] in one syllable is quite different in another syllable. Human speech is thus quite different from alphabetic orthography; it is not segmented at the acoustic level. This inherent lack of segmentation is however, not a liability. It is one of the advantages of human speech as a means of vocal communication. The rate at which meaningful sound distinctions are transmitted in human speech is about 20 to 30 segments per second. That is, phonetic distinctions that differentiate meaningful words, e.g., the sounds symbolized by the notation [b], [æ], and [t] in the word *bat*, are transmitted, identified, and put together at a rate of 20 to 30 segments per second. It is obvious that human listeners cannot simply transmit and identify these sound distinctions as separate entities. The fastest rate at which sounds can be identified is about 7 to 9 segments per second (Miller, 1956). Sounds transmitted at a rate of 20 per second merge into an undifferentiable "tone." How, then, is speech transmitted and perceived?

Speech Encoding

The results of the past 20 years of research on the perception of speech by humans demonstrates that the individual sounds like [b], [æ], and [t] are encoded, that is "squashed together" into the syllable-sized unit [bæt] (Liberman et al., 1967). A human speaker in producing this syllable starts with his supralaryngeal vocal tract in the shape characteristic of [b]. However, he does not maintain this articulatory configuration, but instead moves his tongue, lips, etc., towards the positions that would be attained if he were instructed to produce an isolated, sustained [æ]. He never reaches these positions because he starts towards the articulatory configuration characteristic of [t] before he reaches the "steady state" (isolated and sustained) [æ] vowel. The articulatory gestures that would be characteristic of each isolated sound are never attained. Instead the articulatory gestures are melded together into a composite, characteristic of the syllable. The sound pattern that results from this encoding process is itself an indivisible composite. Just as there is no way of separating with absolute certainty the [b] articulatory gestures from the [æ] gestures (you can't tell when the [b] ends and the [æ] begins), there is no way of separating the acoustic cues that are generated by these articulatory maneuvers.

The traditional concept of "coarticulation" which derives from classical experimental studies (Rousselot, 1901) cannot, in an absolute sense, account for the encoding of speech. It is possible to locate and isolate segments of the acoustic signal and articulatory gestures that can be closely related to a particular segment, e.g., the vowel [æ] in [bæt]. Speech however, really does not appear to be either perceived, produced, or neurally "programmed" on a segmental basis. There are, for example, no invariant motor commands that correspond to the segments of speech (Harris, 1974). If the syllable [bæt] were recorded on a magnetic tape, it would be impossible to isolate either the [b] or the [t]. You would always hear the [æ] vowel. The acoustic cues that, in fact, transmit the initial and final consonants are the modulations of the formant frequency pattern of the [æ] vowel. The process is, in effect, a time-compressing system. The acoustic cues that specify the initial and final consonants are transmitted in the time slot that would have been necessary to transmit a single, isolated [æ] vowel.

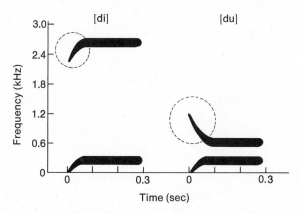

FIGURE 7-4. *Two formant patterns that will produce the sounds* [di] *and* [du]. *Note that the second formant frequency transitions are quite different.* (*After Liberman, 1970.*)

In Figure 7-4 we have reproduced two simplified spectrographic patterns that will, when converted to sound, produce approximations to syllables [di] and [du] (Liberman, 1970).[1] The dark bands on these patterns represent the first and second formant frequencies as functions of time. Note that the formants rapidly move through a range of frequencies at the left of each pattern. These rapid movements, which occur in about 50 msec, are called formant transitions. The transition in the second formant, which is encircled, conveys the minimal acoustic information that human listeners interpret as a token of a [d] in the syllables [di] and [du]. It is again impossible to isolate the acoustic pattern of [d] in these syllables. If tape recordings of these two syllables are "sliced" with the electronic equivalent of a pair of scissors (Lieberman, 1963), it is impossible to find a segment that contains only [d]. There is no way to cut the tape so as to obtain a piece that will produce [d] without also producing the next vowel or some reduced approximation to it.

Note that the encircled transitions are different for the two syllables. If these encircled transitions are isolated, listeners report that they hear either an upgoing or a falling frequency modulation. In context, with the acoustic correlates of the entire syllable, these transitions cause listeners to hear an "identical sounding" [d] in both syllables. How does a human listener effect this perceptual response?

[1] It is simpler to start with a single consonant–vowel syllable like [di] or [du], but the principles that we will discuss also apply to longer stretches of speech (Ohman, 1966; MacNeilage, 1970).

The "Motor Theory" of Speech Perception

The formant frequency patterns of speech reflect the resonances of the supralaryngeal vocal tract. The formant patterns that define the syllable [di] in Figure 7-4 thus reflect the changing resonant pattern of the supralaryngeal vocal tract as the speaker moves his articulators from the occlusion of the tongue tip against the palate that is involved in the production of [d] to the vocal tract configuration of the [i]. A different acoustic pattern defines the [d] in the syllable [du]. The resonances of the vocal tract are similar as the speaker forms the initial occlusion of the [d] in both syllables by moving his tongue against his palate (Perkell, 1969); however, the resonances of the vocal tract are quite different for the final configurations of the vocal tract for [i] and [u]. The formant patterns that convey the [d] in both syllables are thus quite different since they involve transitions from the same starting point to different end points. Human listeners "hear" an identical initial [d] segment in both of these signals because they, in effect, "decode" the acoustic pattern using prior "knowledge" of the articulatory gestures and the anatomical apparatus that is involved in the production of speech. The listener in this process, which has been termed the "motor theory of speech perception" (Liberman et al., 1967), operates in terms of the acoustic pattern of the entire syllable. The acoustic cues for the individual "phonetic segments" are fused into a syllabic pattern. The high rate of information transfer of human speech is thus due to the transmission of acoustic information in units that are at least syllable-sized. The phonetic elements of each syllable are "encoded" into a single acoustic pattern which is then "decoded" by the listener to yield the phonetic representation.

In the initial formulation of this theory it was assumed that the listener perceived speech by matching the incoming signal against an internally generated signal. The listener hypothetically generated the internal signal by means of the same neural mechanisms that he used to control his vocal tract in the generation of speech. The process of matching an incoming signal against an internally generated reference was termed "analysis by synthesis" (Halle and Stevens, 1959). Motor theory explanations of various aspects of speech were extended to various aspects of speech perception, including the perception of intonation and stress (Lieberman, 1967). Recent studies, which we will discuss, have replicated the original observations that led to the formulation of the motor theory of speech perception. However, it is not necessary to relate speech perception to the same neural mechanisms that control speech production.

The Speech "Mode" of Perception

When they listen to speech human listeners often appear to behave in what appears to be a "mode" different from the mode for other acoustic signals. The dominant hemisphere of the brain (which is usually the left hemisphere) appears to be more involved in the perception of speech signals than nonspeech signals. The relevant data include studies of the effects of lesions of the brain (Kimura, 1961, 1967; Penfield and Roberts, 1959; Luria, 1961; Geschwind, 1965), which continue in the tradition of Broca's and Wernicke's original observations. Broca (1861) observed that damage to the brain in a particular area of the left hemisphere will result in a loss of speech production ability. Listeners who have suffered various traumas in their left hemispheres also may have difficulty in perceiving human speech (Wernicke, 1874). The nature of the neural mechanisms that are involved in the production and perception of speech is not known, nor is there general agreement on even the general organization of the brain. The functions of the brain may, or may not, be strictly localized (Penfield and Roberts, 1959). We have to wait until we have a better understanding of the brain before we can identify the specific neural mechanisms that are involved in the perception of speech. There is, however, much evidence that some "specialized" neural processing is involved.

When normal human listeners hear speech sounds, greater electrical potentials are recorded by electrodes positioned over their left hemispheres than over their right hemispheres. In contrast, no differences in electrical activity can be noted by the same electrode array when the subjects listen to musical sounds (McAdam and Whitaker, 1971; Wood et al., 1971). The results of hundreds of experiments with dichotically presented speech and nonspeech stimuli (Shankweiler and Studdert-Kennedy, 1967) again demonstrate that the left hemisphere of the brain is somehow crucially involved in the perception of speech. The dichotic experiments involve the simultaneous presentation of two different sounds to a listener. One sound is presented to the subject's right ear through one headphone. The other, "competing" sound is presented to the subject's left ear via a second headphone channel. Under these conditions, consonant–vowel syllables presented to the subject's right ear tend to be heard. The listener doesn't blend the two sounds together; he simply doesn't hear the competing sound. The effect is manifested statistically; that is, subjects sometimes hear instead the sound presented to their left ear. But as long as they are listening to speech stimuli, they tend to hear the sounds presented to their right ears more often.

The effect is most pronounced when speech signals are presented to listeners, but it also occurs for other complex signals (Cutting, 1974;

Molfese, 1972). Its basis seems to be the fact that the right ear is connected to the dominant left hemisphere of the brain by a major contralateral
pathway.[2] This results in speech and other complex signals that are presented to the right ear "going" more readily to the left hemisphere.
The ipsilateral[3] connections of both ears, which transmit signals from
the left ear to the left hemisphere, prevent the effect from being total.
The precise role of the dominant hemisphere in the perception of speech
still is not clear; however, it is clear that whatever is going on probably
does not involve any internal modeling of the articulatory gestures of
speech production or of motor activity. In other words, the classic motor
theory of speech perception does not seem to explain the facts of speech
perception.

Neural Acoustic Property Detectors

A number of researchers have begun to develop and test models of
speech perception that involve neural "property detectors" that
respond to specific acoustic signals. Cutting (1974), for example, found
that frequency transitions in nonspeech signals are perceived in a manner
similar to the formant transitions of consonant–vowel syllables. Human
listeners from the age of two months onwards (Eimas et al., 1973; Cutting
and Eimas, 1975; Morse, 1972; Molfese, 1972) appear to identify speech
signals in a manner that suggests that the human brain has a number of
devices, or property detectors, that respond selectively to particular types
of acoustic signals (Cooper, 1974; Cutting and Eimas, 1975). The plausi-
bility of the original motor theory of speech perception comes from the
fact that many of these neural property detectors respond to signals that
the human vocal tract is adapted to make. In other words, there seems
to be a "match" between the sounds that humans can make and the
sounds that they are specially adapted to readily perceive (Lieberman,
1970, 1973, 1975; Stevens, 1972). People do not have to internally model
the maneuvers of the vocal tract and compute the acoustic consequences
of possible articulatory patterns in order to determine whether they are
listening to a speech sound. They seem to be furnished from birth onwards with neural mechanisms that selectively respond to the acoustic
signals of human speech.

[2] The contralateral pathways are the links that transmit the electrical signal from
the right inner ear to the left hemisphere of the brain and the left inner ear to right
hemisphere. The mechanisms of the ear convert acoustic signals into electrical signals
(Flanagan, 1972).

[3] The ipsilateral pathways link the right ear to the right hemisphere and the left
ear to the left hemisphere. The ipsilateral connections also appear to be effective in
transmitting the electrical signals from the inner ear to the brain.

Electrophysiologic and Comparative Studies

Studies with animals other than *Homo sapiens* have demonstrated that similar mechanisms exist in their brains. Electrophysiological techniques that can not be used in experiments with humans have isolated neural mechanisms that respond to signals that are of interest to the animals. These signals include the vocal calls of the animals in question. Even simple animals like crickets appear to have neural units that code information about the rhythmic elements of their mating songs (Hoy and Paul, 1973). Similar results have been obtained in the squirrel monkey (*Saimiri sciureus*). Wollberg and Newman (1972) recorded the electrical activity of single cells in the auditory cortex of awake monkeys during the presentation of recorded monkey vocalizations and other acoustic signals. The electrophysiological techniques of this experiment involved placing electrodes that could record the electrical discharges from 213 cells in the brains of different animals. Some cells responded to many of the calls that had complex acoustic properties. Other cells, however, responded to only a few calls. One cell responded with a high probability only to one specific signal, the "isolation peep" call of the monkey.

The experimental techniques that are necessary in these electrophysiological studies demand great care and great patience. Microelectrodes that can isolate the electrical signal from a single neuron must be prepared and accurately positioned. The electrical signals must be amplified and recorded. Most importantly, the experimenters must present the animals with a set of acoustic signals that explore the range of sounds they would encounter in their natural state. Demonstrating the presence of "neural mechanisms" matched to the constraints of the sound-producing systems of particular animals is therefore a difficult undertaking. The sound-producing possibilities and behavioral responses of most "higher" animals make comprehensive statements on the relationship between perception and production difficult. We can explore only part of the total system of signaling and behavior. However, "simpler" animals are useful in this respect because we can see the whole pattern of their behavior.

The behavioral experiments of Capranica (1965) and the electrophysiological experiments of Frishkopf and Goldstein (1963), for example, demonstrate that the auditory system of the bullfrog (*Rana catesbiana*) has single units that are matched to the formant frequencies of the species-specific mating call. Bullfrogs are members of the class Amphibia. Frogs and toads compose the order Anura. They are the simplest living animals that produce sound by means of a laryngeal source and a supralaryngeal vocal tract (Stuart, 1958). The supralaryngeal vocal tract consists of a mouth, a pharynx, and a vocal sac that opens into the floor of the mouth in the male. Vocalizations are produced in the same manner as in primates; the vocal folds of the larynx open and close rapidly, emitting "puffs" of air into the supralaryngeal vocal tract, which acts as an acoustic filter. Frogs can make a number of different calls (Bogert, 1960), including mating calls, release calls, territorial calls that serve as warnings to intruding frogs, rain calls, distress calls, and warning calls. The different calls have distinct acoustic properties, and there are obvious differences in the manner in which frogs produce some calls. For example, the distress call is made with the frog's mouth wide open, whereas all other calls are made with the mouth closed. The articulatory distinctions that underlie the other calls are not as obvious. Capranica (1965) has, however, analyzed the acoustic properties of the bullfrog mating call in detail.

The mating call of the bullfrog consists of a series of croaks. The duration of a croak varies from 0.6 to 1.5 sec and the interval between croaks from 0.5 to 1.0 sec. The fundamental frequency of the bullfrog croak is about 100 Hz. The formant frequencies of the croak are about 0.2 and 1.4 kHz. Capranica generated synthetic frog croaks by means of a POVO speech synthesizer (Stevens et al., 1955) a fixed speech synthesizer designed to produce human vowels that serves equally well for the synthesis of bullfrog croaks. In behavioral experiment Capranica showed that bullfrogs responded to synthesized croaks so long as there were energy concentrations at either or both of the formant frequencies that characterize the natural croak. The presence of acoustic energy at other frequencies inhibited the bullfrogs' responses. (The bullfrogs' responses consisted of joining in a croak chorus.)

Frishkopf and Goldstein (1963), in their electrophysiological study of the bullfrog's auditory system, found two types of auditory units. They found cells in units in the eighth cranial nerve of the anesthetized bullfrog that had maximum sensitivity to frequencies between 1.0 and 2.0 kHz and other units that had maximum sensitivity to frequencies between 0.2 and 0.7 kHz. However, the units that responded to the lower frequency range were inhibited by appropriate acoustic signals. Maximum response occurred when the two units responded to time-locked pulse trains at rates of 50 and 100 pulses per second that had energy concentrations at, or near, the formant frequencies of bullfrog mating calls. Adding acoustic energy between the two formant frequencies at 0.5 kHz inhibited the responses of the low-frequency single units.

The electrophysiological, behavioral, and acoustic data all complement each other. Bullfrogs have auditory mechanisms that are structured to respond specifically to the bullfrog mating call. Bullfrogs don't respond to just any sort of acoustic signal as though it were a mating call; they respond to particular calls that have the acoustic properties of those that can be made only by male bullfrogs, and they have neural mechanisms structured in terms of the species-specific constraints of the bullfrog sound-producing mechanism. Capranica tested his bullfrogs with the mating calls of 34 other species of frog, and they responded only to bullfrog calls, ignoring all others. The croaks have to have energy concentrations equivalent to those that would be produced by both formant frequencies of the bullfrogs' supralaryngeal vocal tract. The stimuli furthermore have to have the appropriate fundamental frequency.

The bullfrog has one of the simplest forms of sound-making system that can be characterized by the source-filter theory of sound production. Its perceptual apparatus is demonstrably structured in terms of the constraints of its sound-producing apparatus and the acoustic parameters of the source-filter theory—the fundamental frequency and formant frequencies. The neural property detectors that appear to be involved in the perception of human speech are more complex insofar as human speech involves a greater variety of sounds. The acoustic properties of vowels and of sounds like the stop consonants [b], [p], [d], [g], etc., are, for example, quite different. The discrimination and identification of these different classes of sounds also differ and may reflect the presence of different types of neural acoustic property detectors.

Psychoacoustic Tests

Discrimination Versus Identification of Sounds

Much of the perceptual data that we have cited in connection with the probable existence of neural acoustic property detectors in humans involves the phenomenon of "categorical discrimination." In order to understand the significance of categorical discrimination and indeed to understand the terminology we first must clearly understand the distinction that exists between the *discrimination* and the *identification* of speech sounds and other stimuli. These two terms signify very different perceptual tasks. The examples that follow may perhaps make the distinction clear. Suppose that you have a friend who wishes to test your ability to discriminate between the sounds that the different keys of a piano produce when they are struck. Your friend seats you with your back to the piano and strikes a particular key. He then produces another sound on his piano. You don't know whether he has hit the same key again, or has instead hit a different key. He asks you to tell him whether the second sound is like the first sound or whether it's different. If he sometimes randomly hits the same key twice you can't automatically say that the two sounds are always different. You will have to listen carefully to each pair of sounds that he produces. If the experiment were run using careful controls, e.g., striking the different keys with equal force, your friend would be able to determine your ability to discriminate between the sounds that the different keys of the piano produce. Chances are that you would be able to discriminate between all of the keys of the piano if you had normal hearing and if the piano were in good repair and tune.

The results of an identification test probably would be quite different. Suppose that your friend wanted to test your ability to identify the sounds that the keys of his piano produced. You again might start with your back to the piano. Your friend would strike the keys of the piano in a random order and ask you to identify the note that was produced by each key. He would not strike the keys in an ascending or descending scale. Even if you had musical training you would find the task difficult unless you are one of the rare individuals who has perfect pitch. Psychoacoustic tests with pure sinusoidal tones show that most people can reliably identify no more than about 4 or 5 different tones (Pollack, 1952). If you had normal hearing and could hear the frequency range between 20 and 20,000 Hz, you could, in contrast, discriminate between about 350,000 different sinusoidal tones (Stevens and Davis, 1938). Psychoacoustic experiments have established the dl's (difference limens) for the minimal differences that humans can perceive in fundamental frequency, formant frequencies, vowel amplitude (Flanagan, 1955, 1955a), timing (Hirsch, 1959), etc. The difference between discrimination and identification is similar for other sensory tasks. It is, for example, easy to discriminate between colors but it is hard to make absolute identifications. Consider the problems that you may have when you try to identify the color of a particular shade of paint in a store (to match it with the color of some object at home) and the subsequent ease with which you and others can discriminate between the two slightly different paint colors once you've patched a scratch with the new batch of paint. Discrimination is an easier task than identification; you can readily discriminate between a set of objects that you cannot reliably identify.

Psychoacoustic tests are a necessary part of speech research. Although it is possible to perform precise analyses of speech signals using electronic instruments and computer programs that effect various mathematical transformations of the signal, these analyses are, in themselves, meaningless. We can never be certain that we have actually isolated the acoustic cues that people use to transmit information to each other unless we run psychoacoustic studies in which human listeners respond to acoustic signals that differ with respect to the acoustic cues that we think are relevant. Speech synthesizers are thus very useful tools since they permit us to generate acoustic signals that differ with respect to some particular attribute. It is foolish to assume that you can isolate a linguistically relevant acoustic cue without running psychoacoustic experiments, even when the acoustic cue seems to be very "simple." Bloomfield (1933, p. 110), for example, assumed that the acoustic factor that determined the perceptual "loudness" of a sound was the physical intensity of the speech signal. He was wrong. Humans are not electronic instruments that directly respond to a physical measure like intensity. Human judgments of loudness turn out to be a function of the duration and amplitude of the sound (Lifschitz, 1933). Bloomfield further supposed that the relative loudness of the syllables of words like *re bél* and *ré bel* was the basis of the contrast in linguistic "stress" that differentiates these word pairs. The word that bears "stress" on the first syllable (which is indicated by the symbol ') is the noun form, e.g., *The rebel stood in the doorway*. The verb form bears stress on its second syllable, e.g., *You must rebel from your sorry state*. Many verb and noun forms in English are differentiated, in part, by stress.

Psychoacoustic tests (Fry, 1955; Lieberman, 1965) and acoustic analyses (Lieberman, 1960, 1967; Morton and Jassem, 1965; Atkinson, 1973) show that human listeners make seemingly "simple" stress distinctions by taking into account the total fundamental frequency contour of the utterance, the amplitude of syllabic "peaks," the relative durations of segments of the utterance and the range of formant frequency variations. What seems "simple" to us involves a complex decision-making procedure when we try to make stress decisions with an artificial automaton (Lieberman, 1960). The responses of human listeners to even "simple" nonspeech stimuli like sinusoidal signals is not simple. Psychoacoustic "scaling" experiments show that judgments of the relative pitch of two sinusoids are not equivalent to the arithmetic frequency ratio (Beranek, 1940; Fant, 1973; Nearey, 1975). In other words, if you let a human listener hear a sinusoid whose frequency is 1,000 Hz and then let him adjust the control of a frequency generator until he hears a sound that has twice the pitch of the 1,000 Hz signal, he will not set the control to 2,000 Hz. He will instead select a sinusoid whose frequency is about 3,100 Hz. Judgment of relative perceived pitch can be related to the physical measure of frequency by the use of a "Mel" conversion scale. The Mel scale which relates perceived pitch to frequency is plotted in Figure 7-5. Note that the perceptual ratio between two frequencies depends on the absolute magnitude of the frequencies. Frequency is plotted against the horizontal axis in Figure 7-5. The perceptual Mel equivalent of a frequency is plotted with respect to the vertical axis. A sinusoid whose frequency is 1,000 Hz thus has a Mel value of 1,000 Mel and is twice the pitch of a sinusoid having a pitch of 500 Mel. The frequency of a sinusoid having a pitch of 500 Mel is 400 Hz. A sound whose pitch is 3,000 Mel will have twice the perceived pitch of 1,500 Mel but the frequency ratio of these two sounds is 9,000/2,000. The Mel scale is of particular value in regard to some of the acoustic relations that structure the phonetic theory of vowels that we will discuss in Chapter 8.

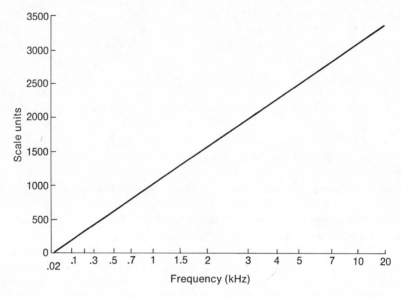

FIGURE 7-5. *The Mel scale which relates perceived pitch to frequency (Adapted from Fant, 1973.)*

Categorical Discrimination

It is straightforward to design psychoacoustic experiments that test either the discrimination or the identification of speech sounds. The speech stimuli can be samples of "real speech," i.e., produced by humans, or "synthetic" speech produced by speech synthesizers that use either terminal or area function analogs of the vocal tract. Whereas certain speech sounds, like vowels, behave like nonspeech stimuli insofar as discrimination is much "better" than identification, the discrimination of other speech sounds is very different. Sounds like the English stop consonants are discriminated no better than they are identified. The graphs of Figure 7-6 illustrate this phenomenon, which has been termed "categorical discrimination." The graphs in the right-hand column show the results of an identification experiment in which listeners had to identify synthesized speech sounds (Liberman, 1970a). The synthesized sounds were produced on a terminal analog with two formants and a fundamental specified. The formant frequency patterns were like those shown in Figure 7-7. The first formant pattern was similar for all of the stimuli. The starting point of the second formant's transition varied. Depending on the starting point of the second formant, the sounds were identified as examples of the syllables [bæ], [dæ], or [gæ]. The starting point of F_2 for stimulus 1 was about 1,700 Hz; about 2,000 Hz for stimulus

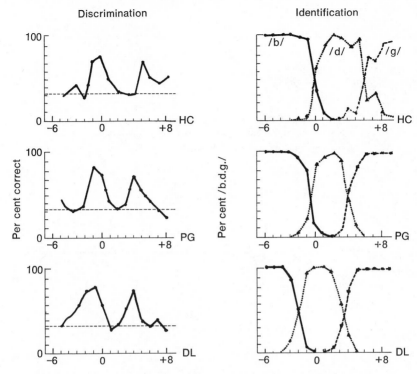

Discrimination   Identification

FIGURE 7-6. *Identification and discrimination functions for three different listeners responding to synthetic speech stimuli that are cued by the second formant transitions schematized in Figure 7-7. The three listeners are HC, PG, and DL. The synthesized sounds are heard as* [bæ], [dæ], *and* [gæ]. *The numbers on the horizontal scale of the figures refer to the second formant frequency transitions numbered in Figure 7-7. (Adapted from Liberman, 1970a.)*

5; 2,200 Hz for stimulus 7; etc. The graphs in the right-hand column in Figure 7-6 show that the listener HC labeled, i.e., identified, stimuli — 6 to — 1 as examples of [bæ]; stimuli 0 to 5 as [dæ]; and stimuli 6 to 9 as [gæ]; etc. The graph shows, for example, that stimulus — 4 was identified 100 per cent of the time as [bæ] by all three listeners, HC, PG, and DC. The boundaries between the identified categories occur where the identification curves for each category fall and overlap.

The graphs in the left-hand column of Figure 7-6 show what happens when these listeners are asked to discriminate between the same synthetic speech stimuli. If the listeners acted as we should expect them to behave they should easily be able to discriminate reliably between all of these stimuli. The graphs in the left-hand column in Figure 7-6 instead

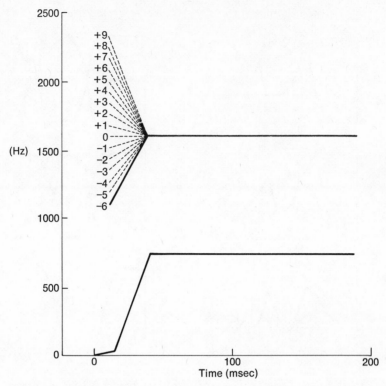

FIGURE 7-7. *Schematic representation of two formant frequency patterns that will produce the sounds* [bæ], [dæ], *and* [gæ]. *The numbers −6 through +9 reference the different signals. (Adapted from Liberman, 1970a).*

show that the listeners are able to reliably discriminate between these sounds *only* when the pair of sounds that they're discriminating between lie across a category boundary. Note that the peaks in the discrimination function occur at the category boundaries. Elsewhere discrimination is at or near the chance level, i.e., the 33 per cent level that we would expect to find if the listeners were simply guessing.

The categorical discrimination of adult human listeners to sounds like the stops [b], [d], and [g] could perhaps be the result of unconscious "training" (Lane, 1965) in which listeners respond differentially to sound distinctions that have great importance. Experiments with 1- to 4-month-old human intants, however, show that this is not the case. The infants' discrimination of these stimuli also appears to be categorical. In other words, the infants also discriminate between pairs of stimuli only when one member of the pair was in the [bæ] category and the other in the [dæ] category (Cutting and Eimas, 1975). These categorical effects disappear when the isolated transitions of the second formant (which are the sole acoustic variables in these experiments) are presented in isolation. Adult (Mattingly et al., 1971) and infant (Cutting and Eimas, 1975) listeners under these conditions are able to discriminate between all the isolated second formant transitions. The adult listeners do not "hear" the isolated second formant transitions as speech signals when they make these fine discriminations.

The discrimination experiment with infants makes use of an ingenious technique in which infants are trained to suck at a rubber nipple when they hear "new" sounds (Eimas et al., 1971; Cutting and Eimas, 1975). The infant is given a hand-held nipple to suck on. Instead of transferring nutrients the nipple contains a pressure transducer which records the force and the rate at which the infant sucks. These signals are recorded on a polygraph and a digital recording. Contingent on the sucking response is the presentation of an auditory stimulus. The rate at which stimuli are presented to the infant can be made proportional to the rate at which the infant sucks. The infant soon learns that more presentations of a stimuli will occur if he sucks more often. What occurs is that infants want more presentations of sounds that they perceive to be different from the sound that they heard before. If the same stimulus is presented many times to an infant, the infant's sucking rate will decrease as he becomes satiated with the sound. If a sound that the infant hears as different is presented, the infant will become interested again and suck more rapidly. The infants' satiation and curiosity make this experiment a discrimination test. The experimenter presents a signal until the infant is satiated. The experimenter then can present a different acoustic signal. If the infant can perceive that the new sound is different, the sucking rate increases abruptly. If the infant is not able to discriminate the new acoustic signal from the "old" acoustic signal he remains satiated and does not increase his sucking rate. The results of these experiments with infants ranging in age from 3 weeks to 4 months is extremely important because they show that the discrimination boundaries of infants and adults appear to be similar for the sounds of human speech. These results are, of course, consistent with a theory that involves innately determined neural property detectors.

Individual Differences and Linguistic "Markedness"

The apparent presence of neural property detectors in human infants and similar devices in other animals lends support to the theory that human language is structured in terms of innately determined mechanisms (Lenneberg, 1967). However, it is apparent that there are great differences between the speech sounds of different languages. If immutable, innately determined mechanisms were all that are involved in the specification of the sounds of speech, we would expect to find that all languages had the same sounds (and the same words, grammar, etc., to the extent that these elements also are the result of innately determined mechanisms). Recent studies with synthesized speech stimuli show that individual differences exist at the perceptual level. Figure 7-8 shows a schematized frequency-time-intensity presentation of stimuli synthesized on a computer-implemented terminal analog model of the vocal tract. The study that made use of these stimuli (Stevens and Blumstein, in press) investigated the perception of the sounds [t], [ṭ], and [k] with particular regard to retroflex sounds like [ṭ]. Retroflexion is defined articulatorily as a maneuver in which the tip of the tongue is curled back and placed posterior to the alveolar ridge of the hard palate. The configuration of the supralaryngeal vocal tract for a retroflex [ṭ] is thus similar to that for a nonretroflex English [t] except for the tongue tip.

Each stimulus started with a burst of noise, which is specified in Figure

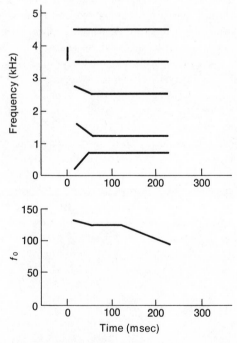

FIGURE 7-8. *Control parameters for synthesis, using five formant frequencies plus burst frequency and fundamental frequency. The burst is specified by the short vertical line that runs between 3.6 and 4.0 kHz. (After Stevens and Blumstein, in press.)*

7-8 by the short, vertically oriented line that runs between 3.6 and 4.0 kHz. The frequency of the burst varies for the vocal tract configurations that generate different sounds. The noise bursts, as we noted in Chapter 6, are the result of the vocal tract's being excited by a momentary turbulent air flow as the stop sound is "released." The noise bursts that are appropriate to different syllables were synthesized in this experiment. The formant frequency patterns appropriate for each syllable were also synthesized. The formant patterns that specify the retroflex consonant involve the third, fourth, and fifth formants. The speech synthesizer was therefore controlled by five formant patterns like that specified in Figure 7-8. The fundamental frequency contour in Figure 7-8 which starts with a downwards perturbation that is a consequence of the — *voiced* (i.e., open glottal) state of the larynx at the start of the voiceless stops [t], [ṭ], and [k] also resulted in more natural speech quality.

The results of this experiment showed that the retroflex consonants were identified less reliably than the nonretroflex consonants although the listeners were native speakers of languages in which these consonants exist. Retroflex articulation can occur for vowels and consonants, but it occurs less often than nonretroflexion (Greenberg, 1963, 1966). The Stevens and Blumstein data suggest that it may occur less often because it is more difficult to perceive. The over-all difference in the identifiability of the retroflex consonant was the result of certain listeners having more difficulty with this category. Other listeners identified the retroflex [ṭ] as well as the nonretroflex [t] and [k].

Experiments with synthesized consonant–vowel stimuli that have noise bursts as well as formant transitions show that some listeners respond to the bursts, whereas other listeners respond to the formant transitions when these cues conflict (Blumstein, in preparation). Listeners will identify the same acoustic signal as a [d] or a [g] depending on whether they respond to the noise burst or the formant transition. These differences may reflect differences in either the nature of the neural property detectors, or the results of interaction with environmental factors of neural property detectors of different individuals.

Phonetic Features

We have already noted certain linguistic theories that describe and classify speech sounds in terms of common attributes or features (Jakobson et al., 1963; Chomsky and Halle, 1968). Some of the experimental evidence that supports these theories involves the analysis of the confusions that occur when listeners are asked to identify speech sounds. Miller and Nicely (1955), for example, analyzed the errors that English-speaking listeners made when they identified short words that were presented mixed with noise and filtered. The noise and filtering made the listeners' task more difficult and it threw into relief effects that might not otherwise be evident. Sounds were confused in consistent patterns. The sounds [p], [t], and [k] for example, as a class were confused with the sounds [b], [d], and [g]. One group is — *voiced* the other + *voiced*. The "confusion matrix" in Table 7-1 shows the particular confusions that were

TABLE 7-1
CONFUSION MATRIX FOR $S/N = +12$ db AND FREQUENCY
RESPONSE OF 2,500–5,000 cps.

	p	t	k	f	θ	s	ʃ	b	d	g	v	ð	z	3	m	n
p	69	30	37	26	16	4	4	21	9	18	13	12	9	3	7	10
t	4	164	9	2	2	2		1	4	4	1	2	2		3	
k	20	35	76	9	11	5	6	3	5	25	5	3	15	11	7	4
f	27	8	7	24	28	7	8	15	8	14	34	14	6	2	11	11
θ	15	19	7	20	49	10	8	12	16	16	13	20	10	5	16	16
s	6	8	2	1	19	160	4		16	10	8	11	27	2	7	11
ʃ	1	1	2	1	5	1	204	1				1	2	44		1
b	23	4	10	13	17		2	48	17	17	34	28	10	1	28	12
d	1	7	6	5	4	2	1	1	128	16	8	6	5	13	5	16
g	6	3	16	5	6	5	2	17	39	85	11	13	6	7	6	13
v	22	6	6	26	18	3	3	33	12	9	32	28	7	2	18	7
ð	21	11	9	16	28	4	2	35	14	22	20	44	10	2	24	22
z	4	5	1	2	9	60	5	1	27	21		12	86	6	2	3
3	2	4	2			3	49	1	7	1	2	1	5	167		
m	18	3	7	11	16	8	2	13	16	12	16	21	3	1	68	37
n	8	4	12	7	9	2		10	22	17	13	8	5	4	16	119

made. Experiments with synthetic speech have yielded similar results (Studdert-Kennedy, 1974). The stimuli that Miller and Nicely used were derived from tape recordings that were made by real speakers; speech perception experiments don't have to always use synthetic stimuli. Experiments on the perception of "natural speech," i.e., speech obtained from human speakers, that make use of this confusion matrix technique also show how speech is "stored" in short term memory (Wickelgren, 1965; 1969).

8
Phonetic Theories

Phonetic theories, like all scientific theories, depend on a particular data base and the research techniques that were used to derive that data base. Phonetic theories relate the physical attributes of sounds with their linguistic function. The linguistic relevance of particular sounds thus must be considered as well as acoustical and articulatory data. We could provide an "exact" recording of the speech sounds of a language by making a set of tape recordings which would preserve all of the acoustic attributes of the signals that served as a medium of vocal communication. We, however, would not have isolated the linguistically significant phonetic elements that were used in this language. We would not, for example, be able to predict the possible words of this language. We could start on a phonetic analysis of these tape recordings by listening to them and attempting to isolate phonetic elements. Of course, we would be abstracting elements from the encoded stream of sounds using our internal speech-decoding devices. Our task would be simpler if we had also recorded native speakers producing isolated words, and it would be much simpler if we had the services of a bilingual "informant" who spoke our language and the language that we were attempting to analyze.

It would be best if we were analyzing our own native language, but we would nonetheless have to remember that we could not derive the acoustic correlates of phonetic elements without making use of acoustic analysis, synthesis, and psychoacoustic experiments. We would know that the encoded nature of speech meant that we could not expect to find isolated acoustic segments that would always directly correlate with phonetic elements. We would know, however, that it is possible to represent speech in terms of a sequence of discrete symbols. All alphabetic, orthographic systems make use of a phonetic or quasiphonetic system. The relationship between a symbol and a sound is sometimes more variable, i.e., more subject to various rules or odd variations, in some languages than in other languages. All alphabetic systems of orthography, however, depend on the fact that it is possible to represent sounds by discrete symbols. Our traditional alphabetic orthography lets us generate sound sequences that convey information, but it does not explain how we are able to produce recognizable sounds when we see these symbols, nor does it tell us how we are able to make these transcriptions.

The ends of a scientific phonetic theory are to "explain" how we produce meaningful sounds, how these sounds may be structured in terms of linguistically relevant units and the biological status of these phonetic units. The only way that we can test a scientific theory is to see what data it "explains." Scientific theories, if they are useful, relate things that previously were thought to be unrelated. Newton thus related the motions of the planets and the motion of objects on Earth when he demonstrated that the same mathematical "rules" would predict the motion of planets and cannon balls. Phonetic theories that predict the possible range of sounds of human languages, the relative frequency of occurrence of various sounds, the sequence of events in the acquisition of speech by infants, the most likely types of sound changes, or the effects of various craniofacial anomalies on speech are thus "better" theories than ones that don't make these predictions. Phonetic theories must relate real physical data, and they may lead to practical and useful applications.

Traditional "Articulatory" Phonetic Theory

The traditional phonetic theory that is most familiar to speech scientists and linguists was developed during the nineteenth century. Melville Bell (1867) did most to develop this theory although he probably derived it from earlier works (Nearey, 1976). Bell was concerned with teaching the deaf how to talk. He thus was concerned with finding a set of articulatory maneuvers that he could teach to deaf people that would enable them to talk. The focus of his system therefore was to find articulatory maneuvers that would serve as "instructions" for producing various sounds. Many of the articulatory maneuvers that are involved in speech production are evident. The position of the lips in sounds like the vowel [u] (the vowel of *boot*), for example, can be observed wihout any special instruments and was noted in many earlier phonetic theories. Some articulatory maneuvers that cannot be directly observed, had also been incorporated in earlier phonetic theories, e.g., the maneuvers of the larynx that produce voicing. The physiologic research of the late eighteenth and early nineteenth century had determined the role of the larynx in producing and regulating phonation. Bell described the sounds of speech in terms of articulatory "features" like the presence or absence of lip rounding, as well as in terms of acoustic features like voicing, which, however, had a known articulatory basis. Bell also used several hypothetical articulatory features that specified the position of a presumed "point of constriction" formed by the tongue against the palate in the oral cavity.

The articulatory theory that derives from Bell's studies has become the "classic" phonetic theory. It has provided the key for significant advances in phonetics, phonology, and speech pathology. The hypotheses that Bell and his successors proposed have been extremely productive; recent research, however, indicates that certain aspects of this theory have to be modified. Although the theory appears to be in accord with articulatory data for consonants, it fails to account for many aspects of vowel production.

Vowels

Bell believed that the phonetic quality of vowels derived from the position and height of the point of constriction of the tongue. The height of the tongue constriction was supposed to be low for a vowel like [a], whereas it was supposed to be high for vowels like [i] and [u]. The position of the point of constriction with respect to the front-to-back dimension of the oral cavity was also specified. The point of constriction was front for [i] and back for [u]. Bell's original articulatory notation was abandoned, but his theory was preserved with comparatively few modifications. A typical vowel diagram that specifies the vowels of English is shown in Figure 8-1. The over-all shape of the presumed vowel space differs somewhat in different versions of this articulatory classification scheme. The "low" vowels sometimes form a quadrilateral space, sometimes a triangle, but the basic dimensions of front–back and high–low are preserved. Individual vowels like [ɪ] (the vowel of *bit*) can be specified in terms of relative position to other vowels. The vowel [ɪ] thus can be described as a front, high vowel somewhat lower than [i] but higher than [e] (the vowel of *bet*). It is also possible to assign numbers to the degrees of height, so [ɪ] could be classified as having height 4 on a scale of 1 to 5, where [i] has 5, the highest value. Bell's theory is essentially preserved in the "generative" theory of Chomsky and Halle (1968) where a number

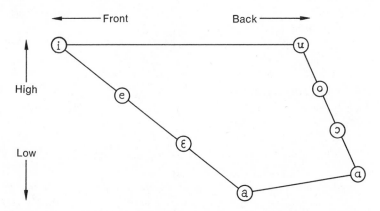

FIGURE 8-1. *The IPA vowel "quadrilateral." The different vowels are defined in terms of the hypothetical position of the tongue. The articulatory dimensions are front versus back, and high versus low.*

of binary features specify the height and position of the tongue. The use of binary notation in itself does not mean that binary values are being assigned to an articulatory parameter. (A binary number system can be used to represent numbers that also can be expressed in terms of other number bases.)

Bell's articulatory features specifying tongue position were made without the benefit of radiographic data. Bell therefore was not aware of the role of the pharyngeal cavity in the production of speech. He was concerned with the position of the presumed "point of constriction" in the oral cavity. Various techniques were employed to obtain data that would test and refine this theory. Direct palatography for example, involved coating the palate with a substance that would wipe off when the tongue came in contact with the palate. A subject would produce a sound after having his palate coated and then open his mouth for inspection. Indirect palatography involved placing a metal form, that generally conformed to the contours of the palate, in the subject's mouth while he produced a sound. The surface of the metal form that would come into contact with the tongue could be coated with lampblack or some other substance that would smudge when it came into contact with the tongue. The metal form could be examined after the speaker had produced the appropriate sound.

Testing the Traditional Vowel Theory

It is relatively simple to test the components of a phonetic theory that describes vowel production in terms of articulatory gestures if X rays are available. It is possible to produce sustained vowels so that the problems of encoding can be avoided. Radiographic techniques made X rays of the supralaryngeal vocal tract possible in the 1920s. Russell (1928) made use of radiographs of sustained vowels spoken by speakers of American English. His radiographic data are not as refined as the data of recent studies, but he correctly noted that the data were not consistent with Melville Bell's hypotheses concerning tongue height and the front–back distinction of vowels. Recent cineradiographic studies that allow the analysis of speech under more natural conditions demonstrate that Russell was correct.

Figure 8-2 is reproduced from a study of Ladefoged and his associates (Ladefoged et al., 1972). Note that the tongue contour is almost identical for the vowels [ɪ], [ɛ], and [e]. The tongue is higher for the vowel /i/, but differences in tongue contour can *not* be the factors that differentiate the vowels [ɪ], [ɛ], and [e]. In Figure 8-3, data for a second speaker are presented. Note that there are differences in tongue contour for all of these "front" vowels. However, the vowel [e] is "higher" than the vowel [ɪ]. In Figure 8-4 we finally see evidence from a speaker whose vowels are produced in accord with traditional vowel theory. It is clear, however, that different speakers behave differently and, except for the vowel [i], which has a consistent contour in these data (Ladefoged et al., 1972) and in the data of Perkell (1969), the acoustic differences that differentiate these vowels must be the result of the total supralaryngeal vocal tract area function. The speakers make small adjustments in the size of their lip opening, the relative protrusion or retraction of their lips, and the height of their larynges.

The formant frequency patterns that specify particular vowels are determined by the shape and size of the total supralaryngeal airway

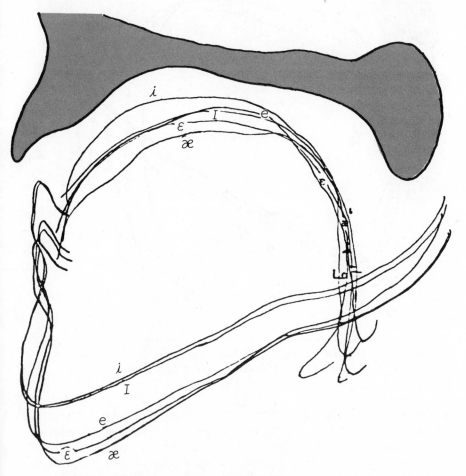

FIGURE 8-2. *Radiographic data derived from an X-ray motion picture of a speaker producing various English vowels. The tongue contours were sketched from motion picture frames that were exposed during the most stable part of each vowel's articulation. Note the lack of differentiation for the different vowels. The contour of the mandible is also sketched. (After Ladefoged et al., 1972.)*

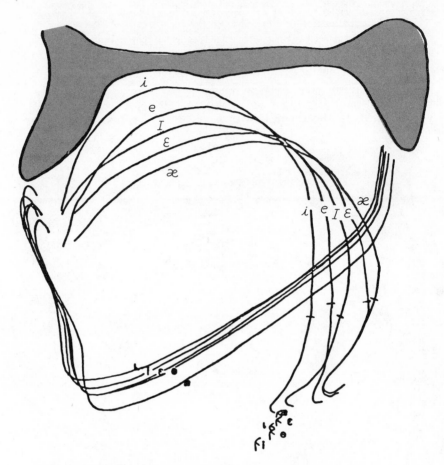

FIGURE 8-3. *Radiographic data for a second speaker. There is more differentiation with respect to the tongue contours, but note that the vowel* [e] *is "higher" than the vowel* [I]. (*After Ladefoged et al., 1972.*)

(Fant, 1960); in other words, the cross-sectional area, as a function of distance from the larynx, of the air passages. The traditional articulatory dimensions of tongue "height" and "frontness" or "backness" would be meaningful if these parameters were significant with regard to specifying the total supralaryngeal vocal tract area functions of different sounds. The data (Ladefoged et al. 1972; Russell 1928), however, show that the tongue contour, in itself, is not an invariant specification of the supralaryngeal vocal tract area functions that generate the acoustic signals of these different vowels. Similar conclusions follow from the cineradiographic data of Perkell (1969) that we mentioned in Chapter 6. As Perkell noted, differences in larynx height and lip protrusion and constriction, are responsible for the formant frequency distinctions that specify vowels like [ɪ], [ɛ], and [e] for the speaker whose utterances he analyzed. Differences in tongue contour can generate appropriate area functions (Figure 8-4), but that is only one possibility.

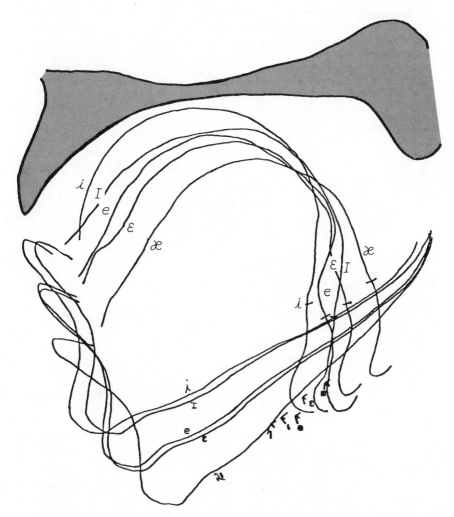

FIGURE 8-4. *Radiographic data for a third speaker, whose tongue contours are in accord with the traditional articulatory classification. All three of these speakers (cf. Figures 8-2, 8-3, and 8-4), however, produced appropriate* acoustic *signals for all of these vowels although they use different articulatory maneuvers. (After Ladefoged et al., 1972.)*

These data are in accord with the predictions of the modeling study of Stevens and House (1955) which we discussed in Chapter 6. That study demonstrated that most vowels can be generated by means of many different articulatory patterns. The only vowels that needed particular tongue contours were ones like [i], [u], and [a], which involved extreme departures from the "neutral" position of the vocal tract. All other vowels can be generated by adjustments of lip opening and total vocal tract length. The human larynx has a vertical mobility of almost 20 mm (Perkell, 1969) so the total range of vocal tract length adjustment is quite great when the effects of lip protrusion and lip retraction are added in. The effects of lip opening are functionally equivalent to adjustments of over-all vocal tract length (Stevens and House, 1955). Human speakers thus, in general, do not generate vowels in accordance with traditional phonetic theory.

It is important to note that a human listener cannot tell whether a speaker produced a vowel like [e] by maneuvering his tongue (like the speaker of Figure 8-4) or by maneuvering his lips and larynx (like the speakers of Figures 8-2, 8-3, and 6-18) unless the "listener" was equipped with X-ray vision or insisted on holding conversations in front of X-ray machines. Inferences that follow from the auditory impression of a "trained phonetician" must be regarded as initial hypotheses. The situation is not very different for samples of speech from speakers of four African languages (Asante Twi, Igbo, Dho-Luo, and Ateso) and German discussed by Lindau et al. (1972). While the tongue shapes that differentiate particular vowel contrasts of some of these speakers seem to be more directly related to a muscular maneuver that shifts the tongue root forward, in some cases the speakers produced similar acoustic contrasts by means of other gestures. As Lindau et al. (1972) noted,

> The nature of some vowel targets is much more likely to be auditory than articulatory. The particular articulatory mechanism that a speaker makes use of to attain a vowel target is of secondary importance only (p. 93).

In summary, the deficiencies of traditional articulation-based phonetic theory thus involve two related points. First, the formant frequency patterns that differentiate many speech sounds are determined by the area function of the supralaryngeal vocal tract. A particular area function will always result in a specified, unique formant frequency pattern. This would seem to support the traditional specification of sounds in terms of invariant articulatory parameters, except that different area functions can generate identical formant frequency patterns. The computer modeling studies of Stevens and House (1955) showed that this was a theoretical possibility. Second, the X-ray studies that we have reviewed, together with many other studies, demonstrate that normal adult speakers actually make use of different articulatory maneuvers to effect similar phonetic contrasts. Although some speakers make use of articulatory maneuvers that afford a reasonable fit with the traditional articulatory parameters (tongue height and the front–back distinction), other speakers produce equivalent acoustic signals by means of very different articulatory maneuvers.

A Physiologic Theory for Vowels

The deficiencies of tradtional vowel theory arise from the fact that phonetic contrasts are directly related to invariant articulatory maneuvers. These particular deficiencies can be avoided by a "unified" theory that is structured in terms of both articulatory and perceptual factors (Ladefoged et al., 1972; Lieberman, 1970, 1976; Lindau et al., 1972)—in other words, the phonetic theory is structured in terms of the biological mechanisms that are involved in the production and the perception of speech. Like most theories, this theory follows from "old" theories and it owes much to the theory proposed in *Preliminaries to Speech Analysis* (Jakobson et al., 1963). Jakobson and his colleagues in *Preliminaries* proposed that the sounds of speech could be specified in terms of a set of "distinctive features," each of which had well-defined acoustic "correlates." The distinctive features, although they were related to articulatory maneuvers that could produce the desired acoustic correlate, focused on the acoustic and linguistic aspects of the sounds of speech. Since the time of the Sanskrit and Greek grammarians of the fourth and fifth centuries B.C., linguists have noted that the sounds of speech are often modified in what appear to be regular patterns. Thus, in English, the final sound of the plural form of a "regular" noun that ends with a stop consonant depends on whether the final stop is, or is not, voiced. Compare, for example, the plural forms of the words *light* and *bag*. As we noted in Chapters 6 and 7 the sounds of speech can either be $+ voiced$ or $- voiced$. Voicing thus appears to be a phonetic feature that specifies a linguistically relevant acoustic property or speech sounds. Jakobson argued for a particlat set of universal phonetic features that could only have binary values. The results of many acoustic and psychoacoustic experiments and recent insights on the possible nature of neural acoustic property detectors are not in accord with the detailed acoustic correlates of many of these initial hypothetical features, nor do they support the view that all phonetic features are necessarily binary (cf. Ladefoged, 1975). However, these data are consistent with the central focus of Jakobson's theory—the focus on acoustic factors that are, in turn, based on the constraints of speech production.

A scientific theory is more powerful if it can relate more facts that seemingly are unrelated. Newton's theories are, as we noted, "better" theories than Kepler's older descriptions of planetary motion, because Newton was able to account for seemingly different phenomena like the motion of the planets and the flight of cannon balls using the same principles. Newton's theory thus "explained" more of the physical universe by offering a more coherent and unified view. The biological or physiologic approach that we shall attempt to develop in this discussion of a phonetic theory for vowels likewise will attempt to "explain" some of the observed properties of vowel sounds. Physiology is the study of biological function. The physiological apprach that we will follow was first proposed by Johannes Müller, who was one of the founders of both modern physiology and psychology. Müller noted (1848) that some of the sounds of human speech appeared to be more basic than others. Purkinje's linguistic studies (1836), for example, showed that certain sounds, like the vowels [i] and [u], appeared to occur more often in different languages. Müller wondered whether this was because of the functional, i.e., the physiologic value of particular sounds, and he stated that the *explanations* for these observations must follow from the functional, i.e., the physiologic attributes of these sounds. Physiology is the science of biological function, and as Müller noted (1848, p. 1044) "It comes within the province of physiology to investigate the natural classification of the sounds of language."

QUANTAL VOWELS. As we have noted before, the shape of the supralaryngeal vocal tract determines the particular acoustic signal, and different speech sounds are specified by different acoustic signals. Each different sound can involve different maneuvers of the tongue, lips, velum, etc., as the speaker talks. If the speaker could produce vocal tract shapes with maximum precision, the acoustic signals that corresponded to particular sounds would always be invariant. The task of speech production would be simplified if it were possible to produce an invariant acoustic signal without having to use precise articulatory maneuvers. The acoustic signals that correspond to various sounds are also more or less distinct from each other. The formant frequencies that specify the vowels [ɪ] and [e] are, for example, closer to each other than the formant frequency patterns of [i] and [a] (Fant, 1960). The task of speech perception thus also would be made simpler if the acoustic signals that were used for vocal communication were maximally distinct. These criteria are captured by the physiological "quantal" factor introduced by Stevens (1972).

The quantal factor can perhaps be illustrated by means of the following analogy. Suppose that an elegant restaurant is to open. The owner decides to employ waiters who will signal the diners' order by means of nonvocal acoustic signals. Shall he employ waiters equipped with violins or with sets of handbells? If he wants to minimize the chance of errors in communication he will opt for the handbells. Each bell produces a distinct acoustic signal without the waiters having to use precise manual gestures. In contrast, violins require comparatively precise maneuvers and will produce graded acoustic signals. The bells produce "quantal" signals, ones that yield distinct acoustic signals by means of relatively imprecise gestures.

Stevens (1972) has demonstrated that certain speech sounds are more quantal than others. Vowels like [i], [u], and [a], for example, are specified by acoustic signals where formant frequencies converge. For [i] the second and third formants F_2 and F_3 are both high; [a] has a low F_2 and a high F_1; while [u] has a low F_1 and F_2. Distinct peaks in the spectrum of the acoustic signal automatically follow from these formant frequency convergences (Fant, 1956). In psychacoustic tests involving English-speaking subjects the vowels [i] and [u] are more reliably identified than vowels like [ɪ], [e], or [ɛ] (Peterson and Barney, 1952; Fairbanks and Grubb, 1961. Stevens, by means of computer-implemented vocal tract modeling, demonstrates that these acoustic signals can be generated by means of imprecise articulatory gestures.

In Figure 8-5A is sketched a stylized model of the cross-sectional area of the supralaryngeal vocal tract for the vowel [a]. The discussion that follows is essentially a paraphrase of K. N. Steven's analysis (1972). Stevens' insights on acoustic stability have provided a new way of looking at the nature of speech sounds. Note that the shape of the supralaryngeal vocal tract for this vowel approximates a two-tube resonator. The posterior portion of the supralaryngeal vocal tract, which corresponds to the pharynx, is constricted and has the cross-sectional area A_1. The anterior, oral cavity is relatively large. The cross-sectional area of the oral cavity A_2 is about ten times as large as A_1 (Fant, 1960). To a first approximation, the first two formant frequencies can be calculated as simple quarter-wavelength resonances of these two tubes. The discussion in Chapter 6 regarding the first resonance of a uniform tube applies to each tube because the coupling between the oral and pharyngeal tubes will be small as long as the cross-sectional areas A_1 and A_2 are substantially different.

The physical reasoning behind this approximation is not difficult to follow. At the closed end of the back tube the air pressure that best "matches" the obstruction of the closed end is obviously a pressure maximum. The air pressure that best matches the end of the constricted tube at point X is zero pressure. This follows from the fact that the cross-sectional area A_2 is ten times greater than T_1. The size of the unconstricted tube is so much greater than that of the constricted tube that it is equivalent to directly connecting the constricted tube to the outside atmosphere. A 10:1 difference in cross-sectional area is enormous. The effect on air pressure can be visualized by imagining what would happen to the members of a crowd as they exited from a passageway that was 3 ft wide to one 30 ft wide. The people in the crowd might be pushing against one another in the 3-ft-wide passage. However, they could spread out in the 30-ft-wide passage and never touch each other. The collision of the gas molecules that generated the air pressure waveform in the constricted tube is thus minimized at point X where the cross-sectional area abruptly changes. The air pressure waveform in the unconstricted tube is also a quarter-wave pattern, because the oral tube is nine-tenths "closed" at point X. The two pressure waveforms are sketched in Figure 8-5.

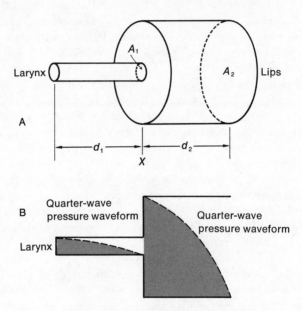

FIGURE 8-5. (*A*) *Two-tube model of the supralaryngeal vocal tract for the vowel* [a]. (*B*) *Area function for two-tube model with air pressure waveforms sketched in.*

The quarter-wave resonance model is only a first approximation to the behavior of the vocal tract for the vowel [a], e.g., the vowel of the word *hod*. It does, however, make evident the salient properties of this sound. The change in cross-sectional area, point X, occurs at the midpoint of the supralaryngeal vocal tract (Fant, 1960). F_1 and F_2, the first and second formant frequencies, therefore, are equal. If we perturbed the position of point X from this midpoint, we would not expect these two formant frequencies to change very abruptly. For example, if we moved point X 1 cm forward or backward we would generate the same first and second formant frequencies. The front tube would be longer and would generate the lower resonance F_1 if point X were moved 1 cm backward. If point X were instead moved 1 cm forward the back cavity would generate the lower first formant. The first formant frequency would be identical for these two situations. It is immaterial whether the front or the back cavity generates the first formant frequency; all that matters is that the same frequency is generated. The second formant frequency would also have the same value for these two cases. It would be generated by the shorter tube. The first and second formant frequencies for the vowel [a] thus won't change too much so long as point X is perturbed about the midpoint of the supraryngeal vocal tract. An increase in the length of the front, oral cavity necessarily results in a decrease in the length of the back, pharyngeal cavity, and the two cavities "trade off" in generating the first and second formant frequencies.

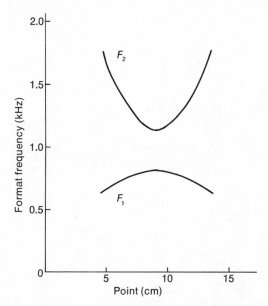

FIGURE 8-6. *The first formant frequency F_1 and the second formant frequency F_2 for the two-tube model of Figure 8-5. The formant frequencies were calculated using a computer model of the supralaryngeal vocal tract in which the position of the area function discontinuity, point X, was shifted forwards and backwards. (After Stevens, 1972.)*

The quarter-wave model for the vowel [a] is, as we have noted, a first approximation because there is actually some coupling between the front and back tubes. In Figure 8-6 calculated values for F_1 and F_2 are plotted for various positions of point X about the midpoint of a 17-cm-long supralryngeal vocal tract. These calculations were made using a computer-implemented model of the supralaryngeal vocal tract (Henke, 1966). The computer program calculates the formant frequencies of the supralaryngeal vocal tract for specified area functions. Note that the first and second formant frequencies converge for $X = 8.5$ cm, the midpoint of the supra-laryngeal vocal tract. The quarter-wave approximation of [a] yields the same frequency for F_1 and F_2, but the coupling between the two tubes results in slightly different formant frequencies. Note that there is a range of about 2 cm in the middle of the curve of Figure 8-6 within which the second formant varies over only 50 Hz and the first formant changes even less. Within this region the two formants are close together. The transfer function for [a] in Figure 8-6 thus has a major spectral peak. In contrast, for the 2-cm range from $X = 11$ to 13 cm, the second formant frequency changes by about 0.4 kHz and the centered spectral peaks would be absent.

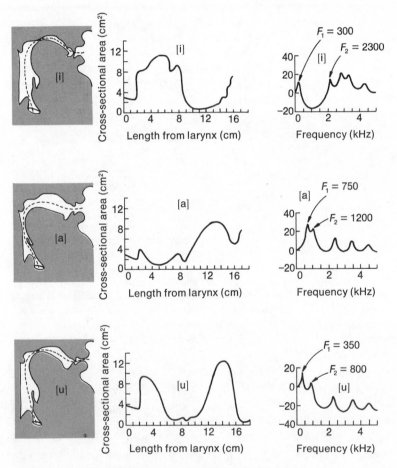

FIGURE 8-7. *Midsagittal sections, cross-sectional area functions, and acoustic transfer functions of the vocal tract for the vowels* [i], [a], *and* [u].

In Figure 8-7 illustrations of approximate midsagittal sections, cross-sectional area functions, and acoustic transfer functions of the vocal tract for the vowels [i], [a], and [u] are presented. Articulatory and acoustic analyses have shown that these vowels are the limiting articulations of a vowel triangle that is language-universal (Trubetzkoy, 1939; Liljencrants and Lindblom, 1972). The body of the tongue is high and fronted to form a constricted oral cavity in [i], whereas it is low to form a large oral cavity ih [a] and [u]. The pharynx is expanded in [i] and [u] and constricted in [a]. The oral and pharyngeal tubes are maximally expanded and/or maximally constricted in the production of these vowels. Further constriction would result in the generation of turbulent noise excitation and the loss of vowel quality (Fant, 1960; Stevens, 1972).

Note that all three vowels have well-defined spectral properties. A central spectral peak occurs at about 1 kHz for [a]. A high-frequency spectral peak occurs for [i] and a low-frequency spectral peak occurs for [u]. All three vowels are acoustically stable. They have well-defined acoustic properties that don't change for small errors in articulation (Stevens, 1972). The small changes in formant frequencies that do occur when the articulatory configuration is perturbed, e.g., the 1-cm perturbations that we discussed for the vowel [a], are not perceptually significant because human listeners cannot differentiate between formant frequencies that differ by less than 60 Hz (Flanagan, 1955). Note that all three of these vowels are produced by means of area functions that involve discontinuities at or near the midpoint of the supralaryngeal vocal tract. The midpoint area function discontinuity has an important functional value. It allows human speakers to produce vowel signals that are acoustically distinct with relatively sloppy articulatory maneuvers.

VOWELS AND NEURAL ACOUSTIC PROPERTY DETECTORS. The quantal vowels [i], [u], and [a], which are also the only vowels that have to be produced using specific vocal tract area functions (Stevens and House, 1955), inherently define and delimit the acoustic vowel space of human speech. Other vowels appear to be defined acoustically in terms of these vowels. In Figure 8-8 the frequency of the first formant of various vowels of Swedish are plotted with respect to the abscissa on a Mel scale. The "effective" second formant frequency is plotted with respect to the ordinate in Mels. The effective second formant frequency takes into account the spectral peaking effect that occurs when the second and third formant frequencies of a vowel approach each other. It thus yields a total spectrum that approximates the spectrum that would result if F_3 were represented when only F_1 and F_2 are used to synthesize a vowel. It therefore takes into account the perceptual effects of the higher formants (Fant, 1969).

The frequency values of these vowels are those derived by Fant (1969). The long vowels of Swedish are spaced out along the peripheral axis

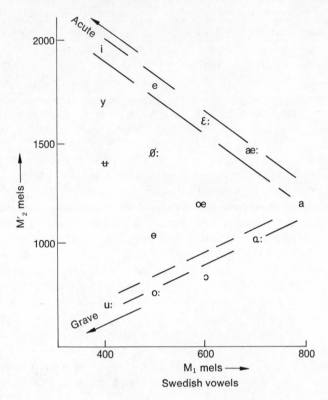

FIGURE 8-8. *Acoustic classification of the vowels of Swedish in terms of Mel values of first formant and "equivalent" second formant frequency. The acoustically defined phonetic features* grave *and* acute *are used to differentiate these two classes of "peripheral" vowels.*

established by the vowels [i] and [a] and [u] and [a] in equal Mel intervals. This is in accord with the predictions of Lindblom (1971) regarding the preferred acoustic spacing of vowels along the peripheral axis established by the quantal vowels [i], [m], and [a]. These quantal vowels tend to occur more often in different languages (Trubetzkoy, 1939; Greenberg 1963, 1966); other vowels can occur in different languages if and only if these vowels also occur. The quantal vowels thus appear to be highly valued for speech communication. The term markedness was introduced by Trubetzkoy (1939) and Jakobson (1940) to convey the natural value of particular sounds. Sounds that are less marked are more prevalent and "natural" sounds. All other things being equal we would expect the least marked, i.e., the most highly valued and natural sounds to occur most often in the inventory of sounds that occur in human languages. This, of course, does not mean that a particular language must make use of the most unmarked sounds. Human societies do not always make use of the simplest or most natural patterns of behavior. However, in a global sense we should expect to find the least marked sounds occurring most often.

All languages do not have the same inventory of peripheral, nonquantal vowels. In Figure 8-9 formant frequencies are plotted in Mels for the average values of the vowels of American English that were measured by Peterson and Barney (1952) and Potter and Steinberg (1950). Note that the [i] to [a] axis is divided up into the same set of vowels as Swedish. Different symbols are used for the vowels of American English and there may be differences in the lengths of some vowels (e.g., [ɪ] and [eː]) but the formant frequency intervals are similar. The situation is quite different for the [u] to [a] axis. The vowels [o] and [oː] line up, as do the vowels transcribed as [ɔ] in English and [aː] in Swedish. However, there

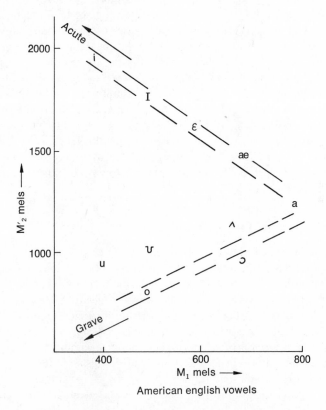

American english vowels

FIGURE 8-9. *Acoustic classification of the vowels of American English. Note that the distribution of vowels is different and that the "same" phonetic symbol, e.g., [ɔ] has different acoustic values in the Swedish than in the American English data.*

is no vowel like Swedish [ɔ] in English. The Swedish [uː] is likewise different from English [u]. These differences point out the dangers of relying too heavily on phonetic studies that compare the sounds of different languages without making use of objective acoustic analysis.

Psychoacoustic data (Stevens et al., 1969) indicate that monolingual speakers of American English are not able to identify the Swedish vowels [y] and [ʉː] with certainty. Swedish listeners, as we might expect, are able to identify these vowels with certainty. What might the psycholological basis for these different vowel distinctions be? The only plausible hypothesis appears to be one that involves either a universal set of neural property detectors that are selectively activated as people are exposed to particular sounds during a "plastic" period, or a completely plastic process that "shapes up" property detectors for sounds of interest. In short, vowels seem to be perceived by means of neural acoustic property detectors that respond to particular acoustic signals. Acoustic rather than articulatory factors thus specify vowels. The range of formant frequencies to which these property detectors can potentially respond, however, is delimited by the quantal vowels [i], [u], and [a]. The acoustic properties of these vowels reflect the constraints of the species-specific supralaryngeal vocal tract anatomy of *Homo sapiens*, which we will discuss in Chapter 9. Like the bullfrogs which we discussed in Chapter 7, we seem to respond to particular vowel sounds by means of neural devices that are "tuned" to particular acoustic signals that reflect the constraints of our speech producing mechanisms. Humans however, unlike frogs, are plastic and will partition the possible range of formant frequencies that the human vocal tract can generate differently, as they grow up in different linguistic environments

Consonants and Phonetic Features

The deficiencies of classical phonetic theory that arise for vowels are not as apparent for consonants. This perhaps reflects the accessibility of relevant articulatory data by means of palatography. The articulatory maneuvers that generate consonants can be measured by palatographic techniques that are still useful in modern computerized forms (Fujimura, et al., 1973). There are still many unresolved problems. The biological nature of the linguistic distinction between consonants and vowels is, for example, still not clear, but the traditional articulatory phonetic theory for consonants is still valid.

Linguists generally maintain a distinction between certain sounds that they classify as vowels and other sounds that they classify as consonants. The distinction is not always disjoint; some sounds like the sounds [h] and [w] in the words *horse* and *cow* are often classified as semivowels or semiconsonants. However, as the protagonist, Monsieur Jourdain, in

Moliere's *Le Bourgeois Gentilhomme* learned, one speaks with both vowels and consonants. A number of attempts have been made to devise articulatory or acoustic definitions of either vowelness or consonantalness. Ẑinkin (1968), for example, defines vowel segments in terms of the amplitude of the speech signal. This definition might work if vowels always occurred between stop consonants or fricatives. The definition, however, clearly does not work. Jakobson et al. (1963) define vowels as voiced sounds that have no "zeros" in their transfer functions. As the discussion of nasality that follows demonstrates, this definition will not work for nasalized vowels. The physiologic insights derived by Stevens (1972) that we discussed in relation to vowels may provide a basis for the vowel–consonant dichotomy. Stevens notes that the physiological mechanisms that are the basis of quantal effects differ for consonants and vowels. The source of acoustic energy for a "true" consonant is generated at a constriction in the supralaryngeal airway above the glottis. Some consonants like the sound [z] (in the word *buzz*) also may involve periodic laryngeal excitation, but consonants like [s] and [f] (the sounds in the words *sat* and *fat*) are "excited" by the noise sources that are generated by the air rushing through the palatal constriction that is sustained through most of the these *continuant* consonants. In consonants like the *stops* [b], [p], [d], etc., noise is generated during the early stages of the "release" of the consonant as the speaker's lips move apart for the *labial* [p] and [b], or as the speaker's tongue moves away from the hard palate in the *dental* [t] or [d]. The noise source is generated by the turbulent air flow through the constriction (Fant, 1960; Flanagan, 1972). The position of the source in relation to the "tubes" of the supralaryngeal airway is thus quite different from vowels excited by a laryngeal source. Computer-implemented modeling studies show that quantal effects occur for consonantal vocal tract configurations when the primary constriction is in one of six positions. Three of these positions—the labial, dental, and velar positions—occur, for example, in the stop consonants [b], [d], and [g] of English (Perkell, 1969). The other three possible quantal positions, which involve constrictions closer to the larynx, occur in other languages. The acoustic signals that result from these quantal positions are resistant to articulatory sloppiness and have well-defined spectral properties. They correspond with the traditional "points of articulation" or "place features" of traditional phonetic theory (Müller, 1848; Jones, 1932). There thus is a physiologic mechanism that defines a class of "true" consonants, a class of sounds that have quantal properties that differ from those of vowels.

The psychoacoustic and perceptual data that we discussed in Chapter 7 show that adult human listeners respond to sounds like [b], [d], and [g] as though they were using neural acoustic property detectors that were "tuned" to perceive these sounds. Similar results occur with 3-week-old infants. The neural mechanisms that seem to be involved in the perception of these sounds furthermore yield differential results in experiments that take note of brain lateralization. The dominant, left hemisphere seems to be more involved in the perception of consonants than vowels. There thus appears to be a neural mechanism or a set of neural mechanisms that are involved in the perception of consonants. The "match" between the quantal possibilities of the supralaryngeal vocal tract and the perceptual distinctions that are manifested with very little exposure to speech in human infants likewise appears to be a result of process of Darwinian natural selection. Humans appear to be predisposed to perceive the quantal acoustic signals that specify these consonants.

Some Phonetic Features for Consonants

CONSONANTAL PLACE OF ARTICULATION. The quantal effects that we have discussed yield the possibility of seven possible "places of articulation" at which quantal effects can occur. In Figure 8-10 an idealized model for the production of a fricative consonant is shown.

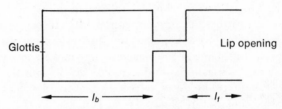

FIGURE 8-10. *An idealized model of the supralaryngeal vocal tract for the production of fricative consonants. The position of the constriction can be shifted by changing the values of the length of the back and front cavities, l_b and l_f.*

The glottis is at the lefthand end of the tube and is considered to be almost closed. The position of the constriction, which is between l_b and l_f can be adjusted to represent different places of articulation. From a simple-minded articulatory point of view there is no reason why a constriction could not be formed at any point in the supralaryngeal vocal tract from the lips down to the pharynx. Human languages, however, make use of a fairly limited number of "places of articulation" (Greenberg, 1963, 1966). Steven's modeling of the acoustic consequences of gradually shifting the constriction to different positions in the supralaryngeal vocal tract "explains" why we use only a limited number of configurations. In Figure 8-11 the length of the back cavity is plotted on the horizontal axis. The length of the constriction is 3 cm and the total vocal tract length is 16 cm. The curved "bars" on the figure indicate the quantal acoustic signals that result as particular formant frequencies generated by the front and back cavities l_f and l_b couple to produce spectral peaks and relative insensitivity to small articulatory perturbations in the two pharyngeal articulations ($l_b = 5$ and 7 cm), the velar articulation ($l_b = 5$ cm), the retroflex articulation, which we discussed in Chapter 7, ($l_b = 10$ cm), and the dental articulation ($l_b = 11$ cm). The labial articulation which occurs for $l_b = 13$ cm always results in formant frequencies lower than the formant frequencies of the unconstricted vocal tract. The

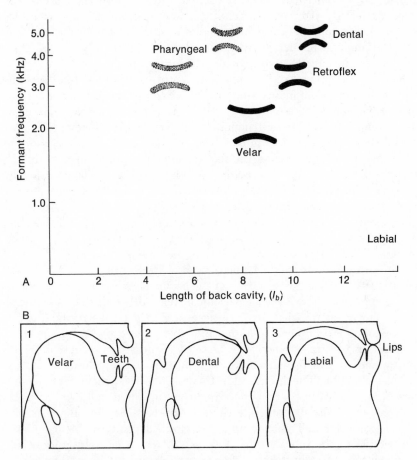

FIGURE 8-11(A)   *Results of a computer modeling of the model of Figure 8-10. The curved bars indicate the* quantal *acoustic signals that are produced at particular "points of articulation."*
FIGURE 8-11(B)   *Sketches of supralaryngeal vocal tract for labial, dental, and velar stops (the stop sounds* [p], [t], *and* [k]). *The retroflex and pharyngeal quantal regions shown in Figure 8-11(A) are not used in English. Further anatomical "landmarks" can be seen in Figure 6-17.*

formant frequencies of a vowel–labial consonant sequence thus always will involve falling transitions. The acoustic signals that specify the pharyngeal points of articulation are stippled in this diagram since these consonants involving these regions do not occur in English and their acoustic properties have not been studied extensively.

The sketch derived from lateral X-ray views in Figure 8-11B show the labial, dental, and velar articulations. There may be minor differences between different speakers and different languages. Steven's model is oversimplified but it points out the salient quantal properties of the consonantal feature *place of articulation*. Note that the feature is multivalued, i.e., a consonant can have one of a number of different places of articulation. This phonetic feature obviously can apply only to consonants that are produced with a supralaryngeal constriction.

STOP CONSONANTS. The phonetic feature *stop* also is relevant only for consonants. Consonants that involve a complete obstruction of the supralaryngeal vocal tract are classified as $+stop$, whereas consonants that do not involve any obstruction can be classified as $-stop$. The phonetic feature *stop* thus is a binary feature, sounds can be either stops or not. The physiologic basis of the feature *stop* is actually not as simple as we might think. The "obstruction" of the vocal tract does not always have to effect an airtight seal. The important factor is to generate the appropriate acoustic signals. The acoustic signals that are important are the formant transitions (which we discussed in Chapter 7) and the noise "bursts" that occur on the "release" of the stop (Halle, et al., 1957; Stevens, 1972; Stevens and Blumstein, in press). Stops often are produced with small air leaks (Yanagihara and Hyde, 1966).

VOICING. The acoustic output of the larynx clearly is binary insofar as the laryngeal air flow is either periodic or not. Although the adjustments of the laryngeal muscles that are necessary to get the larynx into the proper configuration for phonation can involve subtle gradual maneuvers, a sound can be either $+voiced$ or $-voiced$. The acoustic consequence is binary and we can formally take account of its binary character by the $+$ or $-$ notation. The discussion in Chapter 6 of the articulatory maneuvers that are involved in generating the turbulent noise source of a $-voiced$ sound also demonstrate the acoustic basis of the binary nature of this sound signal. The opening of the glottis depends on the size of the constriction in the supralaryngeal airway at which noise excitation is to be generated. The adjustments of the glottal opening thus may vary over a multivalued range, but the acoustic result is again an abrupt binary effect since noise excitation is generated when the air flow exceeds a critical value and becomes turbulent.

The perception of speech also seems to be structured in terms of a binary $\pm voiced$ (voiced or voiceless) distinction. The distinction is apparent in the Miller and Nicely (1954) confusion matrix data as well as in the other experiments which were discussed in Chapter 7.

PHONATION ONSET. The activity of the muscles of the larynx is independent of the muscles that can open your lips or move your tongue when you produce a *stop consonant* like [b], [p], or [d]. The articulatory activity of the supralaryngeal vocal tract is independent of the larynx and is identical for the labial, stop consonants [b] and [p] in similar contexts, e.g., the words *bat* and *pat*. What is different is the activity of the laryngeal muscles with respect to the abrupt lip opening that marks the start of the initial sound in both of these words. In both words the audible acoustic signal commences at the instant when the speaker's lips open. In the case of the word *bat* the speaker's larynx is already in its closed, phonatory position at the moment that the speaker opens his lips. The vocal cords have already moved into their closed, or nearly closed, position and phonation is a consequence of the air flow through the vocal tract. High speed movies of the larynx show that phonation starts about 10 to 20 msec after the start of air flow if the vocal cords are already in their "phonation neutral" position (Lieberman, 1967). When the lips open in the word *bat*, air can flow through the vocal tract and phonation starts shortly thereafter.

In the word *pat* the situation is different. The vocal cords are still open at the instant the speaker's lips open. The sound that initially occurs is not voiced since phonation cannot occur when the vocal cords are open. The open position of the vocal cords instead allows a relatively large air flow and the initial sound is generated by the air turbulence that occurs as the lips are abruptly opened. An initial "burst" of air, therefore, can occur when a [p] is produced, particularly when it occurs in initial position. The speaker producing the word *pat* starts to close his vocal cords after the release of the [p], but it takes about 100 msec for the vocal cords to reach configuration necesssary for phonation (Lieberman, 1967). The distinction between [b] and [p] thus rests on the delay in the start of phonation relative to the opening of the speaker's lips. The sound [p] involves delayed *phonation onset*.

The phonetic feature *phonation onset* which we illustrated with an example drawn from English, simply involves the timing between the onset of phonation and the release of the primary occlusion of the vocal tract. This phonetic feature obviously is relevant only for stop consonants. When a stop consonant occurs in syllable-initial position in the production of an isolated syllable, phonation can start coincident with the release of the stop, after the release of the stop, or before the release of the primary occlusion. In English the sound [p] is produced with *delayed* phonation. The sound [b] in English is produced either with *coincident* or *advanced* phonation. In many languages the *advanced* versus *coincident* contrast is the relevant phonemic distinction (e.g., Spanish). In some languages all three categories are phonemic (e.g., Thai). The exact time intervals that characterize these categories vary from language to language (Lisker and Abramson, 1964, 1971). However, three categories potentially exist. Note that this feature is not a binary feature. There are inherently three possibilities. It is possible to use binary notation to enumerate three levels, e.g., we could set up two binary features $\pm$*advanced* and $\pm$*delayed*. Coincident phonation onset would be indicated by the notation:

$$\begin{bmatrix} -\,advanced \\ -\,delayed \end{bmatrix}$$

Advanced phonation onset would be

$$\begin{bmatrix} +\,advanced \\ -\,delayed \end{bmatrix}$$

The binary nature of this notation would, however, be contrived since the *phonation onset* involves three rather than two possibilities.

The perceptual responses of human listeners to stop consonants bears close inspection, for it reveals a fundamental underlying biological mechanism that structures this phonetic feature. If a large number of examples of the English stops [p] and [b] are measured, it becomes evident that there is a good deal of variation in the timing between the onset of phonation and the release of the stop. Some [b]'s have a phonation delay of 10 msec, others 20 msec, and so on. Some [p]'s have phonation delays of 50 msec, others 60 msec, others 40 msec. The responses of listeners to these stimuli show that there is a sharp "categorical" distinction, i.e., categorical discriminations are occurring (cf. Chapter 7). Stops that have phonation delays less than 25 msec are perceived as [b]. Stops that have phonation delays greater than 25 msec are perceived as [p]. The situation is seemingly odd because these same listeners cannot perceive any difference between versions of [p] that differ as much as 20 msec in their phonation delay. For example, listeners are not able to discriminate between two sounds that have phonation delays of 30 and 50 msec, respectively. But if the phonation delays of two sounds are 10 and 30 msec, one sound will be heard and identified as [b], the other as [p]. In other words, listeners can not differentiate sounds within each phonetic category although they sharply differentiate stimuli across the phonetic boundary on the basis of the same physical parameter, the 20-msec timing distinction. These distinctions occur across many related and unrelated languages (Lisker and Abramson, 1964). The basis of the 20-msec timing distinction appears to rest in a basic constraint of the auditory system. Hirsch (1959) and Hirsch and Sherrick (1961) carried out a series of experiments to determine the difference in time that is required for a listener to judge which of two auditory stimuli with diverse characteristics came first. A time difference of 20 msec was found to be necessary for a variety of stimulus conditions.

The phonetic feature *phonation onset* thus appears to be inherently structured in terms of this perceptual constraint as well as the articulatory constraints of the speech-producing apparatus. The control of the source of excitation for speech is independent of the configuration of the supralaryngeal vocal tract. Speakers thus can change the timing between the laryngeal source and the opening of the supralaryngeal vocal tract. The three simplest categories for timing rest in three simple distinctions—advanced, coincident, and delayed. The magnitude of the time interval that differentiates the categories is a consequence of the minimum temporal resolution of the auditory system.

The 20-msec timing distinction has been shown to mark the perception of stop sounds by 3-week-old infants (Eimas et al., 1971; Eimas and Corbit, 1973). Experiments monitoring their behavior while they listen to artificially synthesized stimuli have shown that they partition the temporal variations that can occur between phonation and the release of the primary occlusion of the supralaryngeal vocal tract at precisely the same 20-msec intervals used by normal adults and older children. There seems to be no way in which month-old infants could "learn" to respond to speech stimuli in this manner. The 20-msec voicing onset interval appears to reflect an innately determined constraint of the auditory system in *Homo sapiens*.

Studies of the responses of chinchillas (Kuhl and Miller, 1974) to stop consonants show that these animals also are sensitive to the same 20-msec threshold. The animals can be taught to discriminate the sound [d] from [t] and their responses appear to be structured by the same 20-msec "temporal resolving" factor that operates in humans. This result is, of course, what we would expect if human language and human speech were the result of a gradual Darwinian process of evolution (Lieberman, 1975). Humans share many biological mechanisms with "lower" animals. We may also share some of our phonetic features with other animals.

NASALITY. There are many phonetic features that are in all likelihood part of human speech communication for which we as yet lack important data. The presence or absence of the acoustic signal that results from opening the nasal cavity to the rest of the supralaryngeal vocal tract is a good example. The articulatory basis of this feature is superficially simple, the speaker simply relaxes his velum, lowering it and thus opening the nasal cavity to the rest of the supralaryngeal vocal tract. The electromyographic data that we discussed in Chapter 6 shows that the situation is not so simple at the muscular level. Different speakers exhibit different patterns of activity. Although some of the acoustic correlates of nasality are known (Fujimura, 1962), the perceptual "value" of various acoustic cues is still not clearly understood. Many sounds can be produced with a significant degree of air flow through the nasal cavity without being perceived as nasal (House and Stevens, 1956). In many instances people will exhibit a nasal quality as they talk, although trained observers find it difficult to agree on the extent of nasal impairment. These problems are aggravated in the treatment of speech pathologies like those associated with cleft palate (Pruzansky, 1973). Despite these uncertainties, it is clear that the presence of the human nasal cavity structures the possibility of generating signals that differ with respect to their nasality.

On the Classification of the Sounds of Speech

Table 8-1 and the accompanying "Illustrations of the Consonant Symbols" in Table 8-2 list the principal consonant letters and chief vowel letters of the International Phonetic Association (1949). These symbols or "letters" for the most part are the result of subjective, auditory analyses of phoneticians supplemented by palatography and some X rays of the supralaryngeal vocal tract (Jones, 1919, 1932). These symbols have been extremely useful for the transcription of both "common" and "unusual" languages, i.e., the languages of cultures that the individual phonetician is familiar or unfamiliar with. In Table 8-3, in contrast, some of the sounds of English are specified in terms of the hypothetical phonetic features that we have discussed. You can see that we have specified only a few phonetic features, that are not sufficient in themselves to characterize all of the sounds that have a linguistic function in English. We could have enlarged the list of hypothetical phonetic features in Table 8-3 and "accounted" for more of the sounds in Table 8-1 by drawing on the results of recent research. We could, for example, introduce a source feature, *periodic noise* that would account for the production of sounds like [z], which involve noise that is generated by the peaks of the glottal air flow (Fant, 1960). The air flow at the peaks of the glottal waveform generates noise at the dental constriction in the supralaryngeal vocal tract. We have not put this sound feature into the matrix since our object is not to provide a complete solution but to point to principles and techniques that may prove useful in devising and evaluating phonetic theories.

In this connection, that is, the evaluation of phonetic theories, there are a few points that we should stress since recent discussions of phonetic theory that derive from the "generative linguistics" school, e.g., Chomsky and Halle (1968) discuss various formal criteria that are supposed to be useful in evaluating different, contrasting theories. These evaluation or "simplicity" procedures essentially take into account the number of symbols that enter into a linguistic description. Theories that make use of fewer symbols are supposed to be "better" theories. The feature matrix of Table 8-3 is a terrible solution taking into account its incomplete nature, if the number of symbols that we use has any bearing on its scientific value. The matrix of Table 8-3 is not parsimonious; it is not symmetric. Different features are relevant if a sound is a vowel or consonant. Consonants, for example, are specified in terms of quantal places of articulation that are not relevant for vowels. This means that the total number of phonetic features that are specified in the theory is greater than would be the case if we made use of a feature matrix like that of Jakobson et al. (1963), in which different values of the same features specified all the sounds of English.

TABLE 8-1

THE INTERNATIONAL PHONETIC ALPHABET.

(Revised to 1951.)

	Bi-labial	*Labio-dental*	*Dental and Alveolar*	*Retroflex*	*Palato-alveolar*	*Alveolo-palatal*	*Palatal*	*Velar*	*Uvular*	*Pharyngal*	*Glottal*
Plosive	p b		t d	ʈ ɖ			c ɟ	k g	q ɢ		ʔ
Nasal	m	ɱ	n	ɳ			ɲ	ŋ	ɴ		
Lateral Fricative			ɬ ɮ								
Lateral Non-fricative			l	ɭ			ʎ				
Rolled			r						ʀ		
Flapped			ɾ	ɽ					ʀ		
Fricative	ɸ β	f v	θ ð | s z | ɹ	ʂ ʐ	ʃ ʒ	ɕ ʑ	ç ʝ	x ɣ	χ ʁ	ħ ʕ	h ɦ
Frictionless Continuants and Semi-vowels	w | ɥ	ʋ	ɹ				j (ɥ)	(w)	ʁ		
							Front *Central*	*Back*			
Close	(y ʉ u)						i y ɨ ʉ	ɯ u			
Half-close	(ø o)						e ø	ɤ o			
								ə			
Half-open	(œ ɔ)						ɛ œ	ʌ ɔ			
							æ	ɐ			
Open	(ɒ)						a	ɑ ɒ			

(Secondary articulations are shown by symbols in brackets.)

OTHER SOUNDS.—Palatalized consonants: ƫ, ȡ, etc.; palatalized ʃ, ʒ: ʆ, ʓ. Velarized or pharyngalized consonants: ɫ, ᵭ, ᵶ, etc. jective consonants (with simultaneous glottal stop): p', t', etc. Implosive voiced consonants: ɓ, ɗ, etc. ɼ fricative trill. σ, ϱ abialized θ, ð, or s, z). ƪ, ƺ (labialized ʃ, ʒ). ʇ, ʗ, ʖ (clicks, Zulu *c*, *q*, *x*). ɺ (a sound between r and l). ŋ Japanese syllabic nasal. ɧ ombination of x and ʃ). ʍ (voiceless w). ɩ, ʏ, ɷ (lowered varieties of i, y, u). ɜ (a variety of ə). ɵ (a vowel between ø and o).

Affricates are normally represented by groups of two consonants (ts, tʃ, dʒ, etc.), but, when necessary, ligatures are used (ʦ, ʧ, ʤ, c.), or the marks ⁀ or ‿ (t͡s or t͜s, etc.). ⁀ ‿ also denote synchronic articulation (m͡ŋ = simultaneous m and ŋ). c, ɟ may occasionlly be used in place of tʃ, dʒ, and ƾ, ƻ for ts, dz. Aspirated plosives: ph, th, etc. r-coloured vowels: eɹ, aɹ, ɔɹ, etc., or eʴ, aʴ, ɔʴ, etc., r ᶒ, ᶏ, ᶗ, etc.; r-coloured ə: əɹ or əʴ or ɹ or ᶕ or ɚ.

LENGTH, STRESS, PITCH.—ː (full length). ˑ (half length). ˈ (stress, placed at beginning of the stressed syllable). ˌ (secondary tress). ˉ (high level pitch); ˍ (low level); ˊ (high rising); ˏ (low rising); ˋ (high falling); ˎ (low falling); ˆ (rise-fall); ˇ (fall-rise).

MODIFIERS.—˜ nasality. ˳ breath (l̥ = breathed l). ˬ voice (s̬ = z). ʻ slight aspiration following p, t, etc. ̫ labializaion (n̫ = labialized n). ̪ dental articulation (t̪ = dental t). ˙ palatalization (ż = ʓ). ̣ specially close vowel (ẹ = a very close e). specially open vowel (ę = a rather open e). ˔ tongue raised (e˔ or e̝ = ẹ). ˕ tongue lowered (e˕ or e̞ = ę). ˖ tongue advanced (u˖ or u̟ = an advanced u, t̟ = t̪). ˗ or ˍ tongue retracted (i˗ or i̠ = ɨ˖, t̠ = alveolar t). ˒ lips more rounded. ˓ lips more spread. Central owels: ï (= ɨ), ü (= ʉ), ë (= ə˔), ö (= ɵ), ɛ̈, ɔ̈. ˌ (e.g. n̩) syllabic consonant. ˘ consonantal vowel. ʃˢ variety of ʃ resembling s, etc.

Reproduced by permission of the International Phonetic Association and Le Maître Phonétique

TABLE 8-2
ILLUSTRATIONS OF THE CONSONANT SYMBOLS

p, b, t, d, k, m, n, l, f and h have their common European values. The values of the other letters are exemplified in the following list.

g. As in Eng. *get*.

j. Eng. *y* in *yet, you*; *j* as in Ger. *Jahr*.

r. Rolled r as in Scottish English, Italian, Spanish, Russian.

s. As in Eng. *see*, Fr. *son*, etc.

v. As *v* in Eng., Fr., Ital.

w. As in Eng. *will, walk*.

z. As in Eng. *zeal*, Fr. *zèle*.

ţ. Swedish *rt* in *kort*.

ḑ. Swedish *rd* in *bord*.

c. Cardinal value, as in dialectal Fr. pronunciation of *quai* (ce).

ɟ. Cardinal value, as in dialectal Fr. pronunciation of *guêpe* (ɟɛ:p).

q. Arabic ق; Eskimo ĸ.

ɢ. The corresponding voiced sound. One value of Persian ق.

ʔ. As in North Ger. *Verein* (fɛrʔain).

ɱ. Ital. *n* in *invidia*; Span. *n* in *anfora*.

ɳ. Marathi ण (ṇ).

ɲ. Fr. and Ital. *gn*; Span. *ñ*.

ŋ. Eng. *ng* in *sing*; Ger. *ng* in *Ding*.

ɴ. As in Eskimo eɴina (melody).

ʇ. Eng. *l* in *table*.

ɬ. Welsh *ll* as in *Llangollen*.

ɦ. Zulu *dhl* as in *dhla* (eat).

 l. Marathi ळ (ḷ).

ʎ. Ital. *gl* in *egli, gli* in *voglio*; Span. *ll* in *allá*.

ɾ. Span. *r* in *pero*.

ɽ. Retroflex flap, starting with retroflexed tongue and moving the tip forwards and downwards so that the under side strikes the teeth-ridge.

R. One variety of Parisian Fr. r.

φ. Frequent Ger. pronunciation of *w* in *Schwester*.

β. Span. *b* as in *saber*.

θ. Eng. *th* in *thing*; Span. *c, z* in *placer, plaza*; Greek *θ*.

ð. Eng. *th* in *this*; Span. *d* in *cada*; Danish *d* in *gade*.

ɹ. Southern Eng. *r* in *dry* (consonantal); Amer. Eng. *ir* in *bird* (vocalic).

ʂ. Swed. *rs* in *tvārs*

ʐ. Pekingese variety of ʒ, as in ˈʒen (man) (narrowly ˈʐən).

ʃ. Eng. *sh*; Fr. *ch*; Ger. *sch*.

ʒ. Eng. *s* in *measure*; in *jour, g* in *géant*.

ç. In occasional pronunciation of Eng. *hue* (çu:); Ger. *ch* in *ich*.

c. Polish ç in *gęś*, *si* in *gęsia*.

ʑ. Polish *ź* in *zle, źi* in *ziarno*.

x. Scottish *ch* in *loch*; Ger. *ch* in *ach*.

ɣ. Span. *g* in *luego*; Danish *g* in *koge*.

χ. Variety of Arabic خ.

ħ. Arabic ح.

ʁ. Variety of Parisian *r*.

ʕ. Arabic ع.

ɦ. Voiced h. Often heard in Eng. between voiced sounds, as in *behave, manhood*.

ɥ. Fr. non-syllabic *u*, as in *nuit*.

ʋ. Dutch *w*.

TABLE 8-3
HYPOTHETICAL PHONETIC FEATURES

Vowels:

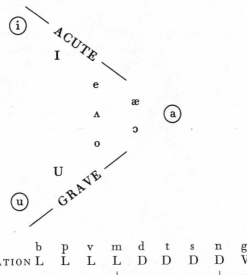

Consonants:	b	p	v	m	d	t	s	n	g	k	ng
PLACE OF ARTICULATION	L	L	L	L	D	D	D	D	V	V	V
NASALITY	—	—	—	+	—	—	—	+	—	—	+
VOICING			+	+			—	+			+
STOP	+	+	—	—	+	+	—	—	+	+	—
PHONATION ONSET	A	D			A	D			A	D	
	C				C				C		

Simplicity metrics, however, have virtually no value in testing scientific theories. There is no logical procedure that we can use to decide which of two different theories is "best." We have to test contending theories against data. The "best" theory is the theory that relates data that were hitherto seemingly unrelated and that points the way to new relationships that we otherwise would not have thought of. Formal, mathematical procedures are useful when we are trying to see whether two theoretical statements are actually different. If we can reduce both statements to the same formal statement then we know that we really have one theory that can be stated in different ways. However, when we have two different theories, e.g., the Ptolemeic and Copernican theories of the universe, there is no logical or formal procedure that can decide which theory is correct. Galileo's data decided the issue for all scientists; formal scholastic logic was not relevant.

The phonetic features in Table 8-3 also are not in any sense adapted to manipulations of phonologic rules that change the binary values of features that can take only one of two values, + or —. Although some features like *voiced* are binary, other features like *phonation onset* have three values, and the consonantal *place of articulation* can take one of three values in English. The different properties of these phonetic features reflect the differing characteristics of the biological mechanisms that these features formally represent. Vowels, for example, appear to be specified in terms of the plastic neural property detectors that we discussed in Chapter 7. Listeners appear to identify vowels in terms of an auditory "map" of the vowel space. Traditional phonetic theories that specify vowels in terms of a vowel triangle (or quadrilateral), e.g., Figure 8-1, thus appear to be better approximations of what is important for human beings than numerical charts like those of Jakobson et al. (1963) and Chomsky and Halle (1968). Table 8-3 therefore specifies vowels in terms of acoustically defined triangle in which the vowels of English are specified as points that bear certain spacial relations to the *quantal* vowels [i], [u], and [a].

The *quantalness* of [i], [u], and [a] is indidated on Table 8-3 by the circles that are placed around these symbols. All of the vowels of English are +*voiced* and —*nasal*. This is a characteristic of English that is part of the detailed "knowledge" of the language that a native speaker would have to "know" in order to produce any of these vowels. These features are therefore not specified for the vowels of English. They form part of the language-specific "implementation rules" of English (Lieberman, 1970). The native speaker has to keep track of many other things that are not directly noted in Table 8-3. The vowels of English, for example, have different durations (cf. Appendix to Chapter 8). This information can be formally specified by means of language-specific implementation rules. Implementation rules afford a method of formally noting some of the differences that exist between different languages and dialects as well as the differences that exist between individual speakers.

The vowels noted in Table 8-3 are valid for a particular hypothetical dialect of English, that of the acoustic studies of Peterson and Barney (1952) and Potter and Steinberg (1950). Different dialects would have different acoustic maps. The relations between vowels that traditional phonetic theories (e.g. Jones, 1932) postulate, have acoustic significance; we therefore could have entered the traditional dimensions of *front* and *back* on the vowel triangle in Table 8-3, bringing it closer to Figure 8-1. The terms *acute* and *grave* as defined by Jakobson et al. (1952) are, however, more appropriate because they convey the acoustic significance of these classifications. The vowels that are spaced between [i] and [a] form the *acute* series, those between [u] and [a], the *grave* series. Recent psycho-acoustic data (Nearey, 1976), as well as the behavior of vowel contrasts in sound changes, appear to justify these classifications. Table 8-3, however, should not be interpreted as though it is making a claim about the "binariness" of *acuteness* or *graveness* or the specification of a vowel like [a] in terms of these properties. A vowel like [a] may be neither *acute* nor *grave* since these attributes may both be secondary, derived classifications based on the sounds and the neural property detectors that are the biological bases of vowel sounds. Acuteness and graveness would still have a psychological reality derived from the acoustic relations between different vowels which might be reflected in higher level property detectors (Cutting and Eimas, 1975; Lieberman, 1976).

The consonants partially specified by the phonetic features in Table 8-3 illustrate the principles that we have discussed. The *places of articulation* that have to be specified for English are the labial (L), dental (D), and velar (V) quantal positions discussed by Stevens (1973) and Stevens and Blumstein (in press). These regions correspond fairly well with the articulatory configurations discussed by traditional phonetic theories like that of Jones (1932) that are noted in Tables 8-1 and 8-2.

Note that the feature *voiced* is not specified for $+stop$ consonants in Table 8-3 because it is not relevant nor is the feature *phonation onset* specified for $-stop$ consonants. The feature *phonation onset* has three values—*advanced*, *coincident*, and *delayed*. The exact value in milliseconds of the timing between the release of the stop and phonation depends on the place of articulation (Lisker and Abramson, 1964). The timing is also different in different languages. Note that sounds like [b], [d], and [g] have the entries A/C. English makes use of only two distinctions with respect to this feature. Some speakers of English make use of *advanced* phonation onset timing when they produce a sound like [b] in utterance-initial position (e.g., in the word *bat*). Other speakers of English use *coincident* phonation onset timing (Lisker and Abramson, 1964). The distinction does not carry any meaning in English; it is not phonemic. Speakers of English can differ with regard to the phonation onset of sounds like [b], [d], and [g] because it doesn't make any difference. Speaker-specific implementation rules can describe how different speakers of English produce these sounds which would have different meanings in a language like Thai where all three categories of phonation onset are phonemic.

Table 8-3, in conclusion, is tentative, hypothetical, and incomplete. Some aspects of the classificatory system like the acoustic vowel space are based on data that have been replicated in many independent experiments over a period of many years. Other aspects, like the sound features *quantal* and *phonation onset* are still fairly novel, although they "explain" and are consistent with the physiologic, acoustic, and perceptual data that we have discussed in the preceding chapters. The primary reason for presenting this table is, however, its very incompleteness. It demonstrates the need for the work that still must be done if we are to understand how humans communicate by means of speech and the relation of speech to language and other forms of communication and behavior.

Prosodic Features

The sounds and phonetic features in Tables 8-1 and 8-3 do not include the prosodic elements of speech. Variations of stress and intonation convey both linguistic and "paralinguistic" or "emotional" information. We discussed some of the acoustic correlates and articulatory maneuvers that manifest and generate the prosodic feature *stress* in Chapter 6. Variations in stress (Daniel Jones (1932) used the term *prominence*) have systematic linguistic functions in many languages and the acoustic correlates and underlying physiology have been carefully investigated in many experiments, e.g., Fry (1955), Lieberman (1960, 1967), Lehiste (1961) Morton and Jassem (1965), Atkinson (1973). We would have to list about 100 references if we wanted to present a comprehensive listing of recent work. *Tone* features which play an important linguistic role in many languages other than English, for example, Swedish and Thai have also been carefully studied (Garding et al., 1970; Erikson, 1975). In Chinese, for example, two words may differ phonetically solely with respect to the tone pattern of fundamental frequency. The study of these "tone" languages reveals that speakers execute deliberate laryngeal maneuvers to produce consistent f_0 contours (Erikson, 1975). There is, however, a second, more general function of the temporal pattern of fundamental frequency that is structured with regard to the biological constraints of respiration. The pattern of fundamental frequency plays a role in signaling the end of a sentence in most, if not all, human languages (Lieberman, 1967). Both traditional and generative grammars (Chomsky, 1957) regard a sentence as the minimal unit from which a complete semantic interpretation can be made. The traditional functional description of a sentence, that it expresses a complete thought, has real validity. It is easy to perform a small experiment that tests this statement. All that one has to do is read a short passage after moving the sentence-final period punctuation one word over. The resulting sequences of words will, for the most part, be unintelligible. The primary function of orthographic punctuation is to indicate the ends of sentences. The sentence-final "period" symbol is essential. Question marks can be optionally replaced by special words in most languages. (English is a special case insofar as some of the options have fallen out of use in comparatively recent times (cf. Lieberman, 1967). Commas are usually optional insofar as the reader would have been able to derive the sentence's meaning if they were omitted.

During normal speech the prosodic content of the message, which is largely determined by the perceived pitch as a function of time, signals the ends of sentences. The phonetic feature that speakers make use of to segment the train of words into sentences is the *breath-group*. The breath-group as a phonetic features has a long history. It derives from the "tune" analysis of Armstrong and Ward (1926) and Jones (1932). Stetson (1951) introduced the concept of a physiologically structured basic prosodic signal. The breath-group probably is one of the most central, basic aspects of language and it, or some equivalent sound signal, would have had to have been present in the earliest forms of hominid language. It is not a question of language being more difficult without signaling the boundaries of sentences. Language would be impossible without this information, for we would be reduced to one-word utterances, each of which would have a fixed, immutable meaning. Language is not a code in which particular signals have fixed meanings. It is impossible to transmit a message in a code if the message is not already in the code book. Language has the potential of transmitting new, unanticipated information. Syntax and the sentence are necessary factors for the presence of language and the *breath-group* is one of the basic, primitive phonetic features that must be present in all languages.

This view of the basic, primitive, status of the breath-group is consistent with the physiologic mechanisms that structure and constrain its form. In the production of normal speech the acoustic cues that characterize the normal breath-group are a consequence of minimal deviation from the respiratory activity that is necessary to sustain life. The primary function of the human respiratory system is *not* to provide air for speech production. Oxygen transfer to the blood stream is the primary vegetative function of the respiratory system. Speech production is a secondary function. Constant respiratory activity is necessary to sustain life, and in the absence of speech there is an ongoing cyclic pattern in which inspiration is followed by expiration as the lungs alternately expand and deflate, forcing air in and out through the nose, mouth, pharynx, and trachea. In Chapter 6 graphs of pulmonary air pressure were presented for both quiet respiration and speech (Figure 6-1). Similar data have been derived for various types of utterances and the details of the pulmonary air pressure function vary. However, one factor is always present. The pulmonary air pressure during the expiratory phase must be greater than the atmospheric air pressure. During the inspiratory phase it must, in contrast, be lower than the atmospheric air pressure. At the end of the expiratory phase of the breath-group, there thus must be a fairly abrupt transition in the pulmonary air pressure from the greater (positive) air pressure necessary for expiration to the lower (negative) air pressure necessary for inspiration.

If a speaker moves his larynx into the phonation position during an expiration and does nothing to change the tensions of the various laryn-geal muscles, then the fundamental frequency of phonation will be determined by the transglottal air pressure drop (Lieberman, 1967; Atkinson, 1973; Collier, 1975). Müller (1848) first noted that the rate at which the vocal cords open and close, which determines the fundamental frequency of phonation, is a function of the air pressure differential across the vocal cords. If a speaker maintains a relatively unobstructed supralaryngeal airway and keeps his larynx in a fixed phonation position, then the fundamental frequency will be determined by the pulmonary air pressure. These conditions are met in the cries of newborn humans (Truby et al., 1965); the supralaryngeal vocal tract's configuration is maintained throughout the cry and phonation occurs until the very end of the breath-group. The fundamental frequency at the end of the breath-group in these cries always falls. The fundamental frequency must fall because, in the absence of increased activity of the laryngeal muscles, the pulmonary air pressure goes from a positive to a negative value at the end of the breath-group. The transition in pulmonary air pressure is a consequence of the act of breathing. The form of the normal breath-group thus is a condition of minimum departure from the constraints of vegetative breathing. A speaker has to generate a negative air pressure in the lungs in order to inspire air. If the muscles that control the larynx simply "set" the proper medial compression and neutral position for phonation, then f_0 will be a function of the transglottal air pressure drop.

There can be various f_0 variations throughout the breath-group. The one certain aspect of the breath-group will be *the fall in f_0 at the breath-group's end*. The pulmonary air pressure must rapidly fall at the end of the expiration from the positive pressure of the nonterminal part of the breath-group to the negative pressure of inspiration. The f_0 contour therefore must fall *unless* the speaker executes compensating maneuvers with his laryngeal muscles. In the absence of compensating maneuvers, f_0 must fall. If the speaker anticipates the beginning of inspiration and opens his larynx towards the end of the breath-group, the f_0 contour will fall still faster. The subglottal pressure will fall because the glottal resistance will decrease; and the tension of the vocal cords will fall as medial compression decreases, causing f_0 to fall still faster. The vibrating mass of the vocal cords will increase, causing f_0 to fall faster; the aero-dynamic and aerostatic forces will fall as the phonation neutral position becomes more open. In short, everything that can occur to hasten the start of inspiration will cause f_0 to fall. This is the basis of the normal or unmarked — *breath-group*. The plots reproduced from Atkinson (1973) in Figure 8-12 show the variations in the f_0 traces of the same person repeating the simple sentence *Bev loves Bob*. Note the variations in the f_0 contours except at the end of the breath-group. Note also the regularity in the duration of each syllable. Many of the perceptual interpretations of

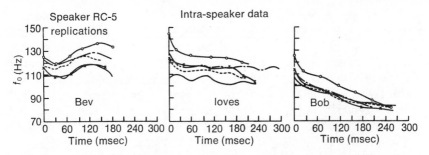

FIGURE 8-12. *Fundamental frequency contours derived from one speaker's production of five tokens of the sentence* Bev loves Bob. *Note that the speaker does not produce the same absolute fundamental frequency contour for each token. Note that the greatest consistency occurs at the end of the sentence where the fundamental frequency falls. (After Atkinson, 1973.)*

prosody that are ascribed to f_0 variations may, in fact, reflect variations in the durations of segments.

Although the "easiest" or "most natural" way of producing a breath-group appears to be the state of minimal control that results in a terminal falling f_0 contour, some speakers produce terminal falling f_0 contours by other means (Lieberman, 1967; Ohala, 1970). The "ordinary" sentences of certain speakers habitually end with a rising or a level f_0 contour. If these speakers are using a language in which ordinary sentences usually end with a normal — *breath-group*, they may be misunderstood because linguistic information is often signaled by using a contrasting variation on the normal breath-group. Many languages, for example, English, make use of a contrasting intonational signal that involves a rising or not-falling terminal f_0 contour (Lieberman, 1967) as well as a slightly higher over-all average fundamental frequency (Hadding-Koch, 1961; Atkinson, 1973). The notation — *breath-group* which implicitly states that the normal breath-group is the unmarked pattern and +*breath-group* can be used to differentiate these patterns. In English, yes–no questions typically are produced with a +*breath-group* (Lieberman, 1967).

The +*breath-group* that is used in normal yes–no questions in English appears to be structured by its acoustic contrast with the —*breath-group*. Whereas the f_0 contour may vary throughout the —*breath-group*'s nonterminal portion, it falls at the end of the breath-group. In the +*breath-group* f_0 does *not* fall at the end. (In a sense the +*breath-group* is structured by physiologic constraints—because it is in opposition to the —*breath-group*, which clearly is structured by the constraints of respiration, being a state of minimum departure from the vegetative function of respiration.) The manner in which a speaker produces a +*breath-group* appears to be quite complex. A number of studies (cf. Chapter 6) have shown that muscles like the sternohyoid, which is one of the muscles that adjusts the hyoid bone, which supports the larynx, is often active when f_0 variations occur during phonation. It is possible that this muscle and the muscles that set the phonation neutral position of the larynx, may act to switch the larynx from the low chest register that is used for a —*breath-group* to a high chest register during a +*breath-group*. The data available at this moment are still rather fragmentary and limited to a few speakers of English, Japanese, and Swedish.

The state of our understanding of the physiologic and perceptual bases of the breath-group is not very different from that of most of the hypothetical phonetic features that we have discussed. We have some good data and several reasonable hypotheses. Many of the studies of the underlying physiology of the prosodic features have derived data that indicate that variations in pulmonary air pressure have only a small effect on the fundamental frequency of phonation (Ohala, 1970; Vanderslice and Ladefoged, 1972). Vanderslice and Ladefoged (1972) also interpret the intonation pattern that corresponds to the normal breath-group as a unified entity. They use the term *cadence* to describe the total pattern that segments a sentence. They, however, ascribe the falling fundamental frequency contour that occurs at the sentence's end to the activity of the laryngeal muscles. The basic acoustic feature of the normal cadence pattern of a sentence would still follow from the vegetative constraints of breathing, because the laryngeal muscles must open the glottis to initiate inspiration. The physiologic basis of the terminal fall of fundamental frequency is however closely correlated with the laryngeal muscles by Vanderslice and Ladefoged. It is hoped that further research will resolve this issue.

The perceptual value of the acoustic phenomena that occur at the end of a breath-group (or cadence pattern) are also still not fully understood. Changes in the tempo of speech, for example, usually appear to typify the end of a breath-group. The duration of segments becomes longer at the breath-group's end. The glottal spectrum also typically loses energy in higher harmonics of the fundamental during the last few glottal periods. All of these events may serve as acoustic cues signaling the end of a breath-group. It is not certain that they actually have much importance, because appropriate perceptual experiments have yet to be performed. It is often possible to isolate acoustic phenomena that are *not* important to human listeners. Irregularities in the fundamental frequency, for example, commonly occur at the start and end of phonation but human listeners are not aware of either the presence or the absence of these "perturbations" (Lieberman and Michaels, 1963).

Linguistic Universals and Biological Structuring

The reader may have noted an apparent inconsistency in the discussion of the breath-group. We first made a strong case for the "naturalness" of the *—breath-group*. We then stated that speakers sometimes do not make use of this pattern of activity and instead produce sounds that have contrasting acoustic properties. The situation would be simple if all languages, and all speakers, behaved like our hypothetical "normal" speaker of English. Most sentences would be produced using the unmarked *—breath-group* by means of the pattern of least muscular control that we have discussed. The more costly, "marked" *+breath-group* would be reserved for fewer sentences. Unfortunately, some speakers of English produce *—breath-group* by means of "odd" patterns of articulatory activity that involve more articulatory control than they could have used (Lieberman, 1967). Worse still is the fact that some languages appear to use *+breath-group* sounds for most of their sentences. If the biological constraints *determined* the sound pattern of all human languages, then we should expect to find a universal invariant pattern.

The answer is that biological constraints *structure* the possible forms of human language although they do not *determine the form* of language. The relation that holds between certain biological constraints and the possible form of the sound pattern may be very strong without being entirely deterministic. The biological mechanisms that underlie *voicing*, for example, appear to be as controling as the biological factors that underlie upright bipedal posture in humans. However, it is possible to devise a human language in which all sounds would be *+voiced*. The key to understanding the properties of human speech is that of determining the biological mechanisms that structure possible phonetic features. We cannot isolate these mechanisms if we insist that the appropriate criterion is that the particular mechanism is always manifested. For example, the biological mechanisms that structure human bipedal posture and locomotion are present in all normal humans. We would not dismiss the significance of these mechanisms if we found a "crucial" case of a normal human being who, like Tom Scott, the assistant to the villianous Quilp in Dickens' Old Curiosity Shop, habitually walked upright on his hands. There is no reason why a structuring principle must be universally manifested. Various groups of people for various peculiar reasons might not make use of some sounds, e.g., bilabials, although they were highly valued and although most languages use these sounds (Jakobson, 1940).

Appendix to Chapter 8

Acoustic Correlates of Sounds and Phonetic Features

We have discussed the sounds of speech in terms of articulatory and acoustic data and theoretical models in this chapter on phonetic theories. Much of the primary data that you might want to review involve the acoustic correlates of various sounds and hypothetical phonetic features. We will therefore review some of the acoustic correlates of various sounds with a view of illustrating the ways in which data are presented and presenting some of the primary data with which you should be familiar. This won't be a comprehensive list of the acoustic correlates of the sounds of human speech or even of the sounds of English but it should be a useful starting point for more detailed study.

Vowels

The first three formants are sufficient acoustic cues for listeners to identify the vowels of English. Differences in vowel duration also are typical of the vowels of English. The "short" vowels [ɪ], [e], [ɛ], [ʊ], and [o] usually have a duration of 150 to 200 msec when produced in syllabic context. The "long" vowels [a], [æ], [i], [u] and [ɔ] have durations of about 250 to 370 msec and are often diphthongized (Peterson and Lehiste, 1960). Some of the short vowels are also diphthongized in various dialects of English. The diphthongization generally consists of the formant frequency pattern going from that of one "pure" vowel to a second vowel or "semivowel," e.g., [ai] or [ay] in the word *bite*.

The formant frequency relations that specify the vowels of English are inherently relational rather than absolute since different sized supralaryngeal vocal tracts will produce different absolute formant frequencies. Perhaps the best way to remember the formant frequency patterns is to start with the *quantal* vowels [i], [u], and [a]. The sketch of the locations of the formant frequencies of these vowels in Figure 8-13 illustrates their quantal properties. The vowel [i] has the highest F_3 of all English vowels. It also has the highest F_2. The convergence of F_3 and F_2 result in a well-defined high frequency peak in the spectrum of the vowel's transfer function. The vowel [i] also has a low F_1. The numbers entered on sketch 8-13 are the means derived from the Peterson and Barney (1952) analysis. The mean values of F_1, F_2, and F_3 respectively of [i] are 300, 2,300, and 3,100 Hz. The quantal vowel [u] also has a F_1 of 300 Hz, but F_2 is also low, about 900 Hz. The vowels [i] and [u] yield two of the vertices of the acoustic vowel triangle in Figure 8-9 where the first and second formant frequencies are plotted in Mels. The quantal vowel [a], which is specified by F_1 and F_2 converging towards each other at 1,000 Hz in the

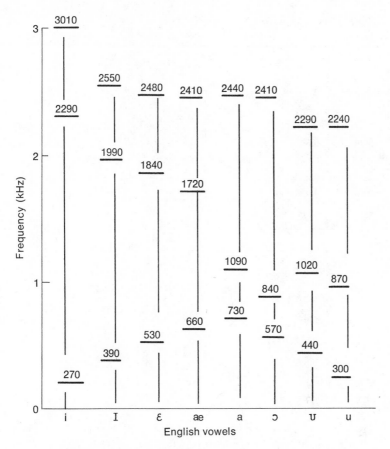

FIGURE 8-13. *Mean values of formant frequencies for adult males of vowels of American English measured by Peterson and Barney (1952).*

middle region of the vowel space forms the third vertex of the vowel triangle. The mean values of F_1 and F_2 of [a] are 700 and 1,100 Hz. Note that the formant frequency pattern of [i] is distinctive; F_3 is highest of all vowels, F_1 lowest. This distinctiveness may account for its perceptual advantages vis à vis other vowels (which we discussed in Chapter 7). When vowels are synthesized by means of two formant frequencies, it is necessary to offset the second formant frequencies to take account of the effect that the missing third formant would have had on the spectrum of the transfer function. The formant frequencies used to synthezsie [i] by Cooper et al. (1952) were, for example, 270 and 2,700 Hz for F_1 and F_2.

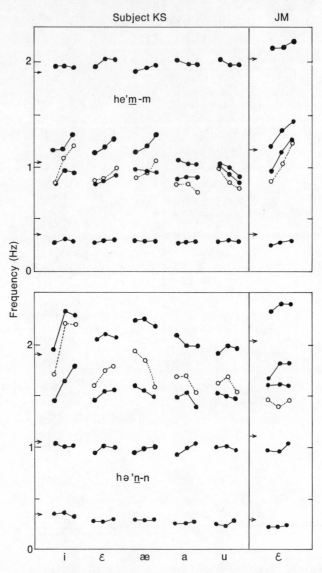

FIGURE 8-14. *Formants and antiformants of* [m] *and* [n] *in inter-vocalic position in different vocalic environments as measured by a computer-implemented procedure for two speakers. The upper graph shows the formants and antiformants of the first* [m] *in the context* [hám V m]. *The closed circles represent formant frequencies, while the open circles represent antiformants. Each sequence of three joined points represents a sequence of three measurements for a given nasal consonant. The sequence of three points thus shows how each formant antiformant changes under the influence of the vowel that follows it. For Speaker KS the formants and antiformants of* [m] *thus, for example, vary least in the context of the vowel* [a] *in the utterance* [hámam].

Nasality

Whereas vowels form a class of sounds that can be described in terms of hypothetical phonetic features like quantal versus nonquantal, etc., *nasality* is itself a phonetic feature that differentiates a class of sounds, the nasals, from their nonnasal equivalents. The acoustic consequences of opening the nasal cavity while a sound is being produced are primarily additional formants and an antiformant or "zero." The lowest nasal formant shows up on sound spectrograms as a "bar" for all nasal consonants. The nasal formant is hard to see in spectrograms of nasalized vowels like [a] because it occurs in the vicinity of the first and second formants of the unnasalized vowels.

The "zero" absorbs acoustic energy. It's effects are often not apparent in a sound spectrogram. In the production of an [m], for example, it shows up as a relatively broad spectrum minimum near 1,200 Hz when the spectrum is carefully measured (Fant, 1960). Computer analyses are necessary to reveal the details of the nasal transfer function. The nasal consonant [m] for example, has formants at 250, 1,100, 1,350, and 2,000 Hz and a zero at 1,000 Hz. The frequencies of formants and antiformants (zeros) are plotted in Figure 8-14 for the sounds [m] and [n] in intervocalic position in a computer-implemented analysis. The spectrogram in Figure 8-15 of the sounds [na] and [da] shows how these effects are manifested by the sound spectrograph. Some of the effects of nasality like formant bandwidth widening are not revealed in the computer display of Figure 8-14. Complete displays of the nasal spectrum derived in the computer analysis are necessary to see such effects (Fujimura, 1962).

Stop Consonants

In Figure 8-11A the formant frequency locations at which quantal signals would result for consonants were plotted. The energy concentrations that occur in the spectrum when two formants converge determine the frequencies of the "bursts" of stop consonants articulated at various of the "points of articulation." The formant transitions that necessarily occur when a stop consonant and a vowel are encoded together in a syllable also will go from the formant frequencies of the stop articulation to those of the vowel in a consonant–vowel syllable. In Figure 8-16 bursts and formant frequency patterns are shown for the consonant–vowel syllables [pa], [ta], and [ka]. The first three vowel formants are plotted. Note that the second and third formants both rise from a lower value for [pa]. The second and third formants diverge from the burst frequency of about 2 kHz for [ka]. For [ta] the burst is located at about 5 kHz and F_3 falls from this high value. The patterning of the second and third formant transitions, in itself, differentiates the labial, dental, and velar consonants in these consonant–vowel syllables. For velars F_2 and F_3 both rise; for

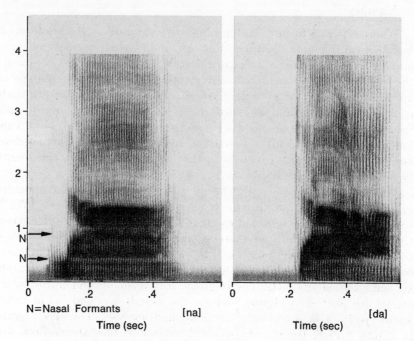

FIGURE 8-15. *Spectrogram of the sounds* [na] *and* [da]. *The wideband spectrogram shows some of the formants of the nasal, but it does not reveal the antiformant that occurs at about 1500 Hz.*

dentals F_3 always falls; for velars F_2 and F_3 diverge or "spread" with F_3 rising. These distinctive patterns are schematized on Figure 8-16.

The first formant frequency is "cut back" with respect to the higher formants in these stops which involved delayed phonation onset. The open glottis that typifies stops produced with delayed phonation onset results in inappropriate "boundary conditions" for the first formant frequency that would have occurred if the glottis had been closed at the moment of stop release. First formant "cut back" is an important acoustic cue for the delayed phonation onset that differentiates sounds like [pa] from [ba]. In Figure 8-17 the *coincident phonation* stops [ba], [da], and [ga] are shown. Note that the first formant frequency transition in all cases rises from the low value that follows from the effective lengthening of the vocal tract by the stop occlusion. (We discussed this phenomenon for bilabials in Chapter 4, cf. Figure 4-12 and its discussion.) The nasal "homorganic" sound [m], which also is articulated using a labial supralaryngeal vocal tract "point of articulation" had a similar formant pattern except for the addition of the nasal formants and zeros.

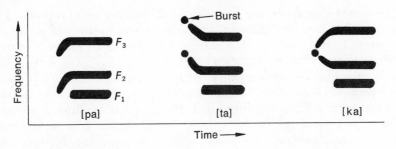

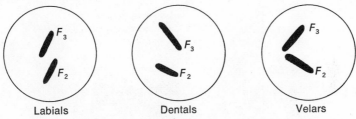

FIGURE 8-16. *Formant transitions and bursts that define the* delayed phonation *stops* [pa], [ta], *and* [ka] *of English.*

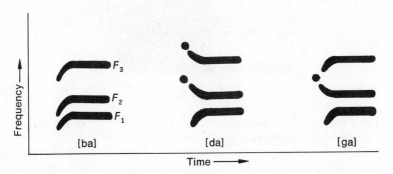

FIGURE 8-17 *Formant transitions and bursts for the* coincident phonation *stops* [ba], [da], *and* [ga] *of English.*

Continuent Consonants with Noise Sources

A homorganic continuant consonant like [f] that is produced by means of noise excitation generated at approximately the same point of articulation in the supralaryngeal vocal tract will involve energy concentrations at frequencies near the corresponding stop "burst" and similar formant transitions (Heinz and Stevens, 1961). Many of the hypotheses of traditional phonetics are in accord with the results of recent data derived from experiments that made use of both speech analysis and synthesis. The traditional concept of consonantal "points of articulation" in particular appears to be well founded. The energy of the particular source or sources of acoustic excitation are modified by the formants and zeros of the transfer functions of the supralaryngeal vocal tract configurations specified by the "point of articulation." Some sounds like [h], however, have acoustic correlates that are not consistent with the claims of traditional phonetic theory. The sound [h], in the syllable [ha] in Figure 8-18 for example, appears to be a noise-excited version of the vowel [a]. This different view

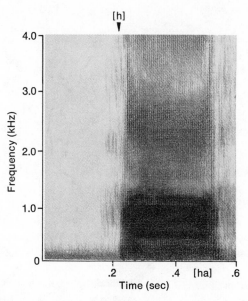

FIGURE 8-18. *Wide-band spectrogram of sound* [ha]. *Note the noise-excited formants at the start of the utterance.*

of the nature of [h] obviously would have important consequences for phonologic theories. Sound sequences transcribed by means of the symbol [h] could be regarded as vowels excited by noise excitation generated at, or near, the level of the glottis. Many of the acoustic cues that differentiate sounds are very subtle. The difference between [r] and [l], for example, appears to rest in the third formant transition (Leidner, 1974). Further study of practically everything is necessary but the general scope of available data should be apparent in these examples.

9
Old Problems and New Directions

ONE of the oldest puzzles about the nature of human existence is the origin of human speech and human language. Human beings talk; they communicate by means of complex languages; animals do not. People of many different cultures and different times have tried to solve this puzzle. Before the general diffusion of the theory of evolution with Charles Darwin's *On the Origin of Species* (1859), the usual explanation of the apparent uniqueness of human language and human speech was that it was one of the endowments to *Homo sapiens* from a higher deity. The presence of human language and speech indeed has been taken as an outward sign that demonstrates the existence of the soul. Descartes claimed that the presence of speech in humans and its absence in apes showed that humans had a soul and that apes lacked a soul. La Mettrie (1749) took this argument so seriously that he proposed that apes be taught to talk. This demonstration if successful would then in La Mettrie's view make the ape "a perfect little gentleman" (La Mettrie, 1749). Attempts to teach apes to talk have persisted until recent years but they have always been unsuccessful (Kellogg, 1968). The lack of success has been puzzling because apes like chimpanzees (*Pan troglodytes*) are close relatives of modern human beings (*Homo sapiens*). The genetic carriers that make up the DNA chains in human beings and chimpanzees are, for example, extremely similar (Sarich, 1974).

The "mystery" concerning the phonetic deficiencies of chimpanzees appears to follow from a lack of understanding of the source-filter theory of speech production. Although the source-filter theory of speech production that we have discussed throughout this book was proposed in the early years of the nineteenth century, a common view is that speech is produced solely by the larynx. There are differences between the larynges of chimpanzees and human beings (Kelemen, 1948, 1969) but they would affect the chimpanzee's ability to sing or his vocal quality rather than speech. Chimpanzees and other nonhuman primates do not have a supralaryngeal vocal tract that would allow them to produce the full range of sounds of human speech. The study of the differences between the human and nonhuman supralaryngeal vocal tract has provided new insights on both the development of speech in human infants and the probable evolution of human speech and its interrelation with human linguistic ability. These studies also constitute a "test" of the source-filter theory of speech production and new methods for treating extreme craniofacial anomalies that affect normal speech production.

Acoustic Analysis of Primate Vocalizations

In Figure 9-1 a sound spectrogram of a vocalization that was made by a gorilla is presented. It is useful to start with this gorilla vocalization since it shows some of the general characteristics of nonhuman primate vocalizations. The spectrogam was made with the normal, 300-Hz bandwidth analyzing filter on the sound spectrograph. The fundamental frequency of phonation of this gorilla vocalization is about 100 Hz, which can be determined from the spacing of the vertical striations on the spectrogram (cf. Chapter 5). The dark bands on the spectrogram thus reflect the formant frequencies of the gorilla vocalization. Note that the formant frequencies occur at approximately 500, 1,500, and 2,400 Hz. The sound thus approximates the formant frequencies of the human vowel /ə/ whose spectrum was noted in Figure 4-4.

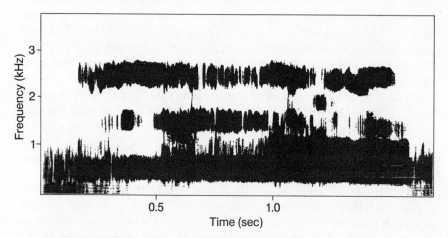

FIGURE 9-1. *Sound spectrogram of a gorilla's vocalization.*

The spectrogram in Figure 9-1 shows that the fundamental frequency of phonation is irregular and that breathy excitation also occurs, but the transfer function of the gorilla's supralaryngeal vocal tract configuration remains that of the vowel [ə]. Acoustic analyzes of the vocalization of nonhuman primates show that they produce cries that can be differentiated in terms of phonetic features (Lieberman, 1967, 1975). Chimpanzee cries, for example, may be produced with periodic or breathy phonation, high or low fundamental frequency, continuous or interrupted phonation, and rising or falling formant transitions (Lieberman, 1975). Animals like gelada baboon may even be producing formant transitions that are analogous to those that occur in the human vowel sequences [æ] to [ɪ]. The only sounds that are not evident in the acoustic analysis of the vocalizations of nonhuman primates are formant frequency patterns like those that specify the vowels [i], [u], or [a] or velar consonants like [g] and [k]. The acoustic analysis of the cries of human newborns also reveals similar deficits (Lieberman et al., 1972). Note the similarities between the spectrogram of the newborn human infant cry in Figure 5-11 and the gorilla vocalization in Figure 9-1.

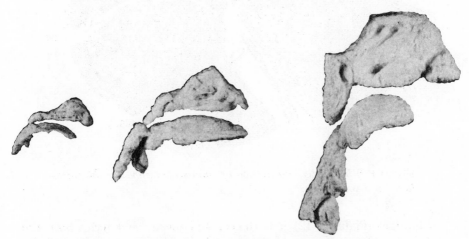

FIGURE 9-2. *Air passages of the supralaryngeal vocal tract of human newborn, chimpanzee, and adult human. Note the similarity between the chimpanzee and the human newborn.*

The computer-modeling techniques that we discussed in Chapter 6 have been used to establish the constraints that the anatomy of the supralaryngeal vocal tract imposes on the phonetic repertoires of these animals. In Figure 9-2 photographs of casts of the air passages of supralaryngeal vocal tracts of human newborn, chimpanzee, and human adult are shown together. The casts were made from cadavers following the technique described in Lieberman and Crelin (1971). In Figure 9-3 a midsagittal section of the chimpanzee from whom the supralaryngeal cast of Figure 9-2 was obtained is shown. Note the differences between the ape and adult newborn supralryngeal vocal tract. The tongue in the chimpanzee is long and thin and forms the lower boundary of the oral cavity, whereas

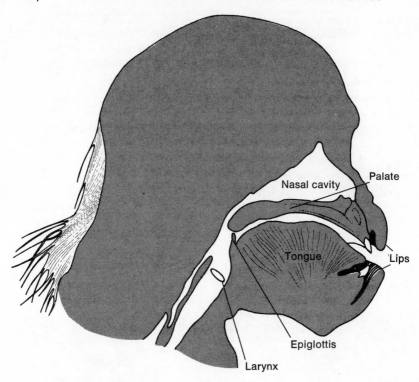

FIGURE 9-3. *Midsagittal section of chimpanzee, showing the supra-laryngeal vocal tract.*

in humans (Figure 6-12) it is thicker and shorter and forms both the lower boundary of the oral cavity and the anterior boundary of the pharynx. The larynx in the chimpanzee is sited higher than is the case in adult humans and opens almost directly into the oral cavity. The non-human pharynx lies behind the larynx and does not form part of the direct airway from the larynx to the lips.

The supralaryngeal vocal tract of newborn human beings is essentially the same as that of the adult chimpanzee. Since the transfer function of the supralaryngeal vocal tract is determined by the shape and size of the air passages, the total inventory of possible formant frequency patterns can be determined in principle, once we know the total range of vocal tract configurations. Cineradiographic data derived from newborn infants (Truby et al., 1965) can be used to determine the total range of vocal tract configurations for newborns and pongids. In Figure 9-4 area functions that were used to control a distributed constant vocal tract analog, are plotted. The area functions are the best approximations of the chimpanzee vocal tract for the quantal vowels [i], [u], and [a]. As we noted in

[i] •——•			[a] ■----■			[u] ▲·······▲		
Formant	Freq.	Freq./ 1.7	Formant	Freq.	Freq./ 1.7	Formant	Freq.	Freq./ 1.7
1	610	360	1	1220	720	1	830	490
2	3400	2000	2	2550	1500	2	1800	1060
3	4420	2600	3	5070	2980	3	4080	2390

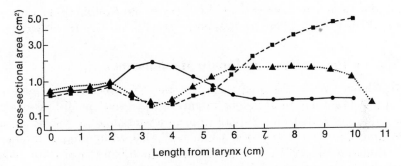

FIGURE 9-4. *Area functions for chimpanzee vocal tract's best approximations to the human vowels* [i], [u], *and* [a].

Chapter 8, these vowels are produced by shifting the body of the tongue up and down and frontwards and backwards. The pharynx is expanded in the sound [i] and the oral cavity constricted by shifting the tongue body forwards and upwards. The oral cavity is expanded and the pharynx contracted in the production of [a] by shifting the tongue downwards and backwards.

The right angle bend of the adult human supralaryngeal vocal tract makes it possible to effect the abrupt 10:1 discontinuities in the area function of the supralaryngeal vocal tract that are necessary to produce these vowels. The modeling study (Stevens and House, 1955) which we discussed in Chapter 6 demonstrated that these vowels can only be produced by means of abrupt area function discontinuities. The supralaryngeal vocal tract of the chimpanzee lacks the right angle bend of the human vocal tract. It thus can not generate extreme discontinuities. The adult human supralaryngeal vocal tract is inherently a "two-tube" system that is well adapted for the production of the shapes that are necessary to produce these quantal vowels. The single-tube vocal tract of the chimpanzee can be perturbed towards these shapes but it can not produce abrupt midpoint discontinuities. The mechanical properties of the tissue of the tongue would prevent it from generating in a single-tube system the abrupt area function changes that are necessary to produce these sounds. The calculated formant frequencies of the chimpanzee vocal tract perturbed towards these vowels in Figure 9-4 show that the chimpanzee and newborn human infant supralaryngeal vocal tracts inherently cannot produce these sounds. The absence of these sounds in the phonetic repertories of nonhuman primates and newborn infants thus can be ascribed to the constraints of their supralaryngeal vocal tracts, as well as to the possible lack of neural control of their vocal apparatus. Recent attempts to assess the speech abilities of extinct fossil hominids (i.e., ancestral forms related to modern humans) indicate that similar phonetic limitations also may have existed (Lieberman and Crelin, 1971; Lieberman, 1975, 1976a). These studies, however, still must be replicated.

Speech Perception and Innate Mechanisms

In Chapter 7 we discussed the perception of speech sounds by 1 to 4-month-old human infants. The infants can perceive the distinctions of phonation onset that differentiate stop consonants like [b] versus [p] at the same 20-msec "categorical boundary" that adult human listeners use (Eimas, et al., 1971). It is unlikely that the infants "learn" to make these distinctions; their behavior must reflect the presence of an "innate" perceptual mechanism. In other words, human beings are born with the neural mechanisms that are necessary for the perception of this phonetic distinction. Linguists have for many years supposed that human linguistic ability involves the presence of innate neural mechanisms. Chomsky (1957), for example, stresses the role of innate "competence" in his transformational theory. The evidence derived from the perception of speech that we discussed in Chapter 7 is consistent with this view. Special neural mechanisms would account for the perception of speech and speech-like sounds by human beings. The special neural mechanisms that are involved in speech perception, however, may not all be species-specific. Although the neural mechanisms that human beings use to perceive speech may be more complex than similar mechanisms present in other species, it is apparent that many animals can also perceive and discriminate the sounds of human speech. Monkeys, for example, can be trained to perceive the formant transitions that differentiate the syllables [da] and [ba] (Sinnott, 1974) or the syllables [dae], [bae], and [gae] (Morse and Snowden, 1975). The ability to perceive human speech sounds is not even restricted to primates. Chinchillas (*Chinchilla laniger*) have been trained to discriminate the sounds [a] versus [i] (Burdick and Miller, 1975) and the stop sounds [d] and [t] (Kuhl and Miller, 1975). Chinchillas, being rodents, are among the "simplest" mammals, yet they can discriminate some of the sounds of human speech. The neural mechanisms that are involved in the perception of speech thus probably have a long evolutionary history. Human beings probably do have some "special" species-specific neural mechanisms that at least facilitate the perception of speech. It would be surprising if this were not so, since even frogs have species-specific mechanisms that shape their responses to the acoustic signals that they produce (cf. Chapter 7). However, the species-specific perceptual mechanisms that underlie human speech communication must be related to analogous mechanisms that exist in other animals. The comparative study of vocal communication in other species, which is still a very new aspect of scientific enquiry, is thus a very promising and exciting area. In conjunction with comparative and evolutionary studies of speech production, the study of the perceptual aspects of vocal communication in other species can provide valuable insights into how we came to be and what we are.

Speech Pathologies and Anomalies

Speech scientists must necessarily be concerned with the causes of speech disabilities. Anatomical anomalies like those involved in cleft palate can interfere with normal speech production. The airway that is opened between the oral and nasal cavities of the vocal tract prevents the cleft-palate speaker from producing normal nasal versus nonnasal speech contrasts. Other craniofacial anomalies also can result in speech production problems (Peterson, 1973). The effective treatment of these anomalies requires a functional analysis of the specific anatomical problem and the compensatory patterns of articulatory gestures that the speaker may have learned. The pathologic speaker develops patterns of articulatory activity that are directed at producing the "best" approximation to the acoustic parameters that specify normal speech. The speaker often has to be retrained to acquire a normal pattern of articulatory activity after surgical intervention has produced a more or less normal anatomical situation.

The study of the behavior of speakers who have particular craniofacial anomalies thus is an important source of data on the hierarchy of acoustic correlates. We can determine what acoustic parameters are most important since the compensatory articulatory gestures often must sacrifice one acoustic quality in order to better approximate another parameter. We also can test our understanding of the physiology of speech production by observing the effects of particular anomalies. As Pruzansky (1973) notes, craniofacial anomalies are in effect, "experiments of nature." The study of these experiments is of interest both for the amelioration of the speech disabilities that follow from specific anomalies and a better understanding of the anatomy and physiology of speech production.

The study of aphasia likewise is an area that has both theoretical and clinical significance. Jakobson (1940) noted that the clinical signs and symptoms of aphasia reflect the destruction of the neural mechanisms that are the bases of speech production, speech perception, and grammar. Aphasia is usually not complete; the victim usually retains some linguistic ability because only a fraction of these neural mechanisms may be destroyed. The study of the effects of various types of aphasia which involve different parts of the brain thus reveals the organization of the neural mechanisms that are the bases of language and speech (Blumstein, 1973).

Old Problems and New Directions

The heading of this last chapter also is a fitting final heading. In discussing various issues throughout this book I tried to indicate the tentative nature of most of the theories involved. Progress in science consists of organizing your best "guesses" as testable theories and then putting them to the test. As we refute "old" theories and formulate "new" theories we hopefully arrive at a better understanding of the phenomena that we are trying to account for. Our understanding of speech science, the physiology of speech production and speech perception, is far in advance of the "old" phonetic theory of the late nineteenth century that still is often taught today. However, we still must find the answers to many of the old questions. How, for example, are the articulatory gestures of speech production organized? The syllable is perhaps the smallest unit for the encoding of speech, but encoding of much longer segments can occur (MacNeilage, 1970). How do children learn the sounds of speech? What are the effects of maturation; what "critical" periods may be involved? These questions only start to probe the list of possible questions. Speech science is an "old" science, but like any science it is also eternally "new."

Bibliography

ARMSTRONG, L. E. and WARD, I. C., 1926, *Handbook of English intonation.* Leipzig and Berlin: B. G. Teubner.

ATAL, B. S. and HANAUER, S. L., 1971, Speech analysis and synthesis by linear prediction of the speech wave; *J. Acoust. Soc. Am.*, 50, 637–655.

ATKINSON, J. R., 1973, Aspects of intonation in speech: Implications from an experimental study of fundamental frequency, unpublished Ph.D. dissertation, University of Connecticut, Storrs.

BELL, A. M., 1867 *Visible speech or self-interpreting physiological letters for the writing of all languages in one alphabet.* London: Simpkin and Marshall.

BELL, C. G., FUJISAKI, H., HEINZ, J. M., STEVENS, K. N., and HOUSE, A. S., 1961, Reduction of speech spectra by analysis-by-synthesis techniques, *J. Acoust. Soc. Am.*, 33, 1725–1736.

BELL-BERTI, F., 1973, *The velopharyngeal mechanism: An electryomyographic study*, unpublished Ph.D. thesis, City University of New York; also Status Report on Speech Research, Supplement, Haskins Laboratories, 270 Crown Street, New Haven, Conn. 06510.

BERANEK, L. L., 1949, *Acoustics*, New York: McGraw-Hill.

BLOOMFIELD, L., 1933, *Language*, New York. Holt.

BLUMSTEIN, S. E., 1973, *A phonological investigation of aphasic speech*, The Hague: Mouton.

BLUMSTEIN, S., (in preparation), "Conflicting cues for the perception of place of articulation."

BOGERT, C. M., 1960, "The influence of sound on the behavior of amphibians and reptiles," in *Animal Sound and Communication*, W. E. Lanyon and W. N. Tavoglga eds., Amer. Instit. of Biological Sciences, Washington D.C.

BOLT, R. H., COOPER, F. S., DAVID, E. E., JR., DENES, P. B., PICKET, J. M., and STEVENS, K. N. 1973, Speaker identification by speech spectrograms: Some further observations, *J. Acoust. Soc. Am.*, 54, 531–534.

BOSMA, J. F., 1957, Deglutition: Pharyngeal stage, *Physiol. Rev.*, 37, 275–300.

BOUHUYS, A., 1974, *Breathing*, New York: Grune and Stratton.

———, PROCTOR, D. F., and MEAD, J., 1966, Kinetic aspect of singing, *J. Appl. Physiol.*, 21, 483–496.

BROCA, P., 1861, Nouvelle observation d'aphemie produite par une lesion de la motie posterieure des deuxieme et troisieme ciconvolutions frontales, *Bull. Soc. Anat. Paris*, 6 (series 2), 398–407.

BURDICK, C. K. and MILLER, J. D., 1975, Speech perception by the chinchilla: Discrimination of sustained /a/ and /i/, *J. Acoust. Soc. Am.*, 58, 415–427.

CAPRANICA, R. R., 1965, *The evoked vocal response of the bullfrog*, Cambridge, Mass.: MIT Press.

CHIBA, T. and KAJIYAMA, J., 1941, *The vowel: Its nature and structure*, Tokyo: Tokyo-Kaiseikan Publishing Co.

CHOMSKY, N., 1957, *Syntactic structures*, The Hague: Mouton.

———— and HALLE, M., 1968, *The sound pattern of english*, New York: Harper & Row.

COLLIER, R., 1975, Physiological correlates of intonation patterns, *J. Acoust. Soc. Am.*, **58**, 249–255.

COOPER, F. S., DELATTRE, P. C., LIBERMAN, A. M., BORST, J. M., and GERSTMAN, L. J., 1952, Some experiments on the perception of synthetic speech sounds, *J. Acoust. Soc. Am.*, **24**, 597–606.

COOPER, W. E., 1974, Adaptation of phonetic feature analyzers for place of articulation, *J. Acoust. Soc. Am.*, **56**, 617–627.

CUTTING, J. E., 1974, Two left hemisphere mechanisms in speech perception, *Perception and Psychophysics*, **16**, 601–612.

———— and EIMAS, P. D., 1975, Phonetic analysers and processing of speech in infants, in *The role of speech in language*. J. F. Kavanagh and J. E. Cutting, eds., Cambridge, Mass.: MIT Press.

DANILOFF, R. and MOLL, K., 1968, Coarticulation of lip rounding, *J Speech and Hearing Res.*, **11**, 707–721.

DARWIN, C., 1859, *On the origin of species*, available as 1967 facsimile ed., New York. Atheneum.

DEJOURS, P., 1963, Control of respiration by arterial chemoreceptors, in *Regulation of respiration*, *Ann. NY Acad. Sci.*, **109**, 682–695.

DELATTRE, P. C., LIBERMAN, A. M., and COOPER, F. S., 1955, Acoustic loci and transitional cues for consonants, *J. Acoust. Soc. Am.*, **27**, 769–773.

DRAPER, M. H., LADEFOGED, P., and WHITTERIDGE, D., 1960, Expiratory pressures and air flow during speech, *Br. Med. J.*, **1**, 1837–1843.

DUDLEY, H., 1936, Synthesizing speech, *Bell Labs. Record*, No. 15, 98–102.

————, 1939, The Vocoder, *Bell Labs. Record*, No. 17, 122–126.

————, 1939, Remaking speech, *J. Acoust. Soc. Am.*, **11**, 169–177.

————, REISZ, R. R., and WATKINS, S. S. A., 1939, A synthetic speaker *J. Franklin Inst.*, **227**, 739–764.

DUNN, H. K., 1950, The calculation of vowel resonances and an electrical vocal tract, *J. Acoust. Soc. Am.*, **22**, 740–753.

EIMAS, P. D., SIQUELAND, E. R., JUSCZYK, P., and VIGORITO, J. 1971, Speech perception in infants, *Science*, **171**, 303–306.

———— and CORBIT, J., 1973, Selective adaptation of linguistic feature detectors, *Cognitive Psychol.*, **4** (1), 99–109.

ERIKSON, D., 1975, A laryngeal description of Thai tones, unpublished paper presented at Annual Meeting of the Linguistic Society of America, San Francisco.

FAIRBANKS, G. and GRUBB, P., 1961, A psychological investigation of vowel formants, *J. Speech and Hearing Res.*, **4**, 203–219.

FANT, G., 1956, On the predictability of formant levels and spectrum envelopes from formant frequencies, in *For Roman Jakobson*, M. Halle, H. Lunt, and D. C. Maclean, eds., The Hague: Mouton.

——, 1960, *Acoustic theory of speech production*, The Hague: Mouton.

——, 1969, Distinctive features and phonetic dimensions, STL-QPSR 2–3/1969; also pp. 1–18 in Fant, G., 1973, *Speech sounds and features*, Cambridge,Mass.: MIT Press.

——, 1973, *Speech sounds and features*, Cambridge, Mass.: MIT Press.

FERREIN, C. J., 1741, *Mem. Acad. Paris*, Nov. 15, 409–432.

FLANAGAN, J. L., 1955, A difference limen for vowel formant frequency, *J. Acoust. Soc. Am.*, 27, 613–617.

——, 1955a, Difference limen for the intensity of a vowel sound, *J. Acoust. Soc. Am.*, 27, 1223–1225.

——, 1957, Note on the design of "terminal analog" speech synthesizers, *J. Acoust. Soc. Am.*, 29, 306–310.

——, 1972, *Speech analysis, synthesis and perception*, 2nd ed., Springer, New York, Heidelberg, Berlin.

——, COKER, C. H., RABINER, L. R., SCHAFER, R. W., and UMEDA, N., 1970, Synthetic voices for computers, *IEEE Spectrum*, 7, 22–45.

——, ISHIZAKA, K., and SHIPLEY, K. L., 1975, Synthesis of speech from a dynamic model of the vocal cords and vocal tract, *Bell System Technical J.*, 54, 485–506.

FRISHKOPF, L. S. and GOLDSTEIN, M. H., JR., 1963, Responses to acoustic stimuli from single units in the eighth nerve of the bullfrog, *J. Acoust. Soc. Am.*, 3c, 1219–1228.

FRY, D. B., 1955, Duration and intensity as physical correlates of linguistic stress, *J. Acoust. Soc. Am.*, 35, 765–769.

FUJIMURA, O., 1962, Analysis of nasal consonants, *J. Acoust. Soc. Am.*, 34, 1865–1875.

——, TATSUMI, I. F., and KAGAYA, R. 1973, Computational processing of palatographic patterns, *J. of Phonetics*, 1, 47–54.

GARDING, E., FUJIMURA, O., and HIROSE, H., 1970, Laryngeal control of Swedish word tones, a preliminary report of an EMG study, *Annual Bull. Res. Inst. Logopedics and Phoniatrics, University, of Tokyo*, 4, 45–54.

GAY, T., 1974, A cinefluorographic study of vowel production, *J. Phonetics*, 2, 255–266.

GESCHWIND, N., 1965, Disconnection syndromes in animals and man, Part I, *Brain*, 88, 237–294; Part II, *Brain*, 88, 585–644.

GOLD, B., 1962, Computer program for pitch extraction, *J. Acoust. Soc. Am.*, 34, 916–921.

GREENBERG, J., 1963, *Universals of language*, Cambridge, Mass.: MIT Press.

——, 1966, *Language universals*, The Hague. Mouton.

GREENEWALT, C. H., 1968, *Bird Song: Acoustics and Physiology*, Washingtob D. C., Smithsonian Institution.

HADDING-KOCH, K., 1961, *Acoustico-phonetic studies in the intonation of southern Swedish*, Lund, Sweden: C. W. K. Gleerup.

HALLE, M., HUGHES, G. W., and RADLEY, J. P. A., 1957, Acoustic properties of stop consonants, *J. Acoust. Soc. Am.*, **29**, 107–116.

―――― and STEVENS, K. N., 1959, Analysis by synthesis, in *Proceedings of the seminar on speech compression and processing*, W. Wathen-Dunn and L. E. Woods, eds., AFCRC-TR-59-198, Dec. 1959, Vol. II, paper D7.

HARRIS, K. S., 1974, Physiological aspects of articulatory behavior, *Current trends in linguistics*, Vol. 12, T. Sebeok, ed., The Hague: Mouton.

HEFFNER, R. M. S., 1949, *General phonetics*, Madison: University of Wisconsin Press.

HEINZ, J. M. 1962, Reduction of speech spectra to descriptions in terms of vocal tract area functions, unpublished Sc.D. thesis, MIT.

―――― and STEVENS, K. N., 1961, On the properties of voiceless fricative consonants, *J. Acoust. Soc. Am.*, **33**, 589–596.

HENKE, W. L., 1966, Dynamic articulatory model of speech production using computer simulation, unpublished Ph.D. dissertation, MIT.

HERMANN, L., 1894, Nachtrag zur Untersuchung der Vocalcurven, *Arch. ges. Physiol.*, **58**, 264–279.

HIROSE, H. and USHIJAMA, T., 1974, The function of the posterior cricoarytenoid in speech articulation, *Status Report on Speech Research*, SR 37/38, Jan–June 1974, 94–102, Haskins Laboratories, 370 Crown St., New Haven, Conn.

HIRSCH, I. J., 1959, Auditory perception of temporal order, *J. Acoust. Soc. Am.*, **31**, 759–767.

―――― and SHERRICK, C. E., JR., 1961, Perceived order in different sense modalities, *J. Exp. Psychol.*, **62**, 423–432.

HOLLIEN, H., 1962, Vocal fold thickness and fundamental frequency of phonation, *J. Speech and Hearing Res.*, **5**, 237–243.

―――― and CURTIS, J. F., 1960, A laminographic study of vocal pitch, *Speech and Hearing Res.*, **3**, 361–370.

―――― and COLTON, R. H., 1969, Four laminographic studies of vocal fold thickness, *Folia. Phon.*, **21**, 179–198.

HOLMES, J. N., MATTINGLY, I. G., and SHEARME, J. N., 1964, Speech synthesis by rule, *Language and Speech*, **1**, 127–143.

HOUDE, R., 1967, *A study of tongue body movement during selected speech sounds*, Speech Communications Research Laboratory Monograph No. 2, Santa Barbara, Calif.

HOUSE, A. S. and STEVENS, K. N., 1956, Analog studies of the nasalization of vowels, *J. Speech and Hearing Disorders*, **21**, 218–232.

HOY, R. R. and PAUL, R. C., 1973, Genetic control of song specificity in crickets, *Science*, **180**, 82–83.

JAKOBSON, R., 1940, Kindersprache, Aphasie und allgemeine Lautgesetze, in Jakobson, R., 1962, *Selected writings*, The Hague: Mouton.

――――, FANT, G. M., and HALLE, M., 1963, *Preliminaries to speech analysis*, Cambridge, Mass.: MIT Press.

JONES, D., 1919, X-ray photographs of the cardinal vowels, *Proc. Royal Inst.*, XXII, 12–13.

――――, 1932, *An outline of English phonetics*, New York: E. P. Dutton.

JOOS, M., 1948, Acoustic Phonetics, *Language*, **24**, Suppl., 1–136.

KELEMEN, G., 1948, The anatomical basis of phonation in the chimpanzee, *J. Morphol.*, **82**, 229–256.

——, 1969, Anatomy of the larynx and the anatomical basis of vocal performance, *Chimpanzee*, **1**, 165–186.

KELLOGG, W. N., 1968, Communication and language in the home raised chimpanzee, *Science*, **162**, 423–427.

KERSTA, K. G., 1962, Voiceprint identification, *Nature*, **196**, 1253–1257.

KIMURA, D., 1961, Some effects of temporal lobe damage on auditory perception, *Can. J. Psychol.*, **15**, 156–165.

——, 1967, Functional asymmetry of the brain in dichotic listening, *Cortex*, **3**, 163–178.

KIPARSKY, P., 1974, The feature advanced tongue root, *NELS V*, Cambridge, Mass.: Harvard University, Linguistics Department.

KIRCHNER, J. A., 1970, *Pressman and Kelemen's physiology of the larynx*, rev. ed., Washington, D. C.: Amer. Acad. Opthalmology and Otolaryngology.

KLATT, D. H., STEVENS, K. N., and MEAD, J., 1968, Studies of articulatory activity and airflow during speech, *Ann. NY Acad. Sci.*, **155**, 42–54.

KOENIG, W., DUNN, H. K., and LACEY, L. Y., 1946, The sound spectrograph, *J. Acoust. Soc. Am.*, **18**, 19–49.

KRATZENSTEIN, C. G., 1780, Sur la naissance de la formation des voyelles, *Acta Acad. Petrograd*, translation in 1782, *J. Phys. Chim. Hist. Nat. Arts*, **21**, 358–381.

KUHL, P. K., and MILLER, J. D., 1974, Discrimination of speech sounds by the chinchilla: /t/ vs /d/ in CV syllables, *J. Acoust. Soc. Am.*, **56**.

——, and MILLER, J. D., 1975, Speech perception by the chinchilla: Voiced-voiceless distinction in alveolar plosive consonants, *Science*, **190**, 69–72.

LADEFOGED, P., 1975, *A course in phonetics*, New York: Harcourt Brace Jovanovich.

——, DeCLERK, J., LINDAU, M., and PAPCUN, G., 1972, An auditory motor theory of speech production, UCLA Phonetics Laboratory, Working Papers in Phonetics, **22**, 48–76.

LA METTRIE, J. O., 1747, *De l'homme machine*, A. Vartanian, ed. critical. ed. 1960, Princetown.: Princeton University Press.

LANE, H., 1965, The motor theory of speech perception: A critical review, *Psychol. Rev.*, **72**, 275–309.

LAWRENCE, W., 1953, The synthesis of speech from signals that have a low information rate, in *Communication theory*, W. Jackson, ed., London. Butterworths Sci. Pub.

LEFRANCOIS, R., GAUTIER, H., PASQUIS, P., and VARGAS, E., 1969 Factors controlling respiration during muscular exercise at altitude, *Fed. Proc.*, **28**, 1296–1300.

LEHISTE, I., 1961, Some acoustic correlates of accent in Serbo-Croatian, *Phonetica*, **7**, 114–147.

LEIDNER, D., 1974, An electromyographic study of American English liquids, unpublished Ph.D. dissertation, University of Connecticut, Storres.

LENNEBERG, E. H., 1967, *Biological foundations of language*, New York: Wiley.

LIBERMAN, A. M., 1970, The grammars of speech and language, *Cognitive Psychol.*, **1**, 301–323.

———, 1970a, Some characteristics of perception in the speech mode, *Perception and Its Disorders*, **48**, 238–254.

———, COOPER, F. S., SHANKWEILER, D. P., and STUDDERT-KENNEDY, M., 1967, Perception of the speech code, *Psychol. Rev.*, **74**, 431–461.

LIEBERMAN, M. R., and LIEBERMAN, P., 1973, Olson's "projective verse" and the use of breath control as a structural element, *Language and Style*, **5**, 287–298.

LIEBERMAN, P. 1960, Some acoustic correlates of word stress in American English, *J. Acoust. Soc. Am.*, **33**, 451–454.

———, 1961, Perturbations in vocal pitch, *J. Acoust. Soc. Am.*, **33**, 597–603.

———, 1963, Some acoustic measures of the fundamental periodicity of normal and pathological larynges, *J. Acoust. Soc. Am.*, **35**, 344–353.

———, 1963, Some effects of semantic and grammatical context on the production and perception of speech, *Language and Speech*, **6**, 172–187.

———, 1965, On the acoustic basis of the perception of intonation by linguists, *Word*, **21**, 40–54.

———, 1967, *Intonation, perception, and language*, Cambridge, Mass.: MIT Press.

———, 1968, Direct comparison of subglottal and esophageal pressure during speech, *J. Acoust. Soc. Am.*, **43**, 1157–1164.

———, 1970, Towards a unified phonetic theory, *Linguistic Inquiry*, **1**, 307–322.

———, 1970, Review of *Physiology of Speech production* by J. A. Perkell, *Language Sciences*, **13**, 25–28.

———, 1973, On the evolution of human language: A unified view, *Cognition*, **2**, 59–94.

———, 1975, *On the origins of language: An introduction to the evolution of human speech*, New York: Macmillan.

———, 1976, "Phonetic features and physiology: a reappraisal," *J. of Phonetics*, **4**, 91–112.

——— and CRELIN, E. S., 1971, On the speech of Neanderthal man, *Linguistic Inquiry*, **2**, 203–222.

———, KNUDSEN, R., and MEAD, H., 1969, Determination of the rate of change of fundamental frequency with respect to sub-glottal air pressure during sustained phonation, *J. Acoust. Soc. Am.*, **45**, 1537–1543.

——— and MICHAELS, S. B., 1963, On the discrimination of missing pitch pulses, *Proceedings of the Speech Communications Seminar*, Stockholm: Royal Institution of Technology.

LIFSCHITZ, S., 1933, Two integral laws of sound perception relating loudness and apparent duration of sound impulses, *J. Acoust. Soc. Am.*, **7**, 213–219.

LILJENCRANTS, J., and LINDBLOM, B., 1972, Numerical simulation of vowel quality systems: The role of perceptual contrast, *Language*, **48**, 839–862.

LINDAU, M., JACOBSON, L., and LADEFOGED, P., 1972, The feature advanced tongue root, UCLA Phonetics Laboratory, *Working Papers in Phonetics*, **22**, 76–94.

LINDBLOM, B., 1971, Phonetics and the description of language, in *Proceedings of the VIIth International Congress of Phonetic Sciences*, Montreal. A. Rigault and R. Charbonneau, eds., The Hague: Mouton., pp. 63–97.

LISKER, L. and ABRAMSON, A., S., 1964, "A cross language of voicing in initial stops: acoustical measurements" *Word*, **20**, 384–422.

———, 1971, Distinctive features and laryngeal control, *Language*, **47**, 767–785.

———, COOPER, F. S., and SCHVEY, M. H. 1969, Transillumination of the larynx in running speech, *J. Acoust. Soc. Am.*, **45**, 1544–1546.

LUBKER, J. F., FRITZELL, B., and LINDQUIST, J., 1970, Velopharyngeal function: An electromyographic study, Speech Translation Lab., Royal Institute of Technology, Stockholm. QPSR 4, 9–20.

LURIA, A. R., 1961, The pathology of directive function of speech, *Reports at the VIIth International Congress of Neurology*, Rome, pp. 601–603, The Hague: Mouton.

MACNEILAGE, P. F., 1970, Motor control of serial ordering in speech, *Psychol. Rev*, **77**, 182–196.

——— and DECLERK, J. L., 1969, On the motor control of coarticulation in CVC monosyllables, *J. Acoust. Soc. Am.*, **45**, 1217–33.

MATTINGLY, I. G., LIBERMAN, A. M., SYRDAL, A. K., and HALWES, T., 1971, Discrimination in speech and nonspeech modes, *Cognitive Psychol.* **2**, 131–157.

McADAM, D. W. and WHITAKER, H. A., 1971, Language production: Electroencephalic localization in the normal human brain, *Science*, 499–502.

MEAD, J., BOUHAYS, A., PROCTOR, D. F., 1968, Mechanisms generating subglottic pressure, *Sound Production in Man, Ann. NY Acad. Sci.*, **155**, 177–181.

MILLER, G. A., 1956, The magical number seven, plus or minus two: Some limits on our capacity for processing information, *Psychol. Rev.*, **63**, 81–97.

——— and NICELY, P. E., 1955, An analysis of perceptual confusions among some English consonants, *J. Acoust. Soc. Am.*, **27**, 338–352.

MINIFIE, F. D., HIXON, T. J., KELSEY, A. A., and WOODHOUSE, R. J., 1970, Lateral pharyngeal wall movement during speech production, *J. Speech and Hearing Res.*, **13**, 584–594.

———, KELSEY, C. A., and HIXON, T. J., 1968, Measurement of vocal fold motion using an ultrasonic Doppler velocity monitor, *J. Acoust. Soc. Am.*, **43**, 1165–1169.

MOLFESE, D. L., 1972, Cerebral asymmetry in infants, children, and adults: Auditory evoked responses to speech and noise stimuli, unpublished Ph.D. dissertation, Pennsylvania State University.

MORSE, P. A., 1972, The discrimination of speech and nonspeech stimuli in early infancy, *J. Exp. Child Psychol.*, **14**, 477–492.

———— and SNOWDEN, C. T., 1975, An investigation of categorical speech discrimination by rhesus monkeys, *Percept. Psychophys.*, **17**, 9–16.

MORTON, J. and JASSEM, W., 1965, Acoustic correlates of stress, *Language and Speech*, **8**, 159–181.

MOSLIN, B. and COWPER, E., 1975, Identification of CVC syllables in single and multispeaker ensembles, unpublished Working Paper, Brown University, Linguistics Department, Providence, R.I.

MÜLLER, J., 1848, *The physiology of the senses, voice and muscular motion with the mental faculties*, W. Baly, trans., London: Walton and Maberly.

NEAREY, T., 1976, *Features for vowels*, unpublished Ph.D. dissertation University of Connecticut, Storres.

NEGUS, V. E., 1949, *The comparative anatomy and physiology of the larynx*, Hafner.

OHALA, J., 1966, A new photoelectric glottograph, UCLA Phonetics Laboratory, *Working Papers in Phonetics*, **4**, 40–52.

————, 1970, Aspects of the control and production of speech, UCLA Phonetics Laboratory, *Working Papers in Phonetics*, **15**.

———— and HIROSE, H., 1970, The function of the sternohyoid muscle in speech, *Annual Bull., Res. Inst. Logopedics and Phoniatrics, University of Tokyo*, **4**, 41–44.

OHMAN, S. E. G., 1966, Coarticulation in VCV utterances: Spectrographic measurements, *J. Acoust. Soc. Am.*, **39**, 151–168.

PENFIELD, W. and ROBERTS, L., 1959, *Speech and brain-mechanisms*, Princeton, N.J.: Princeton University Press.

PERKELL, J. S., 1969, *Physiology of speech production: Results and implications of a quantitative cineradiographic study*, Cambridge, Mass.: MIT Press.

PETERSON, G. E., 1951, *Language*, **27**, 541–553.

———— and BARNEY, H. L., 1952, Control methods used in a study of the vowels, *J. Acoust. Soc. Am.*, **24**, 175–184.

PETERSON, G. E. and LEHISTE, I., 1960, Duration of syllable nuclei in English, *J. Acoust. Soc. Am.*, **32**, 693–703.

————, WANG, W. S-Y., and SIVERTSON, E., 1958, Segmentation techniques in speech synthesis, *J. Acoust. Soc. Am.*, **30**, 739–742.

PETERSON, S., 1973, Speech pathology in craniofacial malformations other than cleft lip and palate, in *ASHA Report 8, Orofacial anomalies: Clinical and research implications*, American Speech and Hearing Association.

POLLACK, I., 1952, The information of elementary audio displays, *J. Acoust. Soc. Am.*, **24**, 745–749.

POTTER, R. K., KOPP, G. A., and GREEN, H. C., 1947, *Visible speech*, New York. D. van Nostrand.

———— and STEINBERG, J. C., 1950, Toward the specification of speech, *J. Acoust. Soc. Am.*, **22**, 807–820.

PROCTOR, D. F., 1964, Physiology of the upper airway, in *Handbook of physiology, respiration*, vol. 1, W. O. Fenn and H. Rahn, eds., Washington, D. C.: American Physiological Society.

PRUZANSKY, S., 1973, Clinical investigations of the experiments of nature, *ASHA report 8, Orofacial anomalies: Clinical and research implications*, American Speech and Hearing Association.

PURKINJE, K., 1836, Badania w przedmiocie fizylolgil mowy Ludzkiej, Krakow.

ROSEN, G., 1958, Dynamic analog speech synthesizer, *J. Acoust. Soc. Am.*, 30, 201–209.

ROUSSELOT, P. J., 1901, *Principes de Phonétique Expérimentale*, Paris, H. Welter.

RUSSELL, G. O., 1928, *The vowel*, Columbus, Ohio. Ohio State University Press.

SARICH, V. M., 1974, Just how old is the homonid line? in *Yearbook of Physical Anthropology*, 1973, Washington, D. C.: American Association of Physical Anthropologists.

SAWASHIMA, M. 1974, Laryngeal research in experimental phonetics, *Current trends in linguistics*, Vol. 12, T. Sebeok, ed., The Hague: Mouton.

——— and HIROSE, H., 1968, New laryngoscopic technique by use of fiber optics, *J. Acoust. Soc. Am.*, 43, 168–169.

——— and MIYAZAKI, S., 1973, Glottal opening for Japanese voiceless consonants, *Annual Bull., Res. Inst. Logopedics and Phoniatrics, University of Tokyo*, 7, 1–9.

SHANKWEILER, D. and STUDDERT-KENNEDY, M., 1967, Identification of consonants and vowels presented to left and right ears, *Quart. J. Exp. Psychol.*, 19, 59–63.

SHIPP, T. and McGLONE, R. E., 1971, Laryngeal dynamics associated with vocal frequency change, *J. Speech and Hearing Res.*, 14, 761–768.

SIMADA, Z. and HIROSE, H., 1970, The function of the laryngeal muscles in respect to the word accent distinction, *Annual Bull. Res. Inst. Logopedics and Phoniatrics, University of Tokyo*, 4, 27–40.

SINNOTT, J. M., 1974, A comparison of speech sound discrimination in humans and monkeys, unpublished Ph.D. dissertation, University of Michigan, Ann Arbor.

STETSON, R. H., 1951, *Motor phonetics*, 2nd ed., Amsterdam: North Holland.

STEVENS, K. N., 1972, Quantal nature of speech, in *Human Communication: A unified view*, E. E. David, Jr., and P. B. Denes, eds., New York: McGraw-Hill.

———, BASTIDE, R. P., and SMITH, C. P., 1955, Electrical synthesizer of continuous speech, *J. Acoust. Soc. Am.*, 25, 207.

——— and BLUMSTEIN, S. E., in press, Quantal aspects of consonant production: A study of retroflex stop consonants, *J. Phonetics*.

——— and HOUSE, A. S., 1955, Development of a quantitative description of vowel articulation, *J. Acoust. Soc. Am.*, 27, 484–493.

——— and HOUSE, A. S., 1961, An acoustical theory of vowel production and some of its implications, *J. Speech and Hearing Res.*, 4, 303–320.

———, KASOUSKI, S., and FANT, C. G. M., 1953, An electrical analog of the vocal tract, *J. Acoust. Soc. Am.*, 25, 734–742.

———, LIBERMAN, A. M., and STUDDERT-KENNEDY, M., 1969, Cross-language study of vowel perception, *Language and Speech*, 12, 1–23.

STEVENS, S. S. and DAVIS, H., 1938, *Hearing*, New York: John Wiley and Sons.

STUART, R. R., 1958, *The anatomy of the bullfrog*, Denoyer-Geppert.

STUDDERT-KENNEDY, M., 1974, The perception of speech, in *Current trends in linguistics, Vol.* 12, T. Sebeok, ed., The Hague: Mouton.

TIMCKE, R., VON LEDEN, H., and MOORE, P., 1958, Laryngeal vibrations: Measurements of the glottic wave, *AMA Archives of Otolaryngology*, 68, 1–19.

TOSI, O., OYER, H., LASHBROOK, W., PEDREY, J., NICHOL, J., and NASH, E., 1972, Experiment on voice identification, *J. Acoust. Soc. Am.*, 51, 2030–2043.

TRUBETZKOY, N. S., 1939, Grundzüge der phonologie, *Travaux du Cercle Linguistique de Prague*, 7, Prague.

TRUBY, H. M., BOSMA, J. F., and LIND, J., 1965, *Newborn infant cry*, Almquist and Wiksell.

VAN DEN BERG, J., 1958, Myoelastic-aerodynamic theory of voice production, *J. Speech and Hearing Res.*, 1, 227–244.

————, 1960, Vocal ligaments versus registers, *Current Problems in Phoniatrics and Logopedics*, 1, 19–34.

————, 1962, Modern research in experimental phoniatrics, *Folia Phoniatrica* 14, 81–149.

VANDERSLICE, R. and LADEFOGED, P., 1972, Binary suprasegmental features and transformational word-accentuation rules, *Language*, 48, 819–838.

VON KEMPELEN, W. R., 1791, *Mechanismum der menschlichen Sprache nebst der Beschreibung seiner sprechenden Maschine*, Vienna: J. B. Degen.

WERNICKE, C., 1874, *Der aphasische Symptomenkomplex*, Breslau: Cohn and Weigert.

WICKELGREN, W. A., 1965, Distinctive features and errors in short term memory for English vowels, *J. Acoust. Soc. Am.*, 38, 583–588.

————, 1969, Context-sensitive coding, associative memory and serial order in (speech) behavior, *Psychol. Rev*, 76, 1–15.

WILLIAMS, J. T., 1965, A static model of the tongue during vowel articulation, unpublished M. S. thesis, MIT.

WOLLBERG, Z., and NEWMAN, J. D., 1972, Auditory cortex of squirrel monkey: Response patterns of single cells to species-specific vocalizations, *Science*, 175, 212–214.

WOOD, C. C., GOFF, W. R., and DAY, R. S., 1971, Auditory evoked potentials during speech perception, *Science*, 173, 1248–1251.

YANAGIHARA, N. and HYDE, C., 1966, An aerodynamic study of the articulatory mechanism in the production of bilabial stop consonants, *Stud. Phonet.*, 4, 70–80.

ZEMLIN, W. R., 1968, *Speech and hearing science, anatomy and physiology*, Englewood Cliffs, N.J.: Prentice Hall.

ŽINKIN, N. I., 1968, *Mechanisms of Speech*, Mouton, The Hague.

Index

A

Abramson, A., 160, 167
Acoustic cues
  isolation of, 128
Acoustic filter, 49–50, 51, 52, 53, 58–59, 61, 62
Acoustic stability, 146–147, 155
Adult human supralaryngeal vocal tract, 3–4, 13, 14, 29–30, 33–36, 39–40, 42–45, 59, 94, 95–104, 107, 141, 142, 144, 147, 159, 181, 185
Air pressure, 6, 8, 53, 73–74, 75, 83, 147, 169
  pulmonary, 8, 53, 73–74, 75, 77, 84, 85, 169–170
  subglottal, 11, 85, 88, 89, 90
  transglottal, 95, 170
  waveform in uniform tubes, 40–44, 147–151
Alveolar air pressure
  see Air pressure, pulmonary
Amplitude of a waveform, 18–19, 25–26, 48
Analysis by synthesis, 46, 122
Antiformants or zeroes, 107, 177
Apes
  see Nonhuman primates
Aphasia, 187–188
Area function, 40, 104, 108, 141, 142, 143, 144, 185
  of chimpanzee vocal tract, 184
  of human newborn vocal tract, 184
  midpoint discontinuity, 151, 184, 185
Armstrong, L. E., 169
Atal, B. S., 71n
Atkinson, J. R., 33, 75, 81, 86, 87, 90, 94, 129, 168, 170, 171
Automatic response patterns, 78

B

Band pass filter, 29
Bandwidth of filter, 51, 52, 53, 58, 59,

Bandwidth of filter [cont.]
  62, 65
Barney, H. L., 1, 37, 67, 94, 110, 147, 153, 166, 174, 175
Bell, A. M., 110, 138, 139, 140
Bell, C. G., 37
Bell-Berti, F., 99, 100
Beranek, L. L., 45, 129
Bernoulli force, 11, 83–84, 89
Bilabial stops, 155
Binary phonetic features, 93, 94, 145, 160
Bloomfield, L., 128–129
Blumstein, S., 5, 134, 135, 158, 167, 188
Body plethysmograph, 79
Bodybox, 79
Bogert, C. M., 126
Bolt, R. H., 47
Bosma, J. F., 97
Bouhuys, A., 8, 74, 75, 77, 78, 79
Brain
  lateralization, 123–124, 156
  localization of functions, 14, 123
Breath-group, 169–172, 173
Breathy phonation, 91–92
Broca, P., 14, 123
Bursts, in the production of stop sounds, 134–135, 158, 177
Bullfrogs, laryngeal physiology and selective auditory response of, 14, 125–127

C

Capranica, R. R., 14, 125, 126
Caruso, Enrico, 90
Categorical perception of speech, 127–128, 130–133, 160
Center frequency, 30, 34, 49, 59
  see also Formant frequencies
Cerebral dominance, 123–124, 156
Chiba, T., 1, 35, 104